Think Ahead
to First Certificate

DAILY MAIL

Jon Naunton

LONGMAN

Addison Wesley Longman Limited
Edinburgh Gate, Harlow, Essex, CM20 2JE, England
and Associated Companies throughout the world.

First published by Addison Wesley Longman Limited 1997

Set in Horley OS MT 11/13pt

Printed in Spain by Gráficas Estella

ISBN 0 582 30248 X

We are grateful to the following for permission to reproduce
copyright material:

Fourth Estate for an extract *Dog Eat Dog* by Wensley Clarkson.
Copyright © 1990; MCA Music Ltd for an extract from the
lyrics 'Vincent' (Don McLean). © 1971, 1972 Music Corp. of
America Inc and Benny Bird Music; Music Sales Ltd for 'She's
Leaving Home', words and music by John Lennon and Paul
McCartney © 1967 Northern Songs; Random Century Group
on behalf of the authors, Sting and John-Pierre Dutilleux, for an
adapted extract from *Jungle Stories: The Fight for the Amazon*
(Pubd. Barrie & Jenkins); Random House Inc for extracts from
'Credo' in *All I Really Need to Know I Learned in Kindergarten*
by Robert Fulghum. Copyright © 1986, 1988 by Robert
Fulghum. Reprinted by permission of Villiard Books, a division
of Random House; Rex Features/News International for
modified extract from the article 'Stopped because I was a black
in a white Porsche' by John Kay and Matthew Cole from *The
Sun* 6.6.90; J Walter Thompson Co Ltd for an extract from
BAA "Body Language" Advertisement; Solo Syndication Ltd for
adapted extracts from the articles 'When all is not what it seems'
by Peter Martin in *You* magazine/*Mail on Sunday* 18.1.87,
'Doctor put woman on Suicide Machine' by Jeremy Campbell in
Evening Standard 6.6.90, and 'Arnie ...' in *Evening Standard*
7.1.92. We have also made reference to *Man after Man* by
Dougal Dixon, published by Cassell PLC.

We are grateful to the following for their permission to
reproduce copyright material and photographs:

Aardman Animations for page 23. ADAGP Paris and DACS for
page 140. Alex for page 10. Aquarius for page 125. Ashmolean
Museum, Oxford for page 143. John Birdsall for pages 63
(centre), 66 (left centre), 82, 83, 127 (bottom left centre). Martin
Black for pages 10/11. Bridgeman Art Library for pages 40,
/Giraudon 57 (top), /Giraudon 57 (bottom), /Giraudon 58, 128,
129. J. Allan Cash for pages 76 (centre right), 108. Chronicle
Features for page 112 (top left) The Far Side cartoon by Gary
Larson is reprinted by permission of Chronicle Features, San
Francisco, CA. All rights reserved. Bruce Coleman for pages
/Mary Plage 18 (centre right), 50, 99 (bottom). Colorific/Lori
Grinker/Contact for page 87. Dewynters PLC for page 76
(bottom left). 4th Estate/Keith McMillan for page 105 (left).
The Ronald Grant Archive for pages 18 (centre bottom), 24.
Sally and Richard Greenhill for page 127 (bottom left). Robert
Harding for pages /Walter Rawlings 96, 99 (top). Veena Holkar

for page 92. Hulton Deutsch for pages 20, 120. Image Bank for
pages /Regine M 14, /David De Lossy 63 (right), /Marc
Romanelli 70 (centre) /Werner Bokelberg 127 (bottom right).
Inspirations/Di Lewis for page 22. The Kobal Collection for page
18 (top right, bottom left). Krolten Muller Museum for page 59
(bottom centre left). B V Lanthuys Foundation for page 59 (centre
right). Life File for pages /Andrew Ward 63 (left), /Tim Fisher
127 (bottom centre right). London Underground for page 77.
Longman Photo Unit for page 17. Mirror Syndication
International for page 105 (right). Museum of London for page 76
(centre left). National Maritime Museum for page 44.
Network/Peter Jordan for page 70 (top left). 19 Magazine/Robert
Harding Syndication for page 9. Observer for page 84.
Photographers Library for page 76 (top left). Popperfoto for page
122. Rex features for pages 18 (top left) /Oxley (top centre), 78,
100, /Hartley/Beine 121, 124, 127 (centre) (top). RMN/H
Lewandowski for page 59 (bottom centre right, bottom left). Solo
Syndication for pages 62, /Evening Standard 86. Tony Stone for
pages /Lamb 32 (left centre), /Ed Pritchard 70 (bottom left), 74
(left) /Sarah Stone (right), /John Lawrence 76 (bottom right), 98
(centre left) /Geary (centre right) /Hilary Kavanagh (bottom
right). Telegraph Colour Library/VCI for page 76 (top right).
Universal Press Syndicate for page 112 (top right, bottom). John
Walmsley for page 63. Zefa for page 70 (bottom right, top right).

Picture research by Veena Holkar.

Designed by Clare Sleven, Route 56.

Illustrated by Tim Archbold, Mike Bambury, Philip Bannister,
Kathy Baxendale, Gary Benfield, John Bradley, Mark Draisey,
Susannah English, Tracy Fennell, David Frankland, Taurus Graphics,
Nick Harris, Rod Holt, Biz Hull, Carol Kemp, Frances Lloyd,
Bethan Matthews, Alan McGowan, Lester Meacham, Andrew Oliver,
Pantelis Palios, Geo Parkin, Chris Pavely, Stephen Player,
Johnathan Satchell, Mary Stubberfield, Katherine Walker, Bee Willey
and Gary Wing.

Cover illustration by Paul Wearing.

Author Acknowledgements

The author would like to express thanks and appreciation to:

- the editorial, design and production team for the new edition,
  especially Judith King, Dave Francis, Jo Stevenson,
  Alaric Cotter, Julie Howard and Yolanda Durham.

- the readers and reporters whose comments and criticisms
  proved invaluable in the development of this new edition, in
  particular Jackie Gresham, Jennifer Bartlett, Beth Neher,
  Sarah Reed and Loukas Ioannou.

- the following people for piloting and reporting on the
  materials for the original edition:
  Richard Acklam, Virginia Garcia, Hara Garoufalia-Middle,
  Sandra Klapsis, Cristina Leito, Tim Oswald, Jeremy Page,
  Sandra Possas, Carol Skinner, Emer Wall and Tricia Watts.

- the editorial, design and production team for the original edition,
  especially Howard Middle, Judith Cunningham, Nicola Witt,
  Delia Greenall, Thérèse Tobin, Hilary Fletcher, Penny Faux,
  Donna Wright and Alison Derbyshire.

Map of book/Contents

Map of book/Contents

*(P) indicates that students have to refer to the Pairwork section on pages 138–145

1 The Art of Deception

SPEAKING

Fashion survey

Ask other students these questions. How far does the class agree about fashion?

1 How important is being fashionable to you?

....

....

2 Which clothes do you like wearing most?

....

....

3 Do you dress up for formal occasions?

....

....

4 Do you ever have to wear things you hate?

....

....

5 Have you ever had arguments about clothes?

....

....

6 Which brands of clothes do you prefer?

....

....

7 Which nationalities do you think are the most/least fashionable?

....

....

VOCABULARY

Clothes and fashion

1 Find the odd one out in each case. There may be more than one answer!

Example: A scarf   B shawl   C gloves

1 **A** hat	**B** cap	**C** tie		
2 **A** skirt	**B** blouse	**C** shirt		
3 **A** vest	**B** socks	**C** tights	**D** stockings	
4 **A** boots	**B** sandals	**C** belt	**D** shoes	
5 **A** jacket	**B** pullover	**C** sweater		
6 **A** tracksuit	**B** suit	**C** trainers		
7 **A** striped	**B** purple	**C** patterned	**D** plain	**E** checked

2 In pairs, now label your dummies.

STUDENT A turn to page 138. STUDENT B turn to page 142.

3 Complete the words using one letter for each space.

1 Lipstick and eye-shadow are both kinds of m_ _ _-_ _.
2 That's a very s_ _ _ _ suit. Are you going for an interview?
3 These jeans are too t_ _ _ _. Have you got a bigger size?
4 I can hardly walk in these h_ _ _-h_ _ _ _ _ shoes.
5 Her clothes are so o_ _-f_ _ _ _ _ _ _ _; she should wear modern things.

LISTENING

Women's fashions since the 1950s

1 Look at the photographs of women in typical British fashions since the 1950s. Which ones do you like the most/the least?

2 Listen to the short descriptions and match them with the photographs. Which photo is missing? Can you draw the clothes?

☐A  ☐B  ☐C  ☐D

3 Listen again and follow the tapescript on page 153. Underline the ways in which the speaker:

• introduces what the women are wearing.
• gives opinions.

WRITING

Describing how someone is dressed

Study this written description of the woman dressed in the fashions of 1951. Use it as a model and write a short description of one of your classmates; then read it out and ask the others to guess who it is.

> She is formally dressed and looks terribly old-fashioned. She is wearing a matching skirt and jacket, a funny little hat, and high-heeled shoes; she is carrying a tiny bag. Her clothes look tight and uncomfortable.

SPEAKING

Look at the cartoon and put the speech bubbles in the right order to make a sensible conversation.

- How does Penny feel about Alex's clothes?
- Why is Alex proud of what he is wearing?
- Whose attitude do you agree with?

READING

The fashion fraud

You are going to read about a detective agency which exposes people who copy famous goods.

1 Read the text quickly and find out who Vincent, Gerry and Miguel are.

2 Read the text again and answer these questions.

1 How does the writer feel about faking fashion goods?
2 Why was Gerry's assignment dangerous?
3 What trap did Miguel set for Gerry?

3 Match each of the following headings **A–D** to the paragraphs you have read (**1–4**).

> **A** Risky business.
> **B** A fairer deal.
> **C** Don't be clever.
> **D** Fighting back.

1

In most markets you can buy fashion goods. They may look like the real thing and carry famous labels but nearly all are fake. But does this really matter if it means we can dress fashionably but cheaply? Don't we pay far too much for fashion goods anyway? Aren't the manufacturers of the genuine articles just exploiting our ridiculous snobbery?

2

Understandably, they don't agree and employ investigator Vincent Carratu to find out who is making the counterfeit goods. Carratu heads his own investigation agency specializing in this kind of crime. Once he knows who the criminals are, he pretends to be a buyer. When he has enough evidence, he contacts the police.

3

It is a dangerous game, so Carratu takes on as his agents ex-policemen with experience of undercover work. They need to be able to act and have nerves of steel, as this example shows. One of Carratu's agents, Gerry, was asked to look into a case involving imitation whisky. Gerry pretended to be a buyer for the American Mafia and made contact with the suppliers. In the meantime, the man who had told Carratu's agency about the factory disappeared. He had almost certainly been murdered by the counterfeiters. Yet, despite the obvious dangers, Gerry continued and persuaded the gang that his story was true.

4

But one member, Miguel, was still suspicious and set a trap. He asked Gerry how whisky was made. Naturally, Gerry knew all about the process but realized that the kind of criminal he was playing wouldn't know. 'How should I know?' he replied. 'I just drink the stuff.' At this, Miguel relaxed. There were no more problems and Gerry obtained information which led to the arrest of the entire network. This included customs officers and policemen! At last the counterfeiters had been taken in.

4 Word search

How many words can you find in the text which express the idea of 'authentic' and 'not authentic'?

VOCABULARY

Phrasal Verbs

1 Study these two sentences.

A *She **took** his photograph **in** the restaurant.*
B *... the counterfeiters had **been** **taken in**.*

In both sentences **take** appears followed by **in**. In sentence **A, in** is a preposition relating to the location. Here is another example of **take** followed by a preposition (**at**): He **took** the photograph **at** a party.

In sentence **B, take** and **in** belong together and express the special meaning of *to deceive* or *trick*. In English, many common verbs combine with prepositions and adverbs in this way to make 'phrasal verbs'.

2 Here are other phrasal verbs from the text and the unit. Match them up with their definitions on the right.

1 find out   A to try to find
2 get on with   B to make known a secret
3 take on   C to start to employ
4 give away   D to see or understand with difficulty
5 look for   E to learn or discover (a fact that was hidden)
6 make out   F to have a friendly relationship with

3 Decide whether the phrasal verbs in these sentences are used correctly or incorrectly.

1 He *found out* some money in the street.
2 She was *taken in* by his false promises.
3 He left home because he couldn't *get on with* his stepmother.
4 What a lovely hat! Where did you *look for* it?
5 The manager *took* him *on* because of his experience.
6 Smoking is bad for you. Why don't you *give it away*?
7 She *found out* that he was lying.
8 It was too dark to *make out* the sign in the distance.
9 He *got on* well *with* his parents.

4 Choose four phrasal verbs and make your own sentences.

LISTENING

handwritten notes in left margin:
- I demand: exijo ver al director.
  to see the manager
- I insist on + Gerundio seeing
  the manager.

Making complaints → to protest. pag 153.

1 Have you ever taken something back to a shop? How did you complain? Were you calm or did you get angry? Were you successful?

2 Colin is taking a sports shirt back to a store. He received it as a present. Listen for the answers to these questions:

1 What is the problem with the shirt?
2 Does he complain successfully?
3 How does he feel at the end?

3 Listen again and try to fill in the gaps in the dialogue. How does Colin introduce and support his complaint?

ASSISTANT:	Can I help you?
COLIN:	Yes, it's (1) .... this sports shirt. I washed it the other day. The colour ran and it shrank.
ASSISTANT:	Oh dear, I see. Do you have the (2) .... ?
COLIN:	I'm (3) ...., but it was in one of your bags.
ASSISTANT:	I'm sorry, (4) .... without a receipt.
COLIN:	(5) .... to the Manageress.
ASSISTANT:	Yes, of course. I'll fetch her for you.
MANAGERESS:	Are you the gentleman who brought this shirt in?
COLIN:	Yes, could you change it? It's (6) ....
MANAGERESS:	Where did you get it? Did you buy it here?
COLIN:	Actually it was a present from my girlfriend. Is (7) .... ?
MANAGERESS:	I'm afraid there is. You see, (8) ....
COLIN:	An imitation? Are you sure?
MANAGERESS:	I'm absolutely positive. The crocodile is even the wrong way round.
COLIN:	I don't know (9) ....
MANAGERESS:	Forget it. But if I (10) .... with my girlfriend!

4 🔲 Intonation in questions

Listen to these two questions again. What do you notice about their intonation patterns?

Where did you get it?   Did you buy it here?

VOCABULARY

Damage

Complete the sentences with the words from the box, which refer to damage.

scratched broken cracked stained torn → TO MAKE BAGS

1 I .... my new white blouse by spilling coffee all over it. It's ruined!
2 Oh, no! That's the third plate you've .... this week.
3 How did this book get .... ? You'll have to buy another one.
4 I'm never going to lend her my CDs again! Can you hear where this one has been .... ?
5 This cup is .... I wouldn't use it, if I were you.

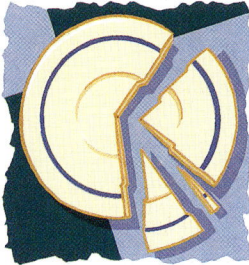

SPEAKING

Making complaints

1 Use these two situations to practise complaining and dealing with complaints.

Situation 1

STUDENT A A CD you bought recently is badly scratched. You haven't got a receipt, but you buy a lot of CDs from the shop.

STUDENT B You have just started working in the shop and don't know what to do. Ask about the receipt. Ask the customer to come back when the Manager is there.

Situation 2

STUDENT A A jacket you bought for £60 is badly stained. You think that someone has already worn it! You would like to keep it but you want some money back to compensate for the damage and to pay for cleaning it.

STUDENT B Examine the item the customer has brought back. Ask for the receipt. Apologize and work out a compromise.

2 How assertive are you? Discuss whether you would complain in these situations and what you would say.

1 You are in a restaurant. When your meal arrives, there is a hair on it.
2 You are on a train in the middle of summer. An old man gets into your carriage and shuts the window. It is extremely hot.
3 You are on a bus. Smoking is prohibited, but a man near you lights a cigarette.
4 You have been queuing in the bank for ten minutes. When it is your turn, someone says, 'Excuse me, I'm in a hurry,' and pushes in front of you.
5 You are in a café. You ordered a glass of mineral water, but when it arrives, you are sure it is ordinary water from the tap.

LANGUAGE STUDY

Tense review

Kirsten is from Sweden. She is working as an au pair for Mr and Mrs Graham, who live in London. She is writing to her German friend, Monika, who is a shop assistant in Newcastle.

1 Quickly read Kirsten's letter and think of a suitable title for her story.
2 Go through it, putting the verbs in italics into a suitable form.

17 Linwood Terrace
London N8 7TW

Dear Monika,

It was so nice to hear from you again. I hope you (1) *get on* better with your boss, she (2) *sound* terrible. If I (3) *be* you I (4) *leave* and come to London. If I (5) *ask* Mrs Graham, she (6) *find* an English family which (7) *need* an au pair.

I (8) *have* a difficult time lately. You (9) *remember* my old boyfriend Victor? Well, yesterday he (10) *send* to prison for (11) *steal* money from foreign girls like us. He (12) *know* I (13) *want be* a model. He (14) *say* he (15) *have* lots of contacts in Paris. After I (16) *give* him money (17) *buy* plane tickets he disappeared. I (18) *think* I (19) *never see* him again. Then one day, I (20) *walk* along Oxford Street when I (21) *see* him with a

Japanese girl. He left, and I introduced myself to her. I (22) *tell* her my story, and at first she (23) *think* I (24) *lie* but I (25) *manage* convince her.

She (26) *tell* the police where he (27) *live* and they (28) *find* a diary full of the names of the girls he (29) *take in* already. If I (30) *know* what he (31) *be* like I (32) *never give* him a penny! I (33) *not trust* another man for a long time!

Anyway, I must go now. I (34) *pick up* the children from school in ten minutes. They (35) *finish* at 4 p.m. every day. I (36) *write* again soon. Be careful.

Love,

Kirsten

P.S. Hope you like my latest photo!

3 Search the letter and find an example of: EXAM

1 the present simple	7 conditional sentences
2 the present continuous	8 the passive
3 the present/past perfect	9 reported speech
4 the past simple	10 constructions using
5 the past continuous	• the infinitive
6 the simple future	• the gerund

Which areas do you find the most difficult?

WRITING

Opening and closing letters (EXAM).

1 Match suitable opening and closing expressions.

D 1 Dear Mum and Dad,   A Yours faithfully,
C 2 Dear Colin and Alan,   B Yours sincerely,
B 3 Dear Mr and Mrs Green,   C With best wishes,
A 4 Dear Sir or Madam,   D Lots of love,

2 Which opening and closing expressions would you use in a letter to:

1 an old school friend?   3 a government department?
2 the head teacher of your school?   4 friends of your parents?

3 Look at Kirsten's letter and find out:

1 where she puts her address.   2 where she puts her signature.

4 Can you find any expressions which would be useful for informal letters?

Example: *It was so nice to hear from you again.*

5 Practice

In her letter, Kirsten tells Monika about her ex-boyfriend, Victor. Write Monika's reply based on the picture story.

Dear Kirsten,

Thank you for your letter – I got it this morning. It made me feel much happier. Please ask Mrs Graham if she can find me a job as an au pair. I want to leave the shop where I am working. The owner is mean and bossy. Your story about Victor is terrible. But let me describe something funny which happened to me...

LAST SATURDAY AT THE DISCO — TOP MODEL — CHAMPION CYCLIST — MONDAY FASHIONS — WINDOW CLEANER — FASHION SALES ASSISTANT — LAUGHED ABOUT IT

So, Kirsten, you aren't the only person to have been taken in!

Love, Monika

LISTENING

A 'Mentalist Act'

Arthur Cross, once a magician's assistant to the 'Great Marvella', is describing one of the acts they performed. The 'Great Marvella' is standing on the stage in the picture. She is wearing a blindfold to stop her from seeing. Listen to the interview and complete the notes.

The mentalist act was a kind of (1) ....
Marvella had to (2) .... of objects while wearing a blindfold.
Members of the audience gave Arthur things like
(3a) .... and (3b) ....
The main reason the act worked was because Marvella could (4) .... !
Arthur helped Marvella by spelling names by
(5) ....
If his head was on the left the object (6) ....
If both arms were bent the object had (7) .... in it.
Arthur tried to mislead the audience by (8) ....
The act worked successfully (9) .... % of the time.
If the act didn't work, Marvella said (10) ....

LANGUAGE STUDY

After and afterwards

1 Study this example from the listening passage.

FIRST ACTION	SECOND ACTION
I put the blindfold on her.	**Afterwards** I went into the audience.

2 Look at these ways of expressing the same thing.

I put the blindfold on her. I went into the audience afterwards.

- *After **I had put** it on her, I went into the audience.*
  After + PAST PERFECT

- *After **putting** it on her, I went into the audience.*
  After + VERB + -ing

- *I put it on her; **after that** I went into the audience.*
  After that + PAST SIMPLE

WRONG: ~~I put it on her, after I went into the audience.~~

It is also possible to say:
*I put it on her **and (then)** I went into the audience.*

3 Practice

Here are some other things the 'Great Marvella' did. Use the ways you have been shown to put them in sequence.

	FIRST ACTION	SECOND ACTION
1	she ate fire	she cut Arthur in half
2	she threw knives	she caught a bullet between her teeth

WRITING

How to perform a trick

Here are Arthur's instructions for the famous trick 'How to make a rabbit appear out of a hat.'

1 Complete the text using the expressions in the box.

> what you do is this   now this is the tricky bit   after that   obviously   and then   first of all   the following   now all you have to do

'You'll need (1) .... for the trick: a rabbit, a chair with a solid back, a top hat and a bag held loosely together by a piece of string. (2) ...., put the rabbit very carefully into the bag. (3) .... hang the bag from a nail on the back of the chair. Make sure that the rabbit is comfortable and that its paws are inside the bag. And now for the trick. (4) .... Invite a member of the audience up on the stage, let him examine the hat, (5) .... ask him to sit down on the chair. (6) ....! As he is sitting down, pass the hat round the back of the chair, lifting the bag with the rabbit into the hat. (7) ...., the audience will be watching the person sitting down, not you! The bag will now open automatically. (8) .... is give the hat to your 'guest' and wait for his reaction.

2 Giving instructions

Look at the pictures and expand the notes to write a simple card trick.

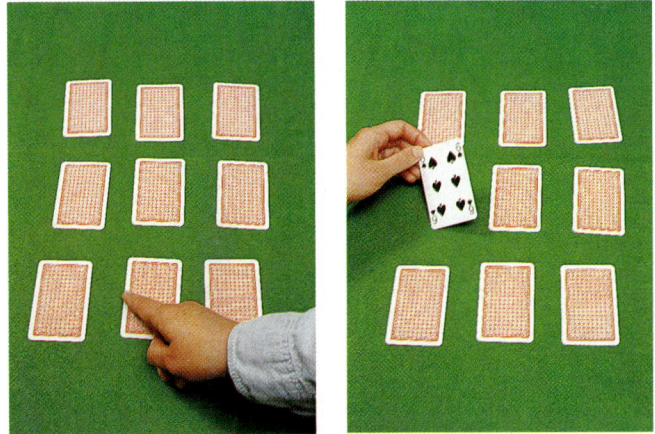

Need an assistant. Nine cards in three rows, face down. Invite member of audience to help you. You leave room. Person chooses card, turns it over and looks at it. You come back. Ask if person has chosen a card. As you ask, watch assistant. Assistant casually places finger on any card to show position of card chosen (e.g. if top right card chosen, assistant touches top right hand corner of card). You close eyes. Think hard. Turn correct card over!

2 Film Fantasy

1 Look at the scenes from different types of film. Match the words with the pictures.

| a western   a thriller   a cartoon   a comedy   a musical   a love story |
| a documentary   a horror story   an adventure   a science fiction film |

2 Main stress in words

Listen to the film types on tape and copy the pronunciation. Then listen again and decide in each case where the main stress is.

Example: Western Oo (two syllables; main stress on first one.)

Think of a film title for each film type.
- What's your favourite type of film?
- Are there any kinds of film that you can't stand?
- Now find out from your classmates what their preferences are.

LISTENING

Organizing an evening out

1 Annabel, Rick and Martin are discussing what to do this evening. Listen to their conversation and answer the questions by writing **A** (for Annabel), **M** (for Martin) and **R** (for Rick) in the boxes.

1 Who suggests having a meal? ☐
2 Who has already seen Robocop? ☐
3 Who wants to change? ☐
4 Who offers something to eat? ☐
5 Who can borrow a car? ☐

2 Listen again and try to complete the tapescript.

ANNABEL: What (1) .... this evening? Have you got any ideas, Martin?

MARTIN: (2) .... go out for a meal? Or maybe we (3) .... go and see a film. What about you, Rick?

RICK: I think I (4) .... go to the cinema.

ANNABEL: So would I.

MARTIN: OK. That's fine by me. (5) .... ?

ANNABEL: Well, there's (6) .... It's (7) .... science fiction thriller.

RICK: Mm, I know. It's great but I've already seen it.

MARTIN: Well, (8) .... go and see *Back to the* (9) .... then.

ANNABEL: That (10) .... a good idea, Martin. I haven't seen it yet.

RICK: (11) .... I. I really enjoyed the first two.

ANNABEL: Look. It's 6 o'clock now and the film doesn't start until 8.30. I'm going home to change.

MARTIN: ... and I'd like to get something to eat!

RICK: Me, too. Why (12) .... for a snack?

MARTIN: Thanks, Rick that (13) ....

RICK: What about you, Annabel?

ANNABEL: Thanks for the offer, but (14) .... and change first. But I can pick you up at Rick's place in my parents' car, if I can borrow it. (15) .... 7.45 be OK?

RICK: Great. We'll see you then. (16) .... if there's a problem?

ANNABEL: I promise. See you later then. 'Bye.

3 Making suggestions and agreeing

What words and expressions are used:
- to ask for and make suggestions?
- to agree with what has just been said?

4 📼 Pronunciation: **don't you/could you**

Listen to the pronunciation of these two sentences again and practise saying them.
Why **don't‿you** come back to my place?
Could‿you give us a ring if there's a problem?

SPEAKING

Complete the telephone conversation between Pat and Jo using the prompts.

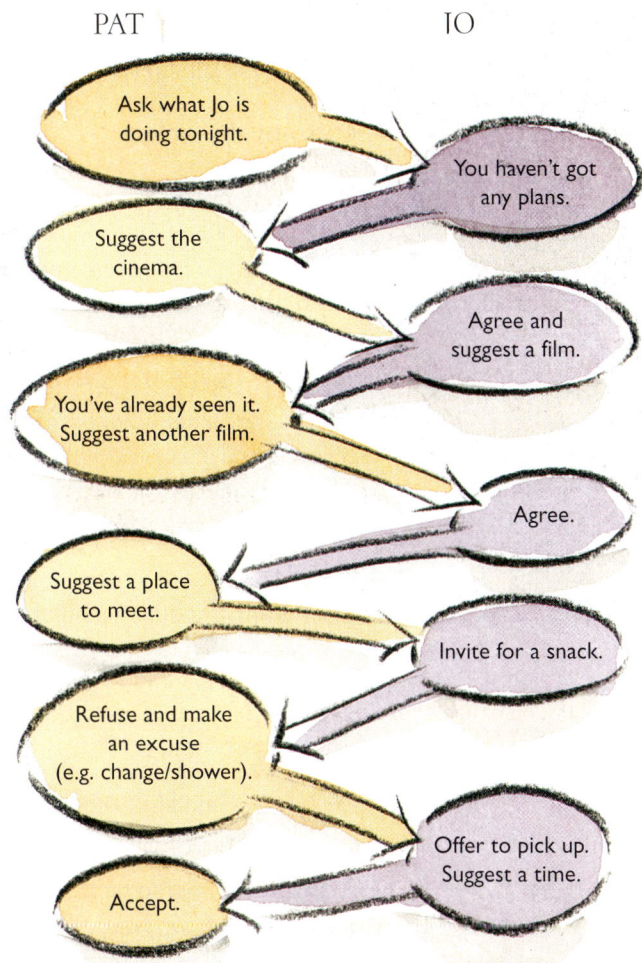

PAT   JO

Ask what Jo is doing tonight.

You haven't got any plans.

Suggest the cinema.

Agree and suggest a film.

You've already seen it. Suggest another film.

Agree.

Suggest a place to meet.

Invite for a snack.

Refuse and make an excuse (e.g. change/shower).

Offer to pick up. Suggest a time.

Accept.

LANGUAGE STUDY

Revision of past forms

1 There are many irregular verbs in English. Revise your knowledge of common irregular verbs by completing the table on page 146, which includes the **infinitive, past simple** and **past participle** forms. When you are sure it is correct, you can use it for reference.

2 Complete this biography of Walt Disney's early career by changing the verbs in italics into the past simple.

Walt Disney (1) *be* born on December 5th, 1901. In his teens he (2) *begin* an art course but World War 1 (3) *break* out and he (4) *drive* for the Red Cross in Europe. When he (5) *get* back to America he (6) *meet* the artist Ub Iwerks and they (7) *go* into business together.

They (8) *make* a series of short cartoons but (9) *lose* all their money. Luckily, Walt's brother Roy (10) *give* him more to start up again. The first talking picture (11) *come* out in 1927 and Disney (12) *see* that sound (13) *hold* the key to the future of film.

He (14) *build* on this success with other cartoons but soon (15) *feel* ready for something more ambitious. He (16) *take* the biggest risk of his career and (17) *spend* a fortune on a full-length cartoon.

He finally (18) *bring* out 'Snow White' in 1935, which the public (19) *pay* millions of dollars to see. By the time he was 40, Disney and his creations (20) *be* household names around the world.

LISTENING

Cartoon characters

1 Two popular cartoon series in English-speaking countries are *Tom and Jerry* and *The Flintstones*. The first one is about a cat and mouse who are always having violent arguments. The second one is based around two Stone Age families, the Flintstones and the Rubbles. What are they called in your country?

2 Three friends, Rachel, John and Barry, are talking about cartoon characters. Rachel has just read an article about Mickey Mouse, the most famous one of all. Listen to their conversation and answer the questions by deciding who says what. Write **R** (for Rachel), **J** (for John) and **B** (for Barry) in the boxes. Who ......

1 used to like Tom and Jerry the best? ☐
2 believes cartoon characters can have a bad influence on children? ☐
3 agrees that cartoon characters do develop over the years? ☐
4 describes the early character of Mickey Mouse? ☐
5 wants to know more about the changes to Mickey? ☐
6 suggests the changes make Mickey look more attractive and appealing ? ☐

3 Listen again and complete the notes and table about the way Mickey has changed.

1 Changes in character
   Before he used to be ....; nowadays he is ....
2 Changes in appearance

	face	eyes	nose
before: now:			

LANGUAGE STUDY

Uses of **used to**

1 Two meanings of *used to*

Rachel says: *I **used to watch** The Flintstones when I was a kid.*
             used to + VERB

John says: *We're not **used to (seeing)** that kind of **Mickey** these days.*
             used to (+ VERB + -ing) + NOUN or PRONOUN

Which sentence describes a present habit? Which one describes a past habit? Which form of **used to** acts as an adjective?

2 Pronunciation of *used to*

Listen to the two sentences again and try to copy the model. What do you notice about the pronunciation of **used to**?

3 How would you make short answers to these two questions?

• Did you use to watch *The Flintstones?* – No, ...
• Are you used to watching a lot of TV? – Yes, ...

4 Study the sentences and change one of the verbs in brackets into **used to + do**, and the other into **be used to + -ing**.

1 In the old days, directors .... (make films) in black and white. These days, we are so .... (see) films in colour that black and white films seem strange.
2 Nowadays, film stars .... (have) stunt men doing anything dangerous. Actors from the 40s and 50s like Kirk Douglas always .... (do) their own.
3 Before television was invented, people .... (go) out to the cinema a lot. Nowadays, they .... (watch) video recordings at home on TV.
4 That restaurant is owned by an actress who .... (be) a famous film star in the 1960s. These days, people in the movie business .... (eat) lunch there.
5 When she first became a star, she .... (run) away if photographers saw her, now she .... (be photographed) and doesn't take any notice.
6 Didn't she .... (be called) Mavis Brown? That's right, but she changed her name to Lola Lamont when she became famous. Now, she .... people (call) her Lola.

SPEAKING

An interview with Chris Caine

Work in pairs.
STUDENT A is Chris Caine, the famous Hollywood movie star (turn to page 138).

STUDENT B is a journalist from *Mondo Movie* magazine (turn to page 142).

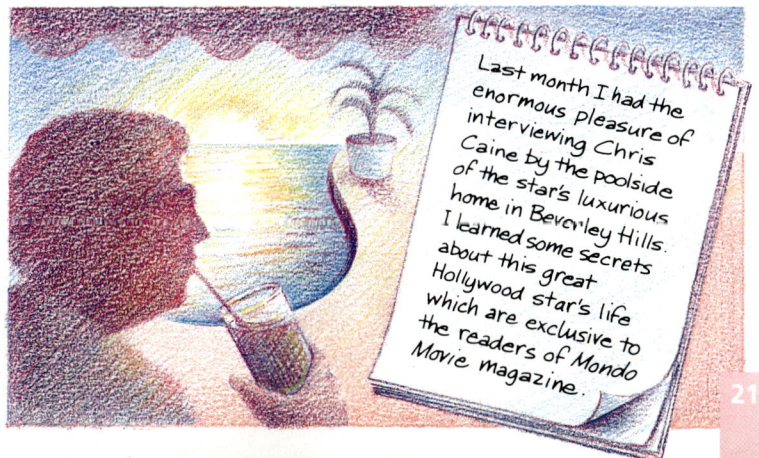

WRITING

A magazine article

Write an article about Chris Caine for *Mondo Movie* magazine. Try to include the different uses of **used to** which have been introduced. Begin the article like this:

Last month I had the enormous pleasure of interviewing Chris Caine by the poolside of the star's luxurious home in Beverley Hills. I learned some secrets about this great Hollywood star's life which are exclusive to the readers of Mondo Movie magazine.

SPEAKING

Look at the photograph of Maxine Guest. What do you think her job is?
Try to describe the picture in as much detail as you can.

READING

1 Skim read the article and see if your assumptions about Maxine were right.

2 The four sentences below (**A–D**) have been taken out of the text. Read the text carefully and decide where they belong in the gaps (**1–4**).

2 **A** Despite its versatility, plasticine is difficult stuff to control.

3 **B** Animators often use mirrors because they need to study the way their mouths make a sound before adjusting the model.

1 **C** Unlike cartoonists who work in two dimensions, Aardman work in three.

4 **D** Once they are completed, the job is far from over.

One of the most famous characters on British TV is Douglas who advertises butter. Douglas is just five inches high and made of plasticine. Yes, that's right, plasticine, the stuff children make models from. However, there is nothing childish about Aardman Animations, the company responsible. Their work has won them three Oscars® and many other awards. **1** C The same principle guides both techniques: tiny changes are made to each drawing or model before every photograph. A forty second advertisement is made up of a thousand frames of film. When the shots are run together at twenty-five frames a second, the brain believes it is watching real action. Maxine Guest is a modelmaker ar Aardman. Maxine has been making models ever since she finished her studies in theatre design. At Aardman, she is responsible for producing the prototypes and solving technical problems. Some are such a challenge, she lies awake at night. Others are simpler to solve: when people say a model keeps falling over she tells them to put metal plates under its feet and place it on a magnetic floor!

2 A Models are built around metal frames in order to keep them rigid. Douglas has joints so that his arms bend just like a real person's. One of the most complicated creations is the *Chewits* sweet commercial monster which has a latex rubber body, eyes that roll, a tongue that flicks in and out and claws that can be moved. That's why he seems so realistic.

Aardman often works with advertising agencies. First of all, the agency presents the story behind the commercial in simple pictures. After that, Aardman takes over to produce an 'animatic', i.e. an animated sequence of drawings showing the moves the characters will make. Depending on their number and complexity, it takes between two and eight weeks to produce all the models. **3** B Animators choreograph the model's movements on sets using the animatic as a guide. They are also given a soundtrack. Making the characters 'speak' poses enormous technical problems. Pablo the parrot has twenty different beaks to represent each different sound he makes. **4** D Just three or four seconds of film can take a day to produce and afterwards it has to be carefully cut and edited. Maxine and the others often have to wait months before finally seeing the finished film on TV or at the cinema. When she hears the laughter and admiration it inspires, she feels it has been worth the wait.

WRITING

1 Imagine you are interviewing an expert about Maxine and Aardman Animations. You are given the answers, what would the questions be?

Q: Could I ask you some questions about Aardman animations and Maxine Guest?
A: Of course, go ahead.
Q: How ..... *had been? recognised their production?*
A: Very successful, their films have won three Oscars®.
Q: What ..... *are made? The main material of the animations?*
A: They are are made of plasticine.
Q: How many ..... *frames are? There in a forty second advert?*
A: A thousand.
Q: How ..... *long has she make models?*
A: Ever since she finished her studies in theatre design.
Q: What ..... *are her? responsibilities in the co.?*
A: She produces the prototypes and solves problems.

2 In pairs, make similar questions and answers based around the last paragraph of the text.

LANGUAGE STUDY

Sequencing/Reason and purpose

1 In Unit 1, you looked at ways of putting actions into a sequence. Look again at the second paragraph of the text about Aardman Animations and Maxine Guest and find the words and expressions which are used for sequencing.

2 Read the paragraph once again and find the words and expressions which introduce a reason or a purpose.

3 Using the expression in **bold type**, rewrite these sentences without changing their meaning.

Example: Chris was so nervous that she was always sick.
because
She was always sick because she was so nervous.

1 Chris went to Hollywood because she wanted to develop her career. *THAT'S WHY*
that's why
2 She wasn't used to driving on the right; that's why she had so many accidents. *BECAUSE*
because
3 She slept in car parks because she wanted to save money.
in order to
4 She's studying very hard because she wants to pass the exam. *so THAT*
so that

4 Study these two sentence patterns. When do we use **such** and when do we use **so**?

a *Some are* **such** *a challenge* **that** *she lays awake at night.*
b *Some are* **so** *challenging* **that** *she lays awake at night.*

RULES { *SO + ADJ or ADV.* *SUCH + ADJ + NOUN*
SUCH + A NOUN.

5 Complete the second sentence so that it means the same as the one above it.

1 The film was so sad that it made us miserable.
such
It ..... film it made us miserable.
2 He gave such a loud scream that everybody jumped.
loudly *screamed so loudly*
He ..... that everybody jumped.
3 It was such a funny film that she laughed until she cried.
because *because it was*
She laughed until she cried ..... funny.
4 There was so much violence that they banned the film.
such *because it's such a*
It was banned ..... violent film.
5 He isn't a famous actor any more.
be *used to be*
He ..... a famous actor.
6 She still finds it strange to sign her autograph.
used *used to signing*
She still is ..... her autograph.
7 They went to Hollywood because they wanted to become film stars.
order *In order to*
They went to Hollywood ..... become film stars.

READING

Describing a film

1 Gary Boorman is on a TV show talking about classic films from the 1980s. Read what he says and match the picture with the right part of the text.

2 Complete the text below by using: **when, who, whose, why, which** and **where**. Which of these words are used to replace: people, things and animals, times, places and reasons?

[handwritten annotations: Possesive Pronoun. where. what. who. whose. which. when.]

3 Word search

Which of the words highlighted in **bold** type in the text means:
- the story? *plot.*
- a person in the story played by an actor? *Character.*
- where (and when) the story happens? *is set in small town in U.S.*
- the words the actors learn? *script.*
- the 'good guy'? *hero.*
- the 'bad guy'? *Villian.*

WRITING

You are going to describe your favourite film.
First of all, use the description of *Back to the Future* as a model and make notes about:
- the name of your favourite film.
- the stars.
- the kind of film.
- where/when it is set.
- the characters (e.g. the hero/heroine/villain).
- the plot.
- the script
- anything special about the film e.g. special effects.

Which tense are you mostly going to use to describe what happens?

'One of my favourite films is *Back to the Future,* (1) ...*Which*... stars Michael J Fox. It's a kind of comedy adventure and science fiction film, (2) *Which* **is set in** a small town in the US. It opens in a house in the suburbs, (3) ...*where*... the **hero**, Marty McFly, lives with his family. Marty's father, George, is a silly man (4) ...*Who*... laughs at old TV comedies, his mother, (5) ...*Whose*... name is Lorraine, is dull and unattractive and a terrible housewife. The **villain** of the film is George's boss Biff, (6) ...*who*... is used to pushing him around. The other main **character** is Dr Emmet Brown, (7) ...*Who*... has invented a time machine (8) ...*Which*... is made from an old sports car. Dr Brown has a dog (9) ...*Which*... is called Einstein.

Marty gets into the car and, by accident, is transported back to 1955, the year (10) ...*where*... his parents fell in love. He meets his father George, (11) ...*Who*... even then is being bullied by Biff. However, Marty fights Biff and his gang and makes fools of them. He also meets his mother, (12) ...*Who*... used to be slim and beautiful. George is madly in love with her and would like to take her to the college dance, but he is such an idiot that no girl will take him seriously.

Marty finds a photograph he has brought from the future and notices that his brother and sister are starting to disappear. This is (13) ...*Why*... he has to make sure that his parents really do get together; otherwise he won't be born!

The rest of the film revolves around how he can bring them together at the dance (14) ...*Where*... they are supposed to fall in love. I won't say anything else because I don't want to spoil it for you if you haven't seen it. All I will say is that the **plot** is clever, the **script** is funny and the acting and special effects brilliant. I highly recommend it to you.'

LISTENING

People in films

1 Look at the list (**A–G**) of people who work in films and find them in the pictures.

A star ☐4   B stuntman/woman ☐5   C cameraman/woman ☐2   D producer ☐⊞
E extra ☐6   F director ☐1   G scriptwriter ☐3

What are their duties and responsibilities?
Which one would you most/least like to be?

2 Listen to the seven people (**A–G**) speak. They were all involved in the film 'Angela' . Decide the order they speak in by writing a number (**1–7**) in the box after each one.

3 Listen to each speaker again and decide which answer (**A or B**) is correct.

1 What does the director want the actors to concentrate on?
Ⓐ Getting the emotions right. *correct .* ✓
B Getting the actions right. ✗

2 Why was the camera shot difficult?
Ⓐ It lasted a long time. ✓ *2 day took a night.*
B There were lots of cameras to organise. ✗

3 What was the scriptwriter's big difficulty?
Ⓐ Making Angela's actions appear logical.
B Making Angela an exciting character. ✓

Leading man = = main actor

4 What was the most difficult thing for the actress?
Ⓐ The actor she played opposite? ✓
B The character of Angela?

5 What does the stuntwoman think about her profession?
Ⓐ People like her will always be needed. ✓
B Technology will eventually replace them. ✗

6 The extra appears in films …
A just for fun. ✗
Ⓑ because he wants to be a star. ✓

7 The producer...
A smokes a lot.
Ⓑ realises people don't like him. ✗ *He's the man that everybody love to hate.*

3 Great Escapes

SPEAKING

Look at the sequence of pictures and make notes of what is happening, then, in pairs, tell the story.

Tara the Tarantula

LANGUAGE STUDY

Prepositions of position and direction

1 Study these prepositions and the illustrations showing their meaning.

2 Revise prepositions of position and direction by completing the text on page 147.

3 Complete this paragraph by deciding which preposition is right in each case.

It was exactly four o'clock when she woke up. She jumped quickly (1) *outside/out* of bed, got dressed and looked (2) *across/through* the window. It was a cold winter's day and snow lay (3) *at/on* the ground. She then took her best clothes (4) *out of/off* her wardrobe and put them (5) *onto/into* her small, dusty old suitcase which was leaning (6) *onto/against* the wall. She took the money which she kept (7) *inside/into* an empty chocolate box hidden (8) *between/against/among* the wardrobe and the wall and put it (9) *to/into* her pocket. She took a note for her parents (10) *out/out of/outside* a drawer and placed it (11) *into/onto* her dressing table. Carefully, she opened the door and crept (12) *by/along* the corridor, (13) *past/behind* her parents' room and (14) *along/down* the dark staircase (15) *onto/into* the hall. She made her way (16) *at/into/towards* the back door and opened it. Closing it quietly (17) *in front of/behind* her, she moved silently (18) *through/across/down* the garden and climbed (19) *under/over/through* the low garden gate. For a few seconds, she stood (20) *from/at/on* the gate and looked back at the sleeping house. Then she turned and walked quickly away to begin a new life.

LISTENING

🔊 **She's leaving home**

Read the completed text, listen to the song and think about these questions.

1 Why is the girl leaving home?
2 Do you think she feels guilty?
3 How old do you think she is?
4 Where is she going?
5 How do her parents react?
6 Do they think they have been good parents?

READING

A bowl of macaroni

1 Read the first paragraph of the text and find out why Casanova was in prison.

2 Look at the objects above and imagine how they helped him escape. Then read the text to check your answers.

3 Read the text again and try to imagine his escape route.

4 Word search

The writer of the text uses certain adjectives and verbs which add to the drama of the escape. Find the words that mean:

Para. 1   famous in a bad way
Para. 2   very angry
Para. 3   clever like a fox
          to move something to another place illegally
Para. 4   to move along on your hands and knees
          to walk slowly and silently to avoid detection
Para. 5   to look very closely
          to walk purposefully, with big steps

Giovanni Giacomo Casanova, history's greatest lover, was extremely nervous. He wasn't waiting for his latest conquest or hiding from an angry husband. Instead he was waiting for the beginning of his greatest adventure: escape from a notorious Venetian prison. In his youth he had written a book which attacked the church. This gave his many enemies an excellent excuse for arresting him and locking him up. Now, fifteen months later, he was ready to win back his freedom ...

Since the beginning of his captivity he had been planning to escape. He managed to obtain a piece of iron which he sharpened into a spike, which he then used to dig a hole in his cell floor. Just when he was about to make his attempt, he was moved to another cell. Inevitably, his furious jailer discovered the hole, but somehow

5 Read the text carefully and decide which of the choices (**A** or **B**) is the best answer to the following questions. Be ready to explain why one of the choices is wrong.

1   What happened when Casanova was moved?
A   His tunnel was found.
B   His jailor reported the escape attempt to the prison governor.

2   Why did Casanova involve Balbi in his plans?
A   Balbi was freer to act.
B   To divert the attention of the guards.

3   How did Casanova and Balbi communicate?
A   By tapping messages on the wall.
B   Through notes.

Casanova managed to keep him quiet. Casanova realised there would be no further opportunity of tunnelling his way out, as his new cell was now regularly searched. Casanova was still determined to escape, but realized he would have to involve someone else in his plans. This person was a monk called Balbi, a prisoner in the cell next door. They managed to plan their escape via messages written in invisible ink made from fruit juice.

One day Casanova asked the jailer to deliver a huge bible to Balbi as a present, together with a large dish of macaroni. The jailer was so busy trying not to spill the macaroni that he didn't notice how heavy the Bible was. The crafty Casanova had managed to smuggle the spike hidden in the book's cover!

Now the waiting was over. On the night of October 31st, 1756, Casanova saw Balbi's hand appear through a hole in the ceiling. The monk had cut through the ceiling of his own cell, crawled along the attic, then made a hole in Casanova's ceiling. Balbi now pulled Casanova up beside him. Together, they succeeded in lifting one of the heavy lead roof-tiles and, with a rope made from knotted bedsheets, crept along the moonlit rooftops looking for a way down. By chance, they came across a window which led directly into the empty Palace. Casanova changed into a suit of elegant clothes he had brought with him. Unfortunately, as he peered out of one of the windows, somebody from below noticed him. A palace keeper unlocked the main door to find out what was going on. Realizing this was their only chance of escape, Casanova and Balbi strode past him and made for the waterfront, where they got a gondola to freedom. Casanova claims that he spent his first night hiding in the Chief of Police's house while the poor man was out searching for him!

4 Casanova presented Balbi with the bowl of macaroni
A to distract the jailer.
B because he had hidden something inside it.

5 When did the escape take place?
A In total darkness.
B After physical hard work.

6 What happened soon after their escape?
A Balbi was quickly recaptured.
B Casanova showed how crafty and disrespectful he could be.

LANGUAGE STUDY

The infinitive and the gerund

Casanova **managed to keep** him quiet.
... they **succeeded in lifting** one of the roof-tiles.

1 Study the two lists of common verbs. The ones in the first list always take the infinitive and those in the second always take the gerund.

Infinitive: manage, pretend, offer, promise, hope, plan
Gerund: succeed in, consider, deny, look forward to, avoid, risk

2 Now use one of these verbs in the correct form to complete each of the following sentences.

1 She finally .... to escape by stealing a key.
2 He .... to carry the old man's suitcase.
3 I've never been to France before. I'm .... going there next year.
4 They .... reaching the frontier the following day.
5 She realized that she .... breaking a leg if she jumped from the window, but she knew there was no other choice.
6 Her mother made her .... to write home every week.
7 It was nice to see you. I .... to see you again soon.
8 When he gets out of prison, he .... to travel.
9 I would like you to .... working for me.
10 He .... stealing the car, although a witness saw him.
11 Give up smoking if you want to .... getting a cough.
12 He .... to be asleep, but in fact he heard everything they said.

VOCABULARY

Phrasal verbs

1 In the listening exercise on page 31 you will hear six new phrasal verbs. They are in **bold type** in this paragraph. From their context, work out which ones mean:

> to leave   to recover consciousness   to finish
> to arrive   to begin suddenly   to escape

War had **broken out** in the desert kingdom and we realized that we had to **get away**. Amanda **turned up** at my apartment three hours late, so we immediately got the car and **set off** across the desert. Soon, our petrol supply **ran out**, but we managed to beg some from a passing lorry. We were within sight of the border, when there was a sudden, loud bang and everything went black. When I **came round**, night had fallen and Amanda was watching over me with a worried expression. It was then that I realized we had driven over a landmine.

2 Complete these sentences by using each phrasal verb once.

1 He is still unconscious; I'll call you when he ....
2 She was so unhappy at home that she just had to ....
3 If you .... late, you won't be allowed into the concert.
4 We'll have to .... really early to catch the ferry.
5 Just use a cheque if your cash ....
6 A flu epidemic has .... at work; I hope I don't catch it.

LANGUAGE STUDY

Subjects, verbs and objects

English verbs are transitive, intransitive or both transitive and intransitive. A transitive verb *must* take a direct object.

Example: *We*   *got*   *the car*.
          SUBJECT   VERB   OBJECT

Get is a transitive verb, so *We got.* by itself is wrong.

Fall is an intransitive verb, so we can say: *Night had fallen.*

Drive is transitive and intransitive, so we can say:
We drove the car. and *We drove over a landmine.*

We cannot use intransitive verbs in the passive.

The phrasal verbs you have just looked at are all intransitive.

Handwritten notes at top:
α I / S took the pen → The pen was taken (by me)
to be + past participle

wait a minute = Hang on a minute.

A narrow escape

1 Key words

The words in the box will help you understand the listening text. In what kind of context would you expect to find words like these?

Handwritten: disturbis.

protest   troublemaker   shield   stadium
exit   police   confusion   violence   riot

2 In pairs or small groups find out:

• if anyone ever goes to pop concerts.
• if pop concerts are good value for money.
• if pop concerts can ever be dangerous.

3 Listen once to get the main points.

Whose fault do you think the riot was?

4 Listen again and decide whether these statements are **true** or **false**.

1 Janice was on holiday. *F She was studying in Rome Italian two years ago.*
2 The concert was outside. *F. in Indoor Stadium*
3 Some people were protesting about the price of entertainment. *T*
4 All the empty seats were taken. *T*
5 The riot police had been at the stadium from the beginning. *F*
6 The riot police blocked off every exit. *F*
7 Some of the audience had come prepared for a fight. *T*
8 The riot police started the violence. *F*
9 Janice was hurt. *F = because she said almost = casi*
10 Janice couldn't understand what one of the policemen said. *T*

Handwritten right margin:
"tear gas" = gas
biru nogas.

The police talked her in Italian and then she answered in English.

5 Speaking

In pairs or small groups, discuss:
• whether you believe Janice's version of the story.
• what you think a representative from the police would say.
• whether this type of event has ever taken place in your country.

1989 to hide = gaardene

The Wall

1 Until the Berlin Wall came down, many East Germans tried to escape into the West. In pairs or small groups, look at the photographs and discuss how people may have succeeded in escaping.

2 Since German unification, Berlin has become a destination for 'weekend escapes'. Look at the brochure and, in groups, work out a plan of how you would spend a weekend there, arriving on Friday evening and leaving on Sunday evening.

SIGHTSEEING YOU SHOULD VISIT THE BRANDENBURG GATE, SO LONG CUT OFF FROM THE WEST. IF YOU LIKE WILDLIFE, VISIT THE WORLD'S BIGGEST ZOO IN THE TIERGARTEN PARK. NO VISIT TO BERLIN WOULD BE COMPLETE WITHOUT GOING THROUGH CHECKPOINT CHARLIE, WHERE PEOPLE USED TO PASS FROM EAST TO WEST. YOU'LL ALSO FIND THERE THE LITTLE HOUSE, A MUSEUM DEDICATED TO THOSE WHO HAVE ESCAPED FROM THE EAST. CHARLOTTENBURG PALACE IS A VERY FINE EXAMPLE OF BAROQUE ARCHITECTURE, AND THERE ARE MANY FASCINATING MUSEUMS AND ART GALLERIES.

EATING OUT BERLIN OFFERS EVERYTHING, FROM GREEK AND TURKISH CUISINE TO ITALIAN, INDIAN AND BALKAN. COFFEE AND CAKES - *KAFFEE UND KUCHEN* - ARE A MUST!

SHOPPING FOR SHOPPING, VISIT BERLIN'S MAGNIFICENT KURFÜRSTENDAMM. BARGAIN-HUNTERS CAN SPEND HOURS EXPLORING THE CITY'S FASCINATING FLEA-MARKETS AND NUMEROUS ANTIQUE AND SECOND-HAND BOOKSHOPS.

NIGHTLIFE AFTER A HARD DAY'S SHOPPING, WHAT BETTER THAN ONE OF BERLIN'S NIGHT SPOTS? THOSE NEAR THE KURFÜRSTENDAMM ARE QUITE PRICEY BUT THERE ARE CHEAPER ONES IN KREUZBERG AND SCHÖNEBERG.

LISTENING

Booking by telephone

Mrs Roberts is telephoning a travel agent to ask about a weekend break in Berlin.

[handwritten annotation: trip]

1 Listen to Part A of the conversation. Imagine you are the telephonist. Write a short note that you would leave for a colleague.

[handwritten note: Sharron — Call Mrs. Roberts on 675982 about weekend break in Berlin a.s.a.p.]

2 Listen again and answer these questions.

[handwritten annotations in left margin: hold the line = mantener o esperar a la línea; return a call = devolver la llamada]

1 How does Mrs Roberts tell the telephonist what she wants to know? *[handwritten: I'm phoning about...]*
2 How does the telephonist:
  a ask Mrs Roberts to wait?
  b ask Mrs Roberts for her name and telephone number?
  c tell Mrs Roberts someone will call her?

3 Listen to Part B of the conversation and correct Mrs Roberts' notes.

[handwritten note on notepad:]
- Berlin 3 nights
- £340 per person
- three-star hotel
- English breakfast
- return charter flight

4 Listen to Part B again and answer these questions.

1 How does Sharon:
  a introduce herself?
  b show that she is trying to find the information for Mrs Roberts?
2 How does Mrs Roberts:
  a show she is pleased that Sharon has returned her call?
  b ask for information?
  c show that she is happy with the information Sharon gives her?

SPEAKING

Booking a hotel

Work in pairs.

STUDENT A You are a receptionist at the Avonbury Hotel. Study the details on page 139.
STUDENT B You are ringing the Avonbury Hotel to find out some information and book a room there. Study the details on page 143.

Now act out the telephone conversation. (Your answers to exercises 2 and 4 above will help you.)

WRITING PREPARATION

Narrative composition

1 Read the story and think of a title for it.

2 The story contains seven words which should not be there. The first one is underlined as an example. Find the other six.

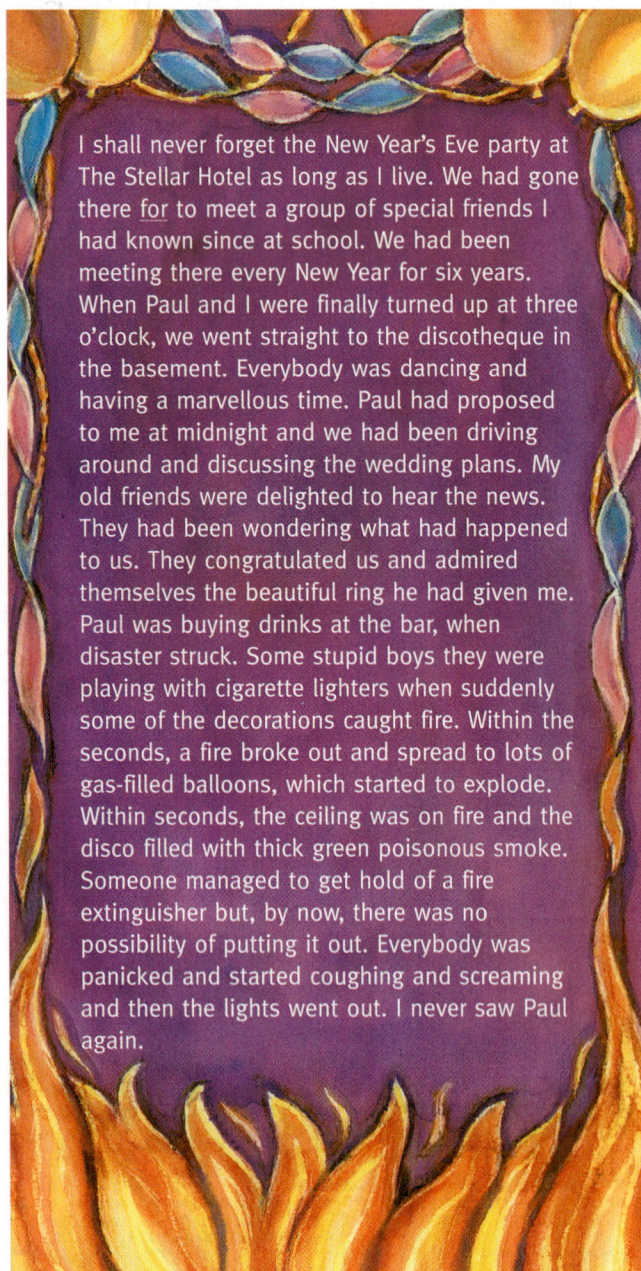

I shall never forget the New Year's Eve party at The Stellar Hotel as long as I live. We had gone there for to meet a group of special friends I had known since at school. We had been meeting there every New Year for six years. When Paul and I were finally turned up at three o'clock, we went straight to the discotheque in the basement. Everybody was dancing and having a marvellous time. Paul had proposed to me at midnight and we had been driving around and discussing the wedding plans. My old friends were delighted to hear the news. They had been wondering what had happened to us. They congratulated us and admired themselves the beautiful ring he had given me. Paul was buying drinks at the bar, when disaster struck. Some stupid boys they were playing with cigarette lighters when suddenly some of the decorations caught fire. Within the seconds, a fire broke out and spread to lots of gas-filled balloons, which started to explode. Within seconds, the ceiling was on fire and the disco filled with thick green poisonous smoke. Someone managed to get hold of a fire extinguisher but, by now, there was no possibility of putting it out. Everybody was panicked and started coughing and screaming and then the lights went out. I never saw Paul again.

• How did the writer of the story escape? Think of an ending to the story and compare your ideas with your classmates.

LANGUAGE STUDY

Narrative tenses

1 The past simple and past continuous

The model composition shows how the PAST CONTINUOUS is used to:
• set the scene. *Everybody was dancing and having a marvellous time.* (ll. 8–9)
• describe how a long action is interrupted by a single action or event. *Paul was buying drinks at the bar, when disaster struck.* (ll. 16–17)

Put the verbs in **bold type** in these sentences into the most suitable of these two tenses.

1 The guard **enter** the cell as he **dig** the tunnel.
2 When they **find** her she **cut** a hole in the fence.
3 He **arrive** while I **try** to phone him.
4 I **walk** in the woods when I **hear** a shot.
5 He **fall** over as he **cross** the road.

Look at the completed sentences and decide when, generally speaking, we use **while, when** and **as**.

2 The past simple and past perfect

When we describe completed actions in their obvious order, we use the PAST SIMPLE.
Within seconds, a fire broke out and spread to lots of gas-filled balloons, which started to explode. (ll. 19–21)
In the composition, the *past perfect* is used to describe things that happened before the main narrative or before a certain point in the past.

Paul had proposed to me at midnight. (l. 9)

Decide if the *past perfect* is used correctly or incorrectly in these sentences.

1 They discovered the tunnel he had dug.
2 After she had crossed the border, she threw away her false papers.
3 He climbed down the rope and had disappeared into the trees.
4 She collected the gun she had left at the cottage.
5 We got dressed, washed and had eaten breakfast.

3 The past perfect continuous

Look at these two sentences from the composition

a *We had been meeting there every New Year for six years.*
Here the PAST PERFECT CONTINUOUS is used to describe a repeated action up to the focus of the narrative.

b *We had been driving around and discussing the wedding plans*
Here the PAST PERFECT CONTINUOUS is used to describe a continuous action up to the focus of the narrative.

Complete the sentences by changing the verbs in brackets into the past simple or the past perfect continuous.

1 They *had been going out* (go out) together for several years before the accident *happened* (happen).
2 Their friends *waited* (wait) for them for three hours when they finally *had been turning up* (turn up).
3 Witnesses *said* (say) the boys who *had been playing* (play) with the lighters were responsible for the tragedy. They *made* (make) a noise and *had been behaving* (behave) stupidly since the party *began* (begin).

• For further practice, turn to page 148.

4 Look back at the story of Casanova's escape. Which tenses are used and why?

SPEAKING

Imagine you are telling the story of how you were kidnapped and your escape from the kidnappers. Working in groups, look at the cues below and take it in turns to add something new to the story, and make notes as the story develops.

WRITING

Narrative composition

Use the notes you have made in your groups and write your own story about how you escaped from the kidnappers. When you have finished, compare your story with the others in your group.

1 Say who you are and why you were kidnapped.
2 Describe your journey to school/work.
3 Describe the car that was waiting at the corner.
4 Describe how the masked drivers got you into the car.
5 Say how it felt when they put a bag over your head.
6 Describe what the journey felt like and how long it took.
7 Say how you knew you were on a farm.
8 Describe the cellar where they put you.
9 Describe what the two kidnappers looked like without their masks.
10 Describe how you found a hole in the roof and tried to escape.
11 Describe what happened when they caught you.
12 Describe the tape recording you had to make for your family.
13 Explain how you heard the conversation where they decided to kill you.
14 Describe how you set fire to the house and escaped.
15 Describe how the woman with the gun fell into the well.
16 Describe your escape by bicycle.
17 Describe the chase and how the second kidnapper crashed his car.
18 Say what happened when the police found you.

4 Treasure

Spot the difference

Work in pairs. Compare the two pictures and find ten differences. What is their connection with treasure?

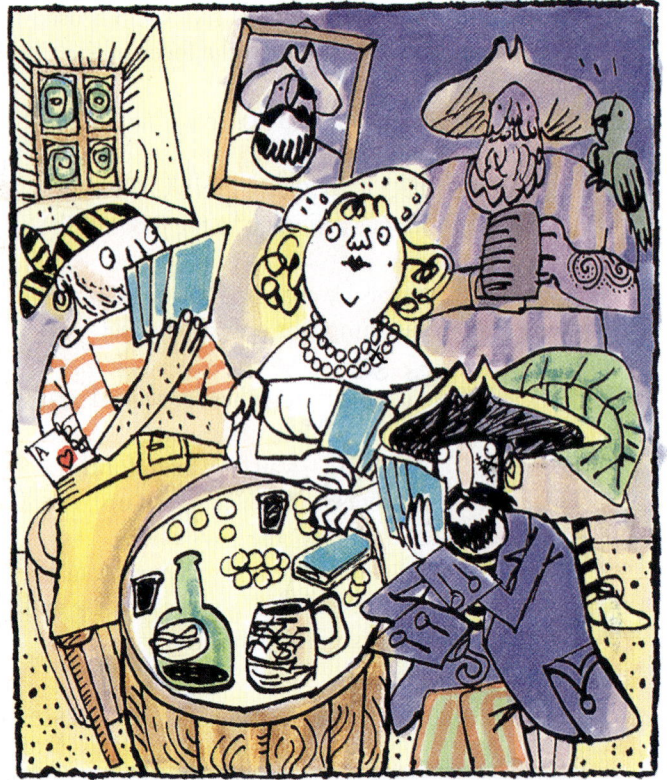

Countable and uncountable

Study this diagram and the explanations. Then do the exercise opposite.

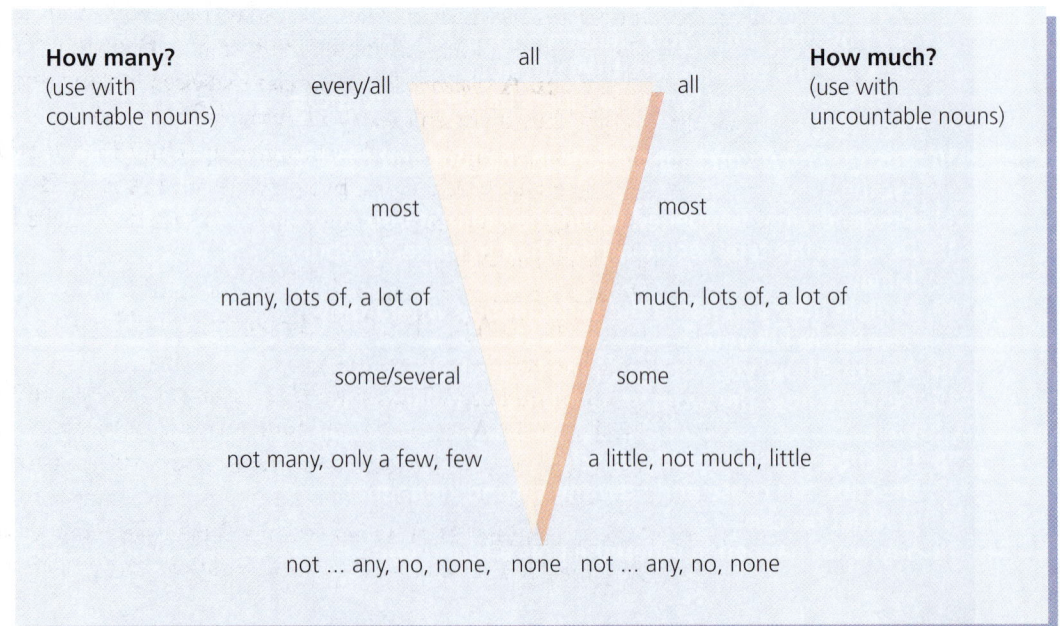

How many? (use with countable nouns)		How much? (use with uncountable nouns)
every/all	all	all
most		most
many, lots of, a lot of		much, lots of, a lot of
some/several		some
not many, only a few, few		a little, not much, little
not ... any, no, none	none	not ... any, no, none

Rose is on the beach talking to Stan, who is using a metal detector to find 'treasure'. Decide which choices can complete the sentences. Often there is more than one correct answer.

ROSE: Hi! What are you doing?

STAN: I'm looking for 1 **A** *some treasure.* **B** *a treasure.* **C** *treasure.*

ROSE: And how 2 **A** *much* **B** *many* luck have you had so far?

STAN: Well, 3 **A** *few* **B** *a little* **C** *little.* I've found 4 **A** *some* **B** *few* **C** *a few* coins and
5 **A** *much* **B** *many* **C** *lots of* **D** *a lot of* silver paper from chocolate bars and cigarette packets!

ROSE: But surely you usually find 6 **A** *anything* **B** *something* valuable 7 **A** *all* **B** *most* **C** *every* day.

STAN: It depends. Last Monday and Tuesday, I looked 8 **A** *anywhere* **B** *everywhere* **C** *nowhere* and found absolutely 9 **A** *nothing* **B** *anything* **C** *none* at all.

ROSE: Perhaps 10 **A** *someone* **B** *anyone* else had been looking, too.

STAN: Maybe, but there isn't really 11 **A** *much* **B** *many* competition. Nearly 12 **A** *all* **B** *each* **C** *every* the enthusiasts who start give up. Only 13 **A** *few* **B** *a few* come regularly enough to become experts, but they waste 14 **A** *much* **B** *many* **C** *lots of* time looking in impossible places. They give up when they don't have 15 **A** *an instant* **B** *any instant* **C** *instant* success.

ROSE: What's the most valuable thing you've found?

STAN: I've found 16 **A** *few* **B** *a little* **C** *a few* rings and bracelets, but I always hand them in to the police.

ROSE: And do you need 17 **A** *special* **B** *any special* **C** *the special* **D** *a special* equipment?

STAN: Well, only 18 **A** *one metal detector* **B** *a metal detector* **C** *metal detector* like this,
19 **A** *some trousers* **B** *trousers* **C** *a trousers* and 20 **A** *a pair* **B** *some pair* **C** *pair* of plastic shoes.

ROSE: Where can I get 21 **A** *an information* **B** *the information* **C** *some information* about it?

STAN: Buy me 22 **A** *some coffee* **B** *coffee* **C** *a coffee* and I'll tell you more !

READING

The history of Captain William Kidd

1 Read the text about the pirate William Kidd and decide whether these statements are **true** or **false**.

1 Kidd was a rough and uncultured man.
2 A 'Privateer' was a pirate who had the support of his government.
3 Kidd became a sort of 'policeman'.
4 Difficult circumstances forced Kidd to become a real pirate.
5 If he had said where the treasure was hidden, he wouldn't have been executed.
6 Kidd's friends tried to save him.
7 One map shows the location of Kidd's treasure.
8 People are still searching for the treasure.

2 Complete the text by using the words in the box once only.

once	employed	most	for	does	the	than	by
several	little	down	since	no	with	him	been

One of the (0) ...*most*... interesting characters from the days of pirates was Captain William Kidd, who has (1)...*been*... the model for romantic tales of adventure on the oceans. He served in (2) ...*the*... Royal Navy and went on to become a successful merchant. He married a wealthy American widow and was a gentleman (3) ...*with*... friends in high places, rather (4) ...*than*... the usual rough sailor. Afterwards, for (5) ...*several*... years, he was a 'Privateer' - a sort of pirate who has a licence from his government to attack enemy merchant shipping.

Later on, he was (6) ...*employed*... by the government to destroy real pirates who were causing problems in the Caribbean. Unfortunately for Kidd, he had such (7) ...*little*... success that it forced (8) ...*him*... to turn to piracy as well. He captured a few ships

but eventually he was arrested and taken back to England (9) ...*for*... trial. He was sentenced to death (10) ...*by*... Parliament. However, the day before his execution, he offered to say where all his treasure was if his life was spared. It made (11) ...*no*... difference; the judge turned his offer (12) ...*down*... and he was hanged on 23rd May 1701. His friends refused to help him.

But this talk of buried treasure caught the public's imagination and, ever (13) ...*since*... then, many searches have been made for Kidd's treasure. In 1929 a man called Palmer came across a map in a desk which, it was claimed, had (14) ...*once*... belonged to Kidd himself. Other articles he found contained further maps giving evidence that perhaps 'Treasure Island' really (15) ...*does*... exist. Nevertheless, so far, nobody has discovered it or its treasure, either.

VOCABULARY

1 Quickly read the text about the adventurer, Colonel Blood, and find answers to these questions.

1 Why did Colonel Blood deserve his name?
2 What was his great adventure?
3 Why was he an extremely lucky man?

2 Now go through the text carefully and underline which of the the words in bold (1–18) are correct. Be ready to explain why the other word is wrong!

fortaleza
traidor / spin

For many centuries the Tower of London acted as a <u>fortress</u> and prison for the enemies of the state. Many <u>traitors</u> met their terrible (0) **destination**/<u>**destiny**</u> within its walls. The nation's coins were once made there and it is still home to the crown jewels. This (1) <u>**priceless**</u>/**worthless** treasure is closely guarded but was almost (2) **robbed**/<u>**stolen**</u> during an (3) <u>**amazing**</u>/**amazed** episode in 1671. The keeper of the jewels - Talbot Edwards - was visited by an apparently honest and (4) <u>**trustworthy**</u>/**trusting** clergyman who claimed his nephew wished to marry Edwards's daughter. In (5) <u>**fact**</u>/**case** the man of God was none other than the appropriately named Colonel Blood, a desperate adventurer. He and his gang brutally attacked Edwards and left him for dead. Blood squashed a crown flat which was then (6) **disappeared**/<u>**hidden**</u> under his large cloak. While the gang were trying to break up the other objects, quite by (7) **luck**/<u>**chance**</u> the keeper's son returned home and discovered his father had almost been (8) **died**/<u>**killed**</u>. By the time the alarm was (9) <u>**raised**</u>/**risen** Blood had almost

(10) **arrived**/<u>**reached**</u> freedom but his horse fell and he was captured.

The adventurer was imprisoned in the Tower to await his (11) **process**/<u>**trial**</u> and (12) **certain**/<u>**certainly**</u> death. However, he refused to speak of his crime to anyone but the king himself - Charles II. Curiosity encouraged the king to meet him. Blood explained that he had *trato* been (13) <u>**unfairly**</u>/**hardly** treated by the crown and had lost his lands. He wanted to steal the jewels as an act of revenge. He had only (14) <u>**come up with**</u>/**come across** the idea of the marriage as a way of winning Edwards's confidence. King Charles II found Blood a (15) <u>**delightful**</u>/**delighted** and amusing individual and listened to his tale (16) <u>**sympathetically**</u>/**comprehensively**. He pardoned the Colonel and even made sure that his property was returned to him. (17) <u>**Nowadays**</u>/**Actually**, millions of visitors to London take the (18) <u>**opportunity**</u>/**possibility** to visit the jewels yet know nothing of this dramatic tale .

SPEAKING

1 Which adventurer was more of a criminal, Captain Kidd or Colonel Blood?
2 How fair was the treatment they received?
3 Are there any characters like Kidd or Blood in your country's history?

READING

Shipwreck!

1 Look at the picture below. The people in the boat have just escaped from a shipwreck. What is happening in the picture? Imagine you could see what else is going on around the picture. What else do you think you could see?

2 Read the text carefully and decide which of the headings (**1–5**) is most suitable for the paragraphs (**A–E**)

> 1 A Change of Identity.   2 No Mercy.
> 3 Fair shares?   4 Off course.   5 A Kind of Justice.

3 Make questions for these answers.

1 Things like storms, enemy warships and pirates.
2 He got his position wrong.
3 I think he must have been cruel and stubborn.
4 They wanted to keep the wreck's position a secret.
5 It may still be there, or else was secretly recovered.

LANGUAGE STUDY

Despite and although

1 **Despite** and **although** both show a contrast of two ideas in a sentence.

The man warned him, but Shovell kept on his course. =
Despite *(hearing) the poor man's warning, Shovell kept on his course.*
Despite + (GERUND +) NOUN/NOUN PHRASE

He escaped drowning, but he was murdered. =
Although *he escaped drowning, he was murdered.*
Although + VERB PHRASE

2 Make sentences using **although** and **despite** based on these details about the career of William Kidd.

1 He was a gentleman, but he became a pirate.
2 He offered to say where his treasure was, but he was hanged.
3 He had important friends, but they refused to help him.
4 There are maps of Kidd's 'Treasure Island', but nobody has found it.

A   As well as dangers at sea, sailors used to face danger on land too. When a ship hit rocks on the coasts of Devon or Cornwall, any survivors were usually murdered. With no witnesses, local people could keep the cargo the ship had been carrying. In bad weather, wreckers even used '*Judas lights' to make sailors steer their ships onto the rocks. By the time captains realized they weren't the welcoming lights of a safe harbour, few were able to turn back.

B   In October 1707, the 'Association' and four other ships were sailing to England, when they were shipwrecked off the Scilly Isles. The 'Association' had been carrying a three-million-dollar cargo of silver. The admiral in charge, Sir Cloudsley Shovell, had believed he was near France and had even hanged a sailor who suggested he might be wrong!

C   Despite the poor man's warning, Shovell kept on his course. This was a terrible error, which cost the lives of two thousand men. A few, including Shovell, reached the shore. Although he escaped drowning, he was murdered by local women who then stole his rings and jewellery.

D   For a short time, the rock where the 'Association' sank was known as 'Shovell Rock'. Later, local people changed the name because they didn't want to give the wreck's position away.

E   Finally, in 1967, the British Royal Navy located the 'Association' and started diving, but other private teams had licences to look for it as well. Under English law, at least half of any of the silver which private teams recovered would have to be given to the government. However, they only rescued a third of the treasure. The rest either still lies at the bottom of the sea, or else was secretly recovered over the years.

*   In the New Testament of the Bible, Judas is the man who betrayed Jesus to the authorities with a kiss.

LISTENING

Sunken treasure

1 Francis Gosling is an expert on treasure exploration. Listen to the interview and complete the notes. *spent what they stole.*

Francis Gosling is unsure about how much treasure is left because *Taken back* pirates either (1) ~~Taken back~~ or it was (2) .... *don't carry out.* His basic advice to people who are interested in searching for it is (3) *not to bother* . Ships mostly sank in (4) *bad weather* and were then covered (5) .... *sand*

• Complete these notes about the three discoveries Francis Gosling discusses.

Name of Ship	Nationality	Cargo	Value
Geldermalsen	(6) ~~Dutch~~	Tea and (7) *porcelaine*	XXXX
La Nuestra Señora de Atocha *(Discovered in (10) 1985 by Mel (11) Fisher)*	Spanish	(8) *silver*	(9) *415 million of dollars*
Admiral Nakhimov	(12) *Russian*	Gold and (13) *platinum* *2 billion of dollar*	(14) *2 billion of dollars* billion

2 Listen again and answer these questions.

1 Why was the cargo of the 'Geldermalsen' in such good condition?
2 How do we know that the discovery of 'La Nuestra Señora de Atocha' wasn't just luck?

VOCABULARY

Phrasal verbs

1 Look at these sentences from this Unit and decide which definition goes with which phrasal verb.

1 A man called Palmer came across a map in a desk. **a** to try to find **3**
2 ... they didn't want to give the wreck's position away. **b** see with difficulty **4**
3 Other teams had licences to look for the wreck as well. **c** tell a secret **2**
4 We can just make out the manufacturer's name. **d** find by chance **1**

2 All four phrasal verbs are transitive, and so they must take an object. Grammatically, there are important differences. Study the sentences.

(i)   He came across a map. CORRECT (iii) He came a map across. WRONG
(ii) He came across it. CORRECT (iv) He came it across. WRONG

• With **come across** we cannot separate the verb **come** from its particle **across**. **Come across** is an inseparable phrasal verb.

(i)   We made out the name. CORRECT (iii) We made the name out. CORRECT
(ii) We made out it. WRONG (iv) We made it out. CORRECT

• We can follow the phrasal verb with a full object (i). We can also separate the verb **make** from its particle **out** with the full object (iii) or object pronoun (iv). However, we cannot place the object pronoun ('it') after the particle (ii). **Make out** is a separable phrasal verb.

VOCABULARY

Personal treasures

1 Match the names in the box with the objects.

2 Compound nouns

The noun 'candlestick' is made up of two nouns with the main stress on the first. Pick out similar words from the list and practise saying them.

3 Shapes and characteristics

Look at the objects again. Which ones are: *shiny, round, curved, oval, rectangular, pointed, spiral*? Which ones would be made of: *wood, china, metal, cloth* or *glass*?

LISTENING

Treasure in our attic

1 Before you listen, how much do you think each of these objects is worth? Imagine you have £5,000. How much would you bid for each one?

1 Teddy
a nothing
b £5
c £50
d £500
e £1,000

2 Golf ball
a nothing
b £25
c £50
d £500
e £4,000

3 Charlie Chaplin
a nothing
b £10
c £100
d £1,000
e £2,000

4 Beatles' record
a nothing
b £10
c £100
d £1,000
e £5,000

2 Listen again and answer these questions.

1 Where did Robin get his teddy?
2 Where was it from and who made it?
3 Where did the man find the golf ball?
4 What was wrong with it?
5 How much did the man pay for Charlie Chaplin?
6 Did he get a bargain?
7 What is special about the Beatles' record?
8 How did the girl's father get it?

golf ball   corkscrew   teddy bear   tennis racket
record   teapot   sea chest   vase   sword   radio
porcelain figure   record player   whistle   fan
silver candlestick

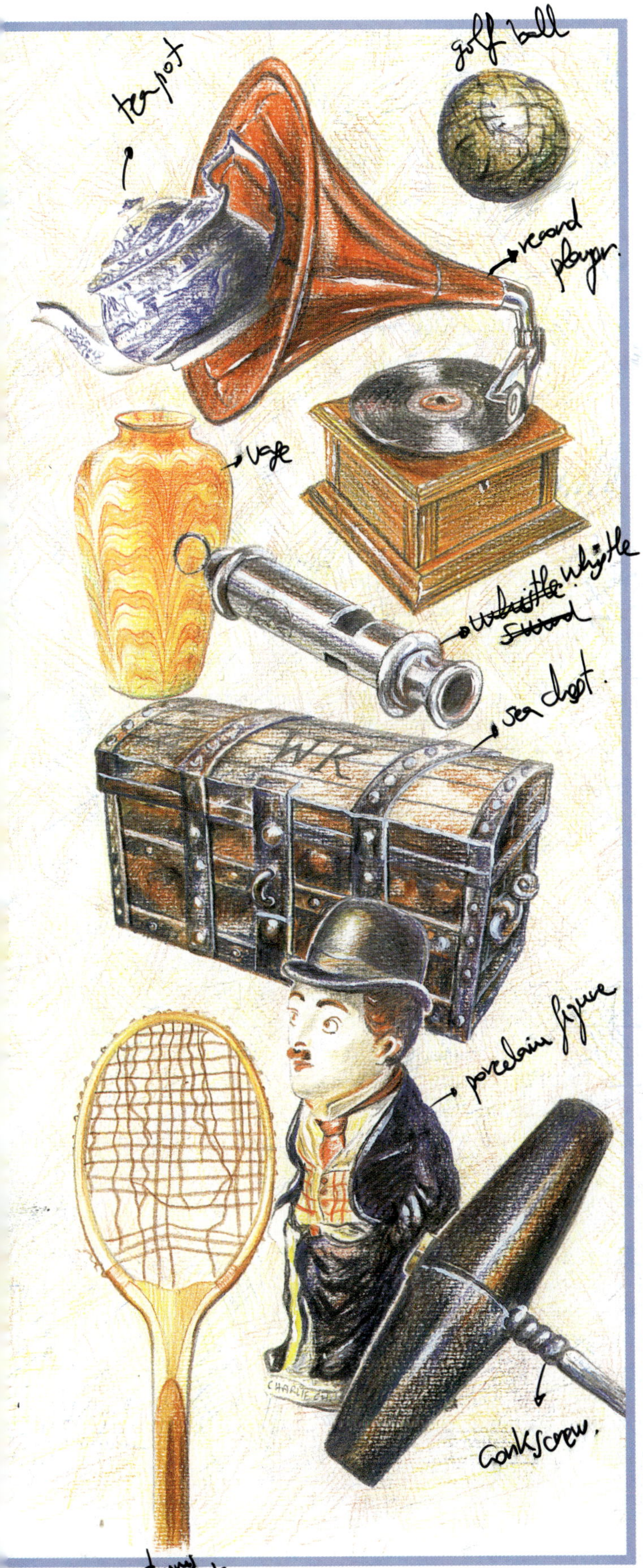

Handwritten labels on illustration: teapot · golf ball · record player · vase · whistle sword · sea chest · porcelain figure · corkscrew · tennis racket · CHARLIE CHAP

LANGUAGE STUDY

Indirect questions

1 Look at these three questions from the recording. How is **a** different in structure from **b** and **c**?

a What have you brought to show us? *DIRECT QUESTION*
b Could you tell me where he was from? *IND. QUESTION*
c Do you know what it's worth? *IND. QUESTION*

2 ▭ **Intonation in questions**

Questions **b** and **c** are indirect questions. We often use them when we want to be polite.
Listen again and try to copy the intonation of all three as closely as you can.

3 Sentences beginning with **I wonder** and **I'm not sure** look like indirect questions in their structure.

I wonder where Alice is. (Where is Alice?)
I'm not sure if this is the house. (Is this the house?)

4 There is another tricky indirect question on the recording.

George Brown asks:
Would you mind telling me how much you paid for it?
Would you mind + VERB + -ing

The man answers:
Not really, I suppose. It cost me £90.
Notice that the reply **not really** means **OK**. Can you think why?
What would the man have said if he hadn't wanted to tell George the price?

5 Look at these sentences and decide if they are right or wrong. Where necessary, correct them.

1 Could you tell me what time is it? *is and I*
2 I wonder what they are doing. ✓ *c*
3 Do you know when does the train leave? *I*
4 I'm not sure where does he work? *I*
5 Does Marion know where the money is? ✓ *a*
6 Could you tell me if the manager is here today? *c*
7 Would you mind to tell me where she lives? *I*
   telling

READING

Pirates!

1 Read the five short texts about women pirates and answer the questions by writing the right letters (**A–E**) in each of the boxes.

Most famous pirates were men but did you know there were women pirates too? We are going to look at the careers of a few of them.

Which one/s....

- was the most powerful? [E]
- dressed up as men? [D], [C]
- was a cannibal? [B]
- do we know the least about? [E]
- was an ex-soldier? [C]
- was the most recent? [E]

- only sailed with women? [A]
- led a revolution? [B]
- were active in the Caribbean? [C][D]
- hated her fiancé? [A][D]
- criticised her lover? [D]
- was considered the best sailor? [E]

A ALVILDA THE GOTH
The earliest female pirate of our selection is Alvilda the Goth. She came from the south of Sweden before the days of the Vikings, who were active from the ninth century and feared for their lightning raids. Unsurprisingly, little is known about Alvilda. According to legend she went to sea with an all-female crew to avoid being forced into marriage with Prince Alf of Denmark!

B CHARLOTTE DE BERRY
Despite her French name, Charlotte was born in England in 1636. As was fairly common in those days, she pretended to be a man so she could go to sea with her husband. However, on one ship bound for Africa she was attacked by the captain. She took her revenge by leading a mutiny and cutting off his head with a dagger. She and the rest of the crew began a life of piracy, preying on the gold ships which sailed up the African coast. By all accounts she was a cruel and ferocious woman. One story claims that when their food ran out, the crew ate two slaves and then consumed Charlotte's husband.

C MARY READ
Mary Read disguised herself as a man in order to join the British army and fought bravely in Flanders. In the middle of the Atlantic her ship was captured by the pirate, 'Calico' Jack Rackham, and she decided to join his crew. She took to her new profession and sailed the Caribbean. She and Rackham became lovers and she even fought a duel on his behalf killing her opponent in a sword fight. Eventually, in 1720, Rackham's ship was surprised by a Royal Navy vessel in the West Indies. Most of his crew were too drunk to fight so Read and Ann Bonny did their best to defend the ship. When her shipmates came out of their hiding places she shot them. Although she escaped the hangman's rope because she was pregnant, she died of a fever in prison.

D ANNE BONNY
Anne Bonny was already married to a sailor but when she met "Calico" Jack Rackham she decided to take up a life of piracy. When Read joined the crew, Anne was taken in by her male disguise and fell in love with her! Mary confessed her secrets and the two women became the best of friends. After their capture, she too escaped hanging as she was expecting a baby. She had cruel words for her lover as he went to his execution. She told Rackham "Had you fought like a man, you need not have been hanged like a dog!"

E CHING SHIH
Even though women captains weren't uncommon, Ching Shih stands out for the enormous size of her pirate fleet and as a brilliant captain. In the early 19th century she dominated the China sea. Her fleet consisted of 1,800 ships and 80,000 pirates and controlled a vast area. Fighting bravely with sword and dagger, she struck terror into the hearts of her victims. In the 1850s the Europeans acted against these huge fleets and by the1860s they had been eliminated.

2 Discuss these questions.

1 Why do you think it was common for women to dress up as men?

2 Which of these female pirates do you think is the most/least terrible?

3 If you could make a film about the life of one of them, who would you choose?

3 Vocabulary in context

1 In parts B, C and D of the text, which phrasal verbs using **take** mean: a *to like something immediately* b *to begin a new activity* c *to trick/decieve.*

2 In part E which words mean *extremely big, extremely clever* and *extremely wide*?

READING

Lost property

Here are two letters which have been jumbled up. One is an informal letter to a friend, the other is more formal and is to a hotel.

1 Try to reconstruct the letters by studying the opening and closing sentences for each letter and choosing from sentences a–s opposite.

Dear Sue,

Just a note to say thank you for a lovely weekend at Pear Tree Cottage.

Lots of love,
May

Dear Sir,

I am writing to say how much I enjoyed my weekend say at your hotel.

Yours faithfully,
Julian January
(Julian January)

---

a I have searched for it but am unable to find it anywhere.

b Or else it could be near the tree where we had the picnic.

c Can't wait to see you at the conference on the 25th!

d You know, it's one of that pair of Victorian silver ones that father gave me for my birthday.

e I look forward to staying with you again on the weekend of the 25th.

f I had a really lovely time and the food was marvellous.

g If you find it, can you pop it in an envelope and send it to me?

h My wife would be most upset if it has been lost since it was a wedding present from her.

i You made me most welcome and the food was excellent.

j I've looked all over and I just can't find it.

k Not only is it valuable, but is of great sentimental value.

l We must find it otherwise he'll start asking questions.

m I would appreciate it if you could check down the side of the sofas in the lounge.

n Failing that, it may be in room 307, where I stayed.

o Have a good look in the bathroom. That's where I probably dropped it.

p However, I believe I may have mislaid my cigarette case somewhere in the hotel.

q Should you discover it, I would be extremely grateful if you could send it to me.

r It is gold with the initials 'JJ' engraved on it.

s By the way, I think I left an earring at your place.

2 Make a list of the informal words and expressions which May uses in her letter.

Can you think what their formal equivalents could be?

WRITING

You recently spent the weekend with friends. However, you think you left something at their home. Write a letter thanking them for the weekend and asking about the lost object.

5 Gods in White Coats

SPEAKING

A monster or a saint?

1 Quickly read the text and find out why Dr Kevorkian – the man in the picture – is in the news.

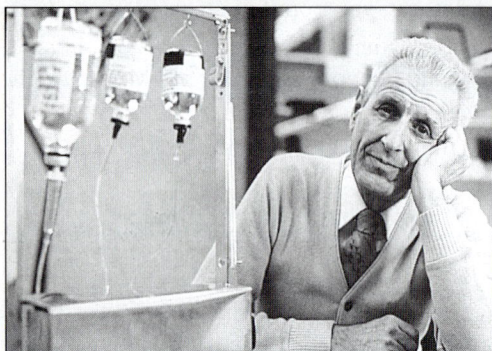

IN THE USA, a doctor is facing trial for helping a woman kill herself. Mrs Atkins, aged 54, contacted Dr Jack Kevorkian and explained that she wanted to end her life because she was suffering from an incurable disease. The doctor put his suicide machine into a van and he drove to a park where he told Mrs Atkins how to administer the fatal injection. If the court decides he killed Mrs Atkins, he could be jailed for life. In his defence, the doctor said: 'She knew what she was doing, she wanted to end her life. I asked her if she knew what that meant. She said, "Yes, I'm going to die. There's nothing for me. There's no life".' The police have taken the machine but Dr Kevorkian will help other people to end their lives unless he is kept in prison. In the doctor's own words he says: 'If they send me to jail, they'd better keep me there, otherwise I'll do it again when I get out.'

2 Discussion points

1 Is Dr Kevorkian a saint or a monster?
2 What 'rights' should a person have over medical treatment? Should they be allowed to choose whether or not to die?
3 What do you think a court in your country would decide in Dr Kevorkian's case?
4 Since this story happened, a cure has been found for Mrs Atkins' disease. Does this change your opinion at all?

LANGUAGE STUDY

If, unless and otherwise

1 **Unless** can often be used to mean **if ... not**.

ACTION	RESULT

Unless you eat more fruit, your teeth will fall out!
If you don't eat more fruit, your teeth will fall out!

Now rewrite these sentences using the words in brackets.

1 You won't get better if you don't rest. (**Unless**)
2 Unless they get here soon, they'll miss the train. (**If**)
3 If he doesn't eat less, he'll get very fat. (**Unless**)
4 I'll report you unless you apologize. (**If**)
5 She won't be a dentist if she doesn't pass her exams. (**Unless**)

2 We can also express the same thing by using **had better** and **otherwise** at the beginning of the result clause.

You'd better eat more fruit, otherwise your teeth will fall out!
Rewrite sentences 1–5 using **otherwise**.

VOCABULARY

Reflexive verbs

*...a doctor is on trial for helping a woman **kill herself**.*

1 Complete these sentences with a reflexive pronoun.

1 Good afternoon, please may I introduce ...myself... ?
2 Bye bye children, have a lovely time and enjoy ...yourself... .
3 The surgeon cut ...itself... with a sharp knife.
4 Be quiet, Gemma. Sit down and behave ...yourself... .
5 The doctors blamed ...themselves... for the accident.
6 Come in Amanda and make ...yourself... at home.

2 Which sentences contain extra and unnecessary reflexive pronouns?

1 How old were you before you could dress yourself?
2 In the evening I like to relax myself by watching T.V.
3 Have you ever hurt yourself by accident!
4 I was hurt myself when I fell off my bicycle.
5 She woke herself up at eight o'clock.
6 Can you amuse the children themselves for half an hour?
7 In the morning I get up, have a shower, get dressed myself and have breakfast.
8 We amused ourselves by playing cards.
9 He did the exercise all by himself.
10 They adapted themselves to the new situation very quickly.
11 They married themselves in that building over there.
12 We were enjoying ourselves until you arrived.
13 What a surprise! He has found himself a job and got himself married.

LISTENING

1 Robert, Jasmine and Thomas are discussing the Kevorkian case. Answer questions **1–7** by writing **R** (for Robert), **J** (for Jasmine) and **T** (for Thomas) in the boxes.

1 Who completely disagrees with what the doctor did? [J] *principal proffeson and the etics.*
2 Who claims that Mrs Atkins killed herself? [T]
3 Who thinks the quality of a patient's life is an important issue? [R]
4 Who thinks sick people aren't always able to make good decisions? [J]
5 Who is worried about what might happen in the future? [T]
6 Who believes doctors already make life and death decisions for patients? [R]
7 Who thinks the doctor may escape justice? [J]

2 Look at the tapescript on page 157 and underline the expressions which are useful for giving opinions and agreeing and disagreeing.

SPEAKING

Guinea pigs → *"Conejillo de Indigo"*

1 Read the text about human 'guinea pigs' and on your own, answer the questions in exercise 2 below.

In some clinics in London, people can agree to be 'guinea pigs' for medical experiments; they stay in hospitals like luxury hotels and earn a lot of money if they are prepared to take the medicines the doctors give them. In one place which experiments with new medical equipment, they pay people £10,000 if they agree to have toes cut off then sewn back on again!

put back

2 In small groups discuss your answers to these questions by using as many of the ways of giving opinions and agreeing and disagreeing as you can.

1 Would you agree to do this?
2 How much money would you want for the 'toe experiment'?
3 In some countries, prisoners serving long sentences can get out of prison sooner if they agree to take part in medical experiments. What do you think of this?

SPEAKING

Food!

- What relationship does each of these people have with food?
- What will happen to the man on the left if he eats any more?
- If you were the brother or sister of the girl, how would you try to help her?

LISTENING

Discussing a problem

Frank is talking to Angie, a student who is helping out at the local youth club.

1 Listen for answers to these questions.

1 What is Frank's problem?
2 Does Angie really understand Frank's problem?

2 Listen again and fill in the gaps.

FRANK: I'm so (1) .... It's (2) ....
ANGIE: So that's it. I thought you looked a bit (3) ....
FRANK: And the more I worry about it the more I seem to eat.
ANGIE: Frank, (4) .... , what have you had to eat today?
FRANK: Well, I didn't have breakfast so I ate a (5) .... on the way to school. Then I had a (6) .... at breaktime.
ANGIE: And what about at lunch?
FRANK: Um .... a (7) .... and a cola.
ANGIE: It's no surprise you're getting fat. (8) .... is a balanced diet.
FRANK: What (9) .... ?
ANGIE: Obviously, you're taking in too many calories. You (10) .... chocolate completely for a time and (11) .... all the snacks you eat. Also, (12) .... of those slimming clubs? You get advice on nutrition and they weigh you each week. It really works.
FRANK: How (13) .... about it?

3 Giving advice

What expressions does Angie use to give advice?

STUDENT A turn to page 139. STUDENT B turn to page 143.

READING

Just puppy fat?

1 Here are three letters to a teenage magazine, but only two replies. Match up the two letters with their replies.

Dear Sally...

B

My main advice is that you should give up these crash diets straight away. Trying to lose weight like this is dangerous. It takes your body a long time to get over this kind of thing and you could be doing yourself long-term damage. You should never miss main meals or allow yourself to feel too hungry. If you starve yourself, you'll pass out, or even worse! So look after your body. Go to a slimming club for some sensible nutritional advice.

A

I'm really overweight but I hate dieting. I find it impossible to cut down on food. I find the best way to lose weight is by going on a crash diet, you know starving myself for a week at a time. I look great afterwards but the only problem is that I put the weight back on really quickly afterwards. What should I do?

D

I adore junk food like chips and hamburgers. My dad says it's really bad for me. Even so I have never felt ill and have got a good figure. I have got away with this so far, so should I take any notice of him? Perhaps I have got the kind of body that lets me do this kind of thing.

C

One reason why you're not losing weight may simply be that you don't need to lose any. Another reason is you have probably got a bit of puppy fat. But whatever the reason, you should check with your doctor. If you are really overweight, you may have to go on a diet or take up some form of exercise. Your doctor will be able to advise you best.

E

Please can you help me? I'm really fed up. With every diet I've tried, I just can't seem to lose more than a couple of pounds. Even though I follow a diet carefully and never cheat, nothing seems to work.

2 Match the headings (**1–5**) to the letters you have just read (**A–E**).

1 Seek medical advice. ☐
2 Eat sensibly. ☐
3 No change. ☐
4 Lucky so far. ☐
5 All or nothing. ☐

VOCABULARY

Phrasal verbs and health

Choose the correct phrasal verb to complete each sentence.
1 A *Look out* B *Look into* C *Look after* your teeth by brushing them regularly.
2 What a bad cough! If I were you I'd A *give out* B *give away* C *give up* smoking.
3 You'd better A *cut off* B *cut down* C *cut out* on the amount of coffee you drink.
4 To stay healthy, people ought to A *take out* B *take in* C *take up* exercise?
5 Has Mrs Brown A *got on with* B *got over* C *got away with* her operation.
6 I feel faint; I think I'm going to A *pass up* B *pass away* C *pass out*.

WRITING

A letter of advice

Make a list of all the words and expressions which are used for requesting and giving advice. Write an answer to the third letter incorporating some of these expressions and some of the phrasal verbs you have studied. Invent a heading to your reply.

READING

It's all in the eye

1 Read the text quickly and find out the connection between an owl and medicine.

Iridology is the study of the eye's iris, used to diagnose someone's state of health and warn patients of potential problems. The underlying theory is that the entire body is reflected in the iris. Iridology is for diagnosis only and not for treatment. However, many iridologists are practising homeopaths, herbalists or acupuncturists. The study of the iris not only indicates current health, but identifies potential weaknesses, many of which we inherit from our parents. By identifying a condition before it becomes a problem, people can minimize it or avoid it through changes to diet and lifestyle. Iridology has a long history. It was practised in Ancient Egypt, and Hippocrates mentions it, too. The Hungarian, Dr Ignatz von Peczely (1822-1911) is the founder of iridology as a modern science. When he was a boy, he accidentally broke the leg of his pet owl and noticed a dark mark appear in the bird's eye. As the leg healed, the mark disappeared. When von Peczely became a doctor, he developed a map showing the relationship of different parts of the body to the iris.

Iridology works because the iris records everything that has happened to the body since the age of six. It also carries genetic information which indicates future problems. The colour of the iris also provides the practitioner with vital information.

2 Choose the best option from the alternatives **A** or **B**.

1 Iridology is
   A a form of treatment.
   B a way of identifying a health problem.

2 Ignatz von Peczely
   A was the first person to notice iris markings.
   B re-established iridology.
3 What did von Peczely notice about the injured bird?
   A A new mark in the owl's eye.
   B The mark disappeared before the leg healed.
4 Iridology
   A can provide an early health warning.
   B is a form of fortune telling.

LISTENING

1 Key vocabulary

Study the simplified iridology diagram of the eye's iris. Can you unjumble the italic letters to find the names of four parts of the body?

2 Annie is interviewing an iridologist called Paola. Listen to their conversation and complete the notes

Paola has been an iridologist (1) ....
She used to be a (2) .... , but gave up for two main reasons:
She noticed people (3) .... by the medicine they are prescribed and can become (4) ....
Problems.
Blue eyes: (5) .... and rheumatism.
Brown eyes: circulation and (6) ....
Hazel eyes and green eyes are both (7) .... colours.
People with green eyes often have problems with their (8) ....
Paola can see Annie has a problem with her (9) .... Annie hurt it while she was (10) ....

LANGUAGE STUDY

The present perfect and past simple

1 Some time in the past

Paola says: *I have been a pharmacist.*
                    I trained as one and practised for a few years.
When we talk about our general experiences, we use the
PRESENT PERFECT.
If we go on to give more detail, or give a specific time,
then we use the PAST SIMPLE. In other words, we move
from the indefinite past to the definite past.
Paola also says: *I have never taken a sleeping pill in my life.*
(= in her life up to now.)

Read the short paragraph about Dr Frederick
Wilberforce and put the verbs in *italics* into the
appropriate form. (Dr Wilberforce is still working.)

Dr Frederick Wilberforce
is now a famous doctor
but in his lifetime he
(1) .... *(be)* a soldier and
an explorer and (2) ....
(live) in many different
countries. When he
(3) .... *(leave)* the army,
he (4) .... *(study)*
medicine and then (5) ..... *(work)* in Africa. His first
wife (6) .... *(be)* a doctor too, but she (7) ....
(die) of malaria. Dr Wilberforce (8) .... *(have)* a
long and interesting career. Over the years, he
(9) .... *(save)* thousands of lives and (10) ....
(perform) hundreds of operations. The medical
profession (11) .... *(give)* him many prizes; he
(12) .... *(win)* the first for the work he did in the
Third World. In addition, he (13) .... *(write)*
several books on surgery. He (14) .... *(publish)*
his latest one last year. He (15) .... *(not become)*
very rich, like many other surgeons, because he
(16) .... *(never believe)* in private medicine.
Instead, he (17) .... *(always work)* in state
hospitals.

2 The unfinished past

Look at these other sentences from the listening.

PAOLA: *There's something wrong with your left knee
             though. I can see that **you have hurt it at some
             time**.* (indefinite past)
ANNIE: *I had quite a bad skiing accident two years ago. I
             had an operation, but **it has bothered me ever
             since**.* (unfinished past)

Decide whether the verb in the following sentences
expresses the idea of the indefinite or the unfinished past.

1   He has smoked since he was eighteen.
2   Johnny has broken his leg three times.
3   He has worked in a London hospital since he returned
     to England.
4   He has travelled widely in Africa.
5   They have lived here for many years.

3 Talking about an activity

When we are talking about an activity which started in
the past and is still going on, we may use the PRESENT
PERFECT CONTINUOUS.

ANNIE: *How long have you been an iridologist?*
PAOLA: *I've been practising for about seven years now.*

How would Paola have answered if she had used **since**
instead of **for**?

4 Complete the second sentence so that it means the
same as the one above it.

1   He passed his dentist's exams ten years ago.
     He has ....
2   They have been dieting for three months.
     They started ....
3   When did you start to train as a doctor?
     How long have .... ?
4   She fell asleep when the doctor left.
     She has ....
5   The children's ward has been open for nine months.
     The children's ward ....

LISTENING

1 Before you listen, discuss these questions.

1 What kind of health care and medical treatment are provided by the government of your country? Is there much difference between private and state (government) medical treatment in your country?

2 How satisfied are people with the medical treatment in your country?

2 You are going to hear five people talking about their local hospital. Read sentences **A–E** which summarise what each has to say. Now listen and decide who says what by writing the number of the speaker (**1–5**) in the boxes.

A The government wastes money. `4`

B His mother does not deserve the way she has been treated. `3`

C Waiting will cause her child educational problems. `2`

D The unions are responsible for the problems. `5`

E The rich don't suffer like ordinary people. `1`

3 Listen again and ask your teacher to stop the cassette each time you hear a word which begins with a negative prefix, e.g. She was really inexperienced. STOP!

4 Complete the article which summarises what you have heard by changing the words in CAPITAL letters into a form that will complete the passage. All the words will need a negative prefix.

Local anger at hospital in crisis.

Local people are more (0 SATISFY) *dissatisfied* than ever with the poor performance of the City hospital. Everybody we interviewed had a story to tell. Major criticisms are that the hospital is (1 EFFICIENT) ...IN... and the staff are becoming more and more (2 EXPERIENCE) ...INEXPERIENCED...

We came across a number of (3 SATISFY) ...UNSATISFACTORY... incidents which included all age groups. A 77 year old grandmother waited six hours to see a doctor after a bad fall. Twelve year old Fiona Post was told it would be (4 POSSIBLE) ...IMPOSSIBLE... to have a minor ear operation for at least four months, the hospital claiming the delay was (5 AVOID) ...UNAVOIDABLE... Ralph Greene said it was (6 FORGIVE) ...UNFORGIVABLE... that his mother's hip operation had been cancelled for a second time. One local man claimed that it was (7 MORAL) ...IMMORAL... to (8 SPEND) ...MISSPENT... so much on weapons and that it should become (9 LEGAL) ...ILLEGAL... to cancel operations. Others felt it was (10 FAIR) ...UNFAIR... that people with money could pay for private treatment and jump the queue.

Local MP Leslie Frobisher claims to understand the (11 SATISFY) ...DISSATISFACTION... felt by local people and continues to condemn the " (12 RESPONSIBLE) ...IRRESPONSIBLE... behaviour of hospital staff in taking (13 NECESSARY) ...UNNECESSARY... industrial action." This paper believes we have had to hear this old excuse too many times. How much longer do ordinary people have to wait before we see an improvement?

5 Notice how the first paragraph summarises the article. The second paragraph gives examples and the third paragraph tells us the newspaper's opinion.

TO HOLD: to celebrate.

READING

Read the six short texts about patients waiting for operations and answer the questions by writing the right letters (**A–F**) in each of the boxes.

to be brave = brave.

A

Richard Bloom "open flower."
Aged 43. An ex-soldier who won medals for bravery. After leaving the army his experiences of combat meant he was unable to adapt to normal life. He has been homeless for the past four years. Mr. Bloom needs a kidney transplant almost immediately and, following a car accident, donor kidneys are available. *Operation time - 3 hours.*

B

Carlos Rodriguez.
Aged 32. He is a refugee forced to flee from his country for political reasons. He is a famous guitar player and songwriter in his own country. He fell and broke his hand and needs immediate surgery if he is to continue playing. If his country becomes a democracy, he will almost certainly have an important position in the new government. *Operation time - 1 hour*

C

Lorna Dobson.
Aged 17. Lorna has had a serious heart problem since she was born. She is getting weaker and will probably only live another year without an operation. Her family could afford private surgery, but her aunt, a politician, is against private health care. *Operation time - 5 hours*

D

Professor Muriel Greene.
Aged 74. Retired professor of medicine. She has been waiting for a replacement hip operation for three years. She is in great pain and her quality of life is poor. Her daughter has had to give up her job to look after her. Her operation has already been cancelled twice. *Operation time - 2 hours*

E

Pauline Bolton.
Aged 36. A housewife and mother of five young children. Six months ago, her face was badly burned in an accident and she needs plastic surgery. She is extremely depressed about her appearance and has threatened suicide. *Operation time - 3 hours*

F

Arthur Griffiths.
Aged 57. Married with two grown-up children. An important and devoted trade union official. He has a serious lung disease caused by his time as a miner. His long-term prospects are poor, but an immediate operation to remove a diseased lung could give him two more years of active life. *Operation time - 2 hours*

Who.....

1 has an important relative? [C]
2 have grown-up children? [D] [F]
3 have problems as a direct result of their work? [A] [F]
4 might have a political future? [B]
5 has been a hero? [A]
6 has the most immediate emotional problems? [E]
7 have lost their homes? [A] [B]
8 has the biggest family responsibilities? [E]

SPEAKING

The six people whose details you have read are expecting operations today. However, for technical reasons, only one operating theatre is available and there is a maximum of eight hours' operating time. The patients who are not operated on today may have to wait at least *another month*. In groups, decide who should receive their operation today. Try to use as many of the ways of giving opinions and agreeing and disagreeing as you can.

WRITING

You are the journalist who wrote the article on page 52 .Write another article on behalf of the people whose operations have been cancelled. Remember to summarise what you have to say in the first paragraph and to give examples in the second.

[handwritten: TO BE OUTSTANDING (IN A DIFFERENT FIELDS) : DESTACAR EN DIFERENTES CAMPOS.]

Famous faces

Try to identify these famous people and say who they are and what they are famous for.

[handwritten annotations on illustration: MARILYN MONROE. STEFFI GRAF. tennis player. ALFRED HITCHCOCK. SALVADOR DALI. it's an ALL-ROUND ARTIST = artista polifacético. SOCRATES. MARÍA CALAS. SHAKESPEARE. a bald man = calvo. PLAYWRIGHT = dramaturgo.]

1 Listen to these four people, all of whom impersonate someone famous, and complete the table.

	John Major	Marilyn Monroe	Elvis Presley	Queen Elizabeth I
Real/ex-job	1	6	11 ..../electrician	16 ....teacher
When did they start?	2 .... years ago	7 when she was	12	17 ....
Why do it?	3	8	13	18 Always admired her ....
Money	4	9 £500 -	14	19 ....
Time and preparations	5 .... and business suit	10 ....hair, ...	15 10 mins - .... and	20 Half an hour make-up, ...

2 Are there any people in your country who make a living as a 'lookalike'?
If you could look like anyone famous who would you choose?

VOCABULARY

Professions

Very often we can make the word for a profession by adding a suffix to the verb, for example, someone who teaches is a **teacher** (teach + **er**). Some professions are based on a verb or noun and end in -**or** (*man*)/-**ess** (*woman*), -**ist** or -**ian**, for example mathemati**cian**. Try to complete the following sentences.

Someone who...

1 is involved in politics is a ....
2 acts in plays is an ....(man) ....(woman).
3 writes stories or novels is a ....
4 sings in opera is an ....
5 plays tennis is a ....
6 explores the world is an ....
7 comes up with inventions is an ....
8 studies science is a ....
9 thinks about the meaning of life is a ....
10 paints or makes statues is an ....
11 composes music is a ....
12 plays a musical instrument is a ....
13 directs films is a ....

LANGUAGE STUDY

The past simple passive

1 Active to passive

*Shakespeare + **wrote** + Hamlet.* → *Hamlet **was written** by Shakespeare.*
SUBJECT + VERB + OBJECT   SUBJECT + *to be* + PAST PARTICIPLE + AGENT

2 Practice: quiz time

In teams, write ten questions about famous people. Take it in turns to ask and answer them. Where you can, use the simple past passive. There will be two points for each answer; one for the correct information and one for perfect English. (There are no points for the wrong information!)

SPEAKING

A party for all time

Work in groups:
You can hold a party for eight guests from today or history.

- Which eight people will you invite and why?
- Who will be the 'guest of honour'? i.e. The most important guest?
- What will the seating arrangement at the dinner table be?
- What will the menu be?
- You can ask ONE guest ONE very important or personal question only. Who would you ask, and what would your question be?

LISTENING

In an art gallery

1 Listen to the conversation between Jane and Phil.

1 Do they have the same taste in painting?
2 Which paintings does Jane like? Which paintings does Phil like?

2 Listen again and put these adjectives in the right order

terrible~~~~ fascinating~~~~ gorgeous~~~~ awful~~~~
fantastic~~~~ marvellous~~~~ *[handwritten: extremely beautiful. Use for woman / physical effect]*

Which adjectives express the ideas of:
very good, *very bad*, *extremely beautiful* and *very interesting!*

3 Stress for emphasis

Listen again to these sentences from the conversation. Notice how Jane and Phil use stress and intonation to emphasize what they say.

I think it's *fascinating*.   All those *gorgeous* colours!

4 Practice

Work in pairs. Discuss the paintings. Say *why* you do or don't like them.

STUDENT A you like painting 1; you hate 2 and 3.
STUDENT B you adore paintings 2 and 3; you hate 1.

LANGUAGE STUDY

Reported speech

1 Look at these two sentences.

DIRECT SPEECH: *'It's awful, I don't like it at all.'*
REPORTED SPEECH: *Jane said (that) it was awful and (that) she didn't like it at all.*

2 Study the examples and then complete the information on tense changes.

[handwritten: THIS → THAT.]

DIRECT SPEECH	REPORTED SPEECH
1 'My memory **is** excellent.'	She said her memory **was** excellent.
2 'I **passed** all my exams.:	She told me she **had passed** all her exams.
3 'I **have worked** very hard.'	She said she **had worked** very hard.
4 '**Will** I **win** a prize, Paul?'	She asked Paul if she **would win** a prize.
5 'What **would** you give me?'	She wanted to know what he **would** give her.

Tense changes: present simple → *[handwritten: simple past]*
[handwritten: simple past] → past perfect
present perfect → *[handwritten: past perfect]*
[handwritten: Future simple] → would

[handwritten: Present cont → past cont.]

✗ **3** Finish each sentence so that it means the same as the one printed above it.

1 'True genius is very rare,' said the expert.
   The expert said that ....
2 Frank told me he had bought a new computer.
   Frank said, '... .
3 'Do you think I'll fail my driving test?' Sally asked.
   Sally asked me ....
4 'Mozart wrote music at the age of four,' she said.
   She said that ....
5 'Alice, I'm leaving soon,' said Tom.
   Tom told ....
6 Mary asked, 'How much is the painting?'
   Mary asked how ....

WRITING

A description of a painting

Which of the two paintings does the text describe? Make any changes you think necessary to describe the other painting.

amapolas.

One of my favourite paintings is *Les Coquelicots* ('poppies') by the Impressionist Claude Monet. It was painted in 1873 and is a charming scene of a <u>stroll</u> through a field full of poppies on a late summer's day. In the foreground we can see a woman and a small child, who seems to be dressed in a sailor's suit. Behind them, further along the way, they are being followed by another woman and child. In the <u>background</u>, there is a row of trees and a house under a cloudy sky. I think I like this picture so much because the artist has managed to capture the time of day and year and moment perfectly. Of course, it was not painted in great detail, like many of the classical paintings that went before; instead it is a <u>delightful</u> → *beautiful* impression of a moment in time.

to go/walking slowly.

campo covered.

campo de trigo

SPEAKING

Work in pairs.

STUDENT A look at the picture on page 140. STUDENT B look at the picture on page 143.
Without showing each other your picture, take it in turns to describe it to your partner, who should try to draw it.

READING

A tragic genius

1 Before you read the biography of Vincent van Gogh, tell each other what you know about him. He painted several self-portraits; this one was painted shortly before his death. What does it say about the artist?

2 Read the story of Vincent Van Gogh and choose the best answer (**A**, **B** or **C**) to the following questions.

1 What do we know about Vincent's childhood?
A There was a lot of unhappiness.
B He spent a lot of time on his own.
C He had a stable personality.

2 Why did Vincent lose his job as a missionary?
A He was too extreme in what he did.
B He had lost his faith.
C He was unpopular among the coal miners.

3 Where did he produce the best of his early work?
A When he was staying with his family.
B In the four years after being a missionary.
C At Mauve's studio.

4 What did Vincent do in Paris?
A He worked for Goupil's again.
B He established his own identity as a painter.
C He decided to imitate the Impressionists.

5 Why did Vincent go to Arles?
A To meet his friend Gauguin.
B To find peace of mind.
C For better painting conditions.

6 What happened in Arles?
A Vincent attacked Gauguin.
B He produced some happy work.
C Gauguin forgave Vincent for their quarrel.

7 Why did Vincent enter the asylum?
A His family had sent him there.
B He feared for his sanity.
C He knew he would be able to paint.

8 Vincent died...
A at the asylum.
B because he took his own life.
C from a knife wound.

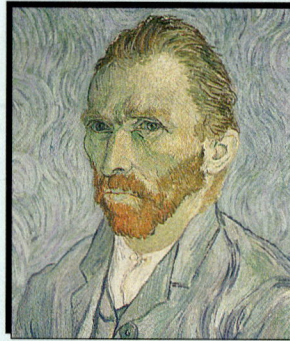

Vincent Van Gogh was born in Holland in 1853. His father was a Protestant pastor. His boyhood was happy although he was a moody and solitary child. (1) .... he was sixteen he joined the art-dealing firm, Goupil, where his uncle was a partner. Four years later he went to London where he had an unhappy love affair and lost his job. Vincent remained single. (2) .... working as a teacher he became a missionary among poor coal miners. He gave away everything he owned and was dismissed (3) .... for taking Christ's teaching too literally. He lost his faith but in 1880 found his vocation as an artist. He worked (4) .... four busy years producing sketches and dark watercolours of peasant life, which capture the lined and weathered faces of his subjects. (5) .... now, he had been self taught, so he went to work with the landscape artist Anton Mauve. After a row he returned to his family. (6) .... his stay with them he produced his best early work: The Potato Eaters. Vincent went to Paris where his brother, Theo, was working for Goupil's. There he was deeply influenced by the Impressionists and the simple but striking design of Japanese prints. This was the turning point of his career. (7) .... he progressed he developed his own style and used brighter colours to express his feelings.

In February 1888 he went to Arles in the south of France, searching for a brighter, 'Japanese' light. He rented a house which he painted yellow, and produced some cheerful pictures. He invited Gaugin to join him and (8) .... a long delay, he came. Vincent had been looking forward to the visit and had even decorated Gauguin's room with paintings of sunflowers. However, they got on badly and had arguments about art. After just one month Vincent threatened to kill his guest with a razor. Gauguin left the same night. As a mark of despair Vincent cut off part of his ear. (9) ...., terrified of madness, he entered the asylum of Saint-Remy de Provence. Despite periods of mental illness, he painted two hundred pictures, including much of his famous work including 'The Starry Night'. The self portrait with its swirling violet background helps us to understand the torment of his soul and inner turbulence. He felt he had to leave the clinic and travelled to Auvers-sur-Oise near Paris where Dr Gachet, a friend of the impressionists Pissarro and Cezanne, kept an eye on him. However, his mental condition worsened and he killed himself with a gun aged just 37. Today, his paintings sell for millions – (10) .... his life he sold just one.

LANGUAGE STUDY

Time expressions

1 Look back at the time expressions in Unit1, Set E and Unit 2, Set C.

2 Now complete the text using each of the following time expressions. Use each one once only.

this time	after	for	until	when
during	as	by now	during	after

LISTENING

1 Van Gogh did a number of paintings of the night sky. As you listen to this extract of the song 'Vincent' complete it by choosing one of the words at the end of the lines.

Starry starry night
Paint your palette blue and grey
Look out on a summer's day
With .... *eyes* .... that know the darkness in my soul. (ice/ eyes)
Shadows on the hills
Sketch the trees and the daffodils
Catch the .... *breeze* .... and the winter chills (freeze/breeze)
In colours on the snowy linen land.

Now I understand
What you tried to say to me
And how you suffered for your .... *sanity* .... (vanity/sanity)
And how you tried to set them free
They would not listen, they did not know how
Perhaps they'll listen now.

Starry starry night
.... *flaming* .... flowers that brightly blaze (framing/flaming)
Swirling clouds in violet haze
Reflect in Vincent's eyes of china blue
Colours changing .... *hue* .... (hue/you)
Morning fields of amber grain
Weathered faces lined in pain
Are .... *soothed* .... beneath the artist's loving hand
(soothed/smoothed)
For they .... *could* .... not love you (could/would)
But still your love was true
And when no hope was left in sight
On that starry starry night
You took your .... *life* .... as lovers often do. (knife/life)
But I could have told you Vincent
This world was never meant for one as beautiful as you.

2 Many famous people seem to have tragic lives. If you had a choice, would you like a happy but unremarkable life or an exceptional but unhappy one?
Does a genius have to be mad or different in some way?

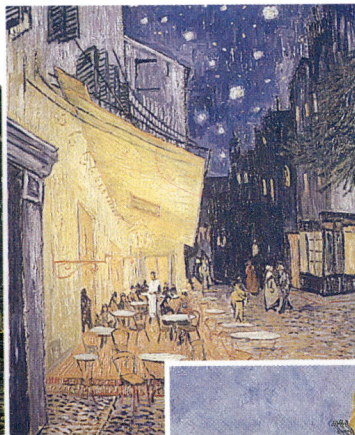

triste

LISTENING

The sad geniuses

Children who are born autistic never really learn normal social skills. However, they sometimes have remarkable abilities, as the case of Ellen Boudreaux shows.

1 Listen to the description of Ellen Boudreaux and tick (✔) her abilities.

1 She could hum a melody when she was still a baby. ✔
2 She was able to walk when she was just four months old. ✔ *no, because four years*
3 She can sense the position of objects. ✔
4 She can use radar equipment. ☐ *no*
5 She can sing any song she has ever heard. ✔
6 She can speak fluently on most topics. ✔
7 She is able to answer any questions of general knowledge she is asked. ☐ *no*
8 She has no idea of time. ✔ *she has an internal clock.*

— to know how to do something.

2 Did you find out anything which you thought was unusual or remarkable? Have you heard of any similar cases?

to hold a conversation = maintener una conversación.

verbs:
— can, could,
— be able to,
— manage + infinitive
— succeed in + gerund
— to be good/bad at something
— to have an ability to do something

LANGUAGE STUDY

1 Listen again and list the different ways in which the speaker describes ability.

2 Tell each other at what age you were able to: walk, speak, tell the time, tie your shoelaces, dress yourself, ride a bicycle, swim, read and write.

Do you think you were 'advanced', 'average' or 'backward' for your age?

3 Expand these notes to tell us about the extraordinary abilities of Alonzo Clemons.

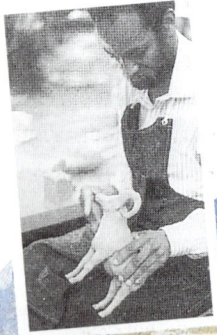

NOTES

- normal baby until age of three
- bad fall and brain damage
- poor speech
- very low intelligence
- aged 25, count to ten
- sculpts constantly
- only needs to see something once
- sculpts in the dark
- makes a horse in twenty minutes
- has sold over 500 pieces

4 🔲 Separable phrasal verbs

When an object comes between the verb and the particle, the particle is normally stressed more than the verb. Listen to these sentences and repeat them.

1 Turn it **off**.
2 Why don't you try them **on**?
3 I can't make it **out**. → *distinguish*
4 Shall we take him **in**?
5 Could you turn it **down**?

6 If I were you, I'd give it **away** → *to reveal a secret/regalar*
7 He made the story **up**.
8 When can you pay me **back**?
9 The operator cut us **off**.
10 The bad weather held us **up**.

to take in
→ to give somebody shelter (dar cobijo, ayudar)
→ to trick/deceive somebody

WRITING

1 Read the biography of the composer Wolfgang Amadeus Mozart and decide when you think he was happiest and most successful.

2 In the text there are twelve words which should not be there, e.g. **been**. Can you find them?

Mozart was born in 1756. He was the son of the composer and violinist Leopold Mozart. He was an extraordinary child who had been learned to play the harpsichord and violin and compose at the age of four. In 1762 his father took him on a tour of the Europe and he was warmly received at its principal courts. People everywhere were enchanted by the child and his extraordinary gifts. In Rome he was challenged for to prove himself; he heard a complicated piece of music twice but was then able to write it down perfectly! Mozart continued to tour and to perform but could not to find a permanent position. Eventually he found one with the Archbishop of Salzburg between 1779 and 1781, but this was an unhappy period because of he argued with his patron. Afterwards, he went to Vienna like as a freelance composer where he wrote much of his most famous work including the operas Marriage of Figaro and Don Giovanni. Despite of being known at the Imperial court this did not help Mozart financially and a lot of his work was poorly received. Much is made of the hatred and a jealousy felt by Salieri, another one court composer. In fact a few people have even accused him of poisoning Mozart. The truth is much more mundane. Mozart had been weakened by a deadly combination of poverty, travel and overwork. He was never able to relax himself because of always having to work so that when he went down with typhus he could not fight the disease and was died. The greatest composer the world has known he was buried in an unmarked grave. Much of Mozart's musical genius rests on his ability to achieve a fusion of German and Italian styles. He wrote 49 symphonies, four famous operas and many concertos and was composed about seven hundred pieces in all.

3 Using the texts about Van Gogh and Mozart as a guide, write a short biography of a famous person you admire. Remember to cover their early lives and to give details of their greatest achievements → *logro.*

SPEAKING

Look at the photograph of the headmistress and pupils of a certain school. What kind of school is it? How do you think the pupils get on with their headmistress?

(handwritten: directora de instituto.)

The last school to cane its girls

(handwritten: to criticize.)
(handwritten: Castigar/golpear con una vara/vergf.)
(handwritten: behave (word comportamiento))

IN NEARLY ALL SCHOOLS IN ENGLAND, pupils who misbehave are just told off by the teacher. However, at the expensive Rodney School naughty girls are punished by caning. The headmistress, Miss Thomas, who has run the school for 47 years, says that she only canes the girls to shame them rather than hurt them.

Surprisingly, the girls back their headmistress up; if they have been up to no good, they believe that they deserve to be punished. One girl, Adele Kirkman, was given three strokes on each hand for going into the nearby town without her school uniform. To be fair, Adele was allowed to choose between writing a long essay, staying in the school grounds for three weeks, or the cane. She chose the cane because it was quicker. Another girl, Nicola Whitely, then twelve, chose to be caned too, because she had been caught in her dormitory with some boys. When she phoned her father, he told her, "Think of all the things you have got away with. This time you have been caught."

(handwritten: to escape/To be free)
(handwritten: doing something bad)
(handwritten: golpes.)

READING

1 Read the text and decide if your assumptions were correct.

2 **Phrasal verbs in context**

Find the four phrasal verbs in the text and match them with the following meanings: *to criticize, to be in the act of doing, to escape punishment for, to support.*

(handwritten: told off)
(handwritten: to be up to / to get away with / back up.)

3 Discuss these questions in groups.

1 What do you think of the girls' attitude to punishment?
2 Which punishment would you have chosen if you'd been Adele?
3 What do you think of Nicola Whitely's father?
4 Do you think the girls will be good adults and parents?
5 What sort of punishment exists in schools in your country?
6 Have you ever been unfairly punished? If so, when?

(handwritten: injustice)

4 Look at these 'crimes' some pupils commit. Which three are the most serious and which three are the least serious?

smoking
being late without a good excuse
cheating in an examination
stealing
playing truant

being rude to the teacher
not doing homework
fighting
not wearing school uniform
bullying

LISTENING

1 Write down Tim's descriptions of Angela and Mr Gilbert.
2 What do you think about Tim, Angela and Mr Gilbert?
3 What do you think happened next and what were the consequences for Tim?

LANGUAGE STUDY

Describing physical appearance

1 Study the tapescript of the listening text on page 160 and notice how **to have, to be** and **with** are used.

2 Imagine that you once knew the people in the photograph below. Use the same sentence patterns and the words in the box to write descriptions of them.

eyelashes   wrinkles   scar   dark   curly   eyebrows   moustache   straight   fair

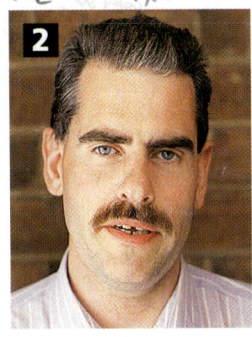
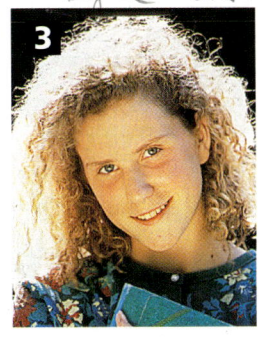

WRITING

'I shall never forget what happened ...'

Like Tim, you have probably had a memorable or embarrassing experience.
Perhaps it was associated with school.
Write a paragraph similar to the one you have heard describing:

* when and where it happened/how old you were.
* the people in the story and what they looked like.
* what happened and how you felt.
* what the consequences were (if there were any).

[handwritten notes at top of page:]

4 1/2 – 7 1/2 – PRIMARY ⎫ OBLIGATORY
7 1/2 – 11 1/2 – JUNIOR ⎭
11 1/2 – 16 1/2 ⎫ OPTIONAL
16 1/2 – 18 1/2 ⎭

Bricklayer = albañil

To pull the chain = Tirar de la cadena

VOCABULARY

Education

1 Look at these names of educational institutions in England and use them to complete the definitions.

> university   college   nursery school
> secondary school   kindergarten   primary school

1 Young children often attend a .... or a ...., where they learn to get on with other children, play educational games, etc.
2 Pupils attend a .... between the ages of five and eleven.
3 Pupils attend a .... between the ages of eleven and sixteen or eighteen. This is where they take their GCSE and/or A level examinations.
4 Older students can attend a .... or .... for higher education and further qualifications (e.g. a degree).

Which educational institutions do you attend in your country and at what ages do you attend them?

2 Match the names with the definitions.

> lecturer   apprentice   professor   coach   instructor

1 someone who trains a sports team
2 someone who teaches a skill like skiing or driving
3 someone who teaches at a university or college
4 someone who works with an experienced person for a number of years to learn a trade or skill
5 someone who heads a university department

Now read these extracts and decide who is speaking in each case. How do you know?

- 'M.S.M. Mirror signal manoeuvre. I want you to turn left at the traffic lights. Look in your mirror. All clear?'
- 'Carefully now. If in doubt measure it again. Remember, if you cut a piece off, you can't put it back!'
- 'I'm very disappointed with your results. If you don't do better when you take them again, you'll have to leave. Degree courses are tough and we can't lower our standards just for you.'
- 'Right, we may be a goal down but everything's to play for. This half, take the game to them.'

READING

All I really need to know...

1 Look at the pictures of kindergarten life. Can you identify what the children are doing?

2 Think about your own early years at school. Did you learn any lessons that have helped you later on? Find out from your partner(s) what they learned from their first experience of school.

3 Read the text about the lessons the writer learned at kindergarten in America.

Which lessons do you think are a) very important; b) quite important; c) not necessary?

All I really need to know about how to live and what to do and how to be, I learned in Kindergarten.
These are the things I learned:
Share everything.
Play fair.
Don't hit people.
Put things back where you found them.
Clean up your own mess.
Don't take things that aren't yours.
Say you're sorry when you hurt somebody.
Wash your hands before you eat.
Flush. 
Warm cookies and cold milk are good for you.
Live a balanced life – learn some and draw and paint and sing and dance and play and work every day some.
Take a nap every afternoon. 
When you go out into the world, watch out for traffic, hold hands, and stick together.
Be aware of wonder. Remember the little seed in the Styrofoam cup; the roots go down and the plant goes up and nobody really knows how or why, but we are all like that.
Goldfish and hamsters and white mice and even the little seed in the Styrofoam cup – they all die. So do we.
And then remember the _Dick and Jane_ books and the first word you learned – the biggest word of all – LOOK.

Handwritten labels on illustration: SPADE, BUCKET (BUCKET AND SPADE). "SAND PIT." seed = semilla. pig Tail = coletas, pony Tail 1 cleta. "gold fish" = pez de colar. fish-bowl "pecera". A fish-Tank = gran pecera.

LANGUAGE STUDY

✗ Indefinite pronouns

1 Some-, any-, no-:

*Say you're sorry when you hurt **somebody**.*
Study these sentences and answer the questions.

A I need **somebody/someone** to talk to, **something** to eat and **somewhere** to sleep.

B I haven't got **anybody/anyone** to talk to, **anything** to eat or **anywhere** to sleep.

C Is there **anybody/anyone** to talk to, **anything** to eat or **anywhere** to sleep?

D There's **nobody/no one** to talk to, **nothing** to eat and **nowhere** to sleep.

Which form (**some-**, **any-**, **no-**) do we use:

1 in questions? C
2 in statements with a positive sense? A
3 in statements with a negative sense but a positive structure? D
4 in sentences with negative structures? B

✗ 2 Every-: *Share **everything**.*

Replace the italic words with an indefinite pronoun beginning with **every-**.

1 We asked *all the people there*. everybody
2 She ate *all there was to eat*. everything
3 I looked *all over the house* for the keys. everywhere

✗ 3 Complete the passage with an appropriate indefinite pronoun.

I had been sleeping when (1) ....Something/Somebody...... woke me up. There was a funny noise coming from downstairs. I went to the top of the stairs and said, 'Is (2) ......anybody...... there?' (3) ......No one...... answered! Feeling a little braver, I looked in the sitting room, in the cupboards and in the dining room. In fact I looked (4) ......everywhere...... Finally I went into the kitchen. I saw (5) ......someone...... standing by the fridge. I screamed and turned on the light. It was my flatmate, Julian. 'Sorry,' he said. 'I got up because I felt like (6) ......something...... to eat so I had a few biscuits but I dropped the tin.' I looked in the tin, there was (7) ......nothing...... there. He had eaten (8) ......everything......

SPEAKING

⌐ Lost lessons

Which lessons have these people forgotten?

1 Peter Jones never tidied his room. His mother had to do it. *clean up his own room*
2 Jenny Brown won the lottery but did not give her family any money. *share everything.*
3 Sam Smith ran across the road and was hit by a car. *watch out before.*
4 Pat Fisher worked so hard that she lost all her friends. *live a balanced life.*
5 Chris Lee always cheated at card games. In the end, no one would play with him. *play fair.*
6 A rich man had his body frozen so that future scientists could bring him back to life, but somebody turned the freezer off by mistake! *don't like things that you don't know.*

READING

Interpreting information

Compulsory education in Britain lasts until the age of 16, when pupils may leave school and start work. Look at the end-of-term reports for four pupils. They take seven compulsory and five optional subjects. Their results are coded A–F.

A = excellent   B = very good   C = good   D = fair   E = below average   F = poor
Answer the questions by writing **BG** (for Belinda Grey); **AR** (for Arnold Roberts); **RP** (for Ratan Patel) and **AD** (for Alison Dukes) in the boxes after each question.

1 Which pupils are best at art? ☐ ☐
2 Whose performance in science subjects is surprisingly poor? ☐
3 Which pupils want to leave school? ☐ ☐
4 Who lacks self-confidence? ☐
5 Who has caused problems in class? ☐ ☐
6 Who is poor at French? ☐ ☒
7 Whose best subjects are English and Geography? RP

BELINDA GREY

Compulsory		Optional	
English	A	Physics	B
Mathematics	A	Biology	C
Science	B	Chemistry	D
French	F	German	
History	D	Spanish	
Geography	C	Handicraft	D
Art	C	Computer Science	A

Class tutor's coments
Belinda is a helpful and co-operative member of the class. She continues to shine at English, Mathematics and Computer Science and could take these subjects at advanced level. Belinda should be proud of her achievements but requires constant encouragement.

ARNOLD ROBERTS

Compulsory		Optional	
English	B	Physics	
Mathematics	B	Biology	E
Science	B	Chemistry	C
French	C	German	B
History	E	Spanish	-
Geography	D	Handicraft	B
Art	A	Computer Science	D

Class tutor's comments
Arnold continues to perform at an above average standard. His work in Art has been outstanding this year. His teachers of History and Geography complain that he becomes easily bored in their classes. We are mystified by his perfomance in Science subjects this year. He appears to have lost much of his enthusiasm. He has some difficult choices to make at "A" level.

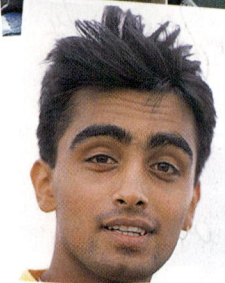

RATAN PATEL

Compulsory		Optional	
English	A	Physics	D
Mathematics	C	Biology	
Science	E	Chemistry	F
French	B	German	B
History	B	Spanish	B
Geography	A	Handicraft	-
Art	E	Computer Science	C

Class tutor's coments
Ratan is an outgoing and extrovert student. Unfortunately this led to some silly and dangerous behaviour in a Chemistry lesson. He is intelligent and articulate and has performed exceptionally well in English, Geography and Languages. We feel that if he leaves school now it will be a decision he will regret in later years. Everyone concerned should encourage him to stay on.

ALISON DUKES

Compulsory		Optional	
English	C	Physics	F
Mathematics	C	Biology	C
Science	D	Chemistry	
French	B	German	D
History	F	Spanish	-
Geography	B	Handicraft	B
Art	A	Computer Science	D

Class tutor's comments
Alison's conduct continues to give concern as she often disrupts classes through her silly behaviour. She is clearly bored with most subjects even though she clearly excels at Art and Handicraft. She should be congratulated on her improvement in French although her performance in History and Physics has been even poorer than before. We are aware that she wishes to find employment at the end of this academic year.

LANGUAGE STUDY

1 Write sentences comparing the performance of Ratan Patel and Alison Dukes at the compulsory subjects. Check the box for help.

Comparatives

Short adjectives:	short**er than**
Long adjectives:	**more** / **less** beautiful **than**
Remember:	**Good** ... **better than**
	Bad ... **worse than**
	as adjective *as* (= the same)

Superlatives

Short adjectives:	**the** short**est**
Long adjectives:	**the** **most** / **least** beautiful
Remember:	**Good** ... **the best**
	Bad ... **the worst**

Example: *Alison Dukes is bad at Science but Ratan is even worse.*

2 Compare the performance of all four pupils at French, History and Science.

VOCABULARY

Adjective + preposition

*Ratan Patel is **good at** languages.*

1 Match the adjectives with the prepositions.

1	good/bad		A	in
2	keen		B	of
3	interested		C	with
4	tired		D	at
5	disappointed		E	on

2 Look at the pupils' results again and complete these sentences with the most appropriate combination of adjective and preposition. In some cases, you will have to use the superlative form of the adjective.

1 Belinda Grey seems to be very *bad* ....at.... French. [*to be poor*]
2 Ratan Patel must be quite .... in languages, after all, he got two Bs.
3 Alison Dukes was probably .... her results in History and Physics. [*keen on / with*]
4 Ratan Patel probably isn't .... Science; if he liked it more, he would probably do better. [*the best at / interested in*]
5 Belinda is the ..*best at*.. Maths and Alison is the ..*worst at*.. Physics.
6 However, Belinda finds languages boring. If she were more ..*interested in*.. them, she would do much better. [*keen on*]
7 Arnold Roberts is ....*tired of*.... Biology; he has been studying it too long!

SPEAKING

Role play

Parents, teachers and pupils are meeting to discuss the futures of the four pupils. Form groups of three. Your teacher will give you each a role – parent, teacher or pupil. Read the notes on the particular pupil and then act out the meeting.

Belinda Grey
Father a successful businessman. Disappointed with his daughter's performance. Belinda wants to study electronic engineering at university but does not have much self-confidence.

Alison Dukes
Parents both want her to stay at school until she is eighteen. She is tired of school, wants to leave. Has been offered an apprenticeship in the fashion business. Would like to accept it.

Ratan Patel
Wants to leave school but his parents want him to stay until he is eighteen. Ratan's ambition – to be a travel agent. Will need A levels for this.

Arnold Roberts
Parents both dentists. Want Arnold to become a dentist and join their practice. Arnold is worried about disappointing his parents. But would he make a good dentist?

LISTENING

A miraculous way to learn?

Kay Able is talking to Dr Brian Green, a lecturer in psychology, about a new approach to language learning. The interview is in three short parts.

1 **Part A** Listen to the first part of the interview and label the diagram to show which functions belong to which half of the brain.

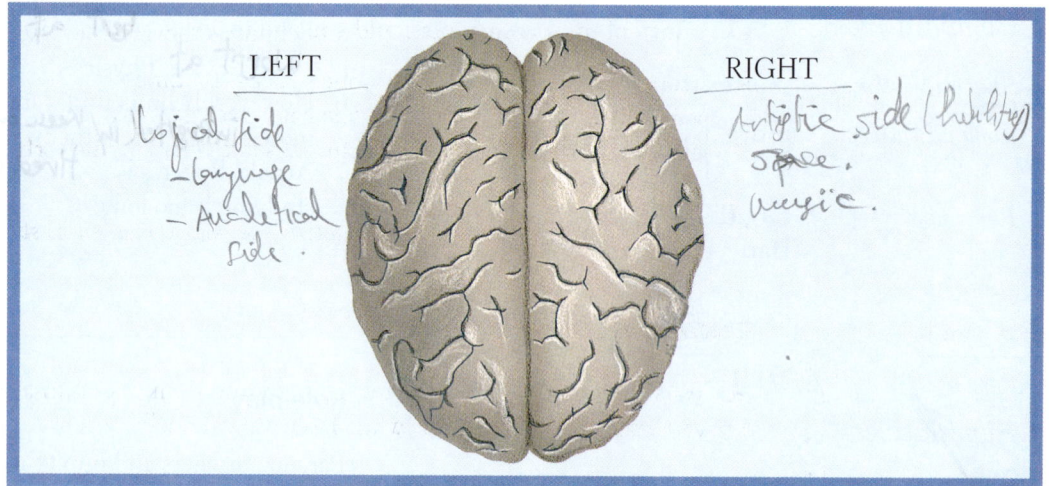

LEFT   RIGHT

2 **Part B** Listen for the answers to these questions.

1 Which side of the brain do most teaching methods use?
2 What is the problem with this?
3 Why does Dr Green mention songs and rhymes? Does the interviewer agree?

3 **Part C** Listen and tick the special features of the method Dr Green describes.

1 It involves singing. ☐
2 Students have to meditate. ☐
3 The teacher speaks in an unnatural way. ☑
4 Students try to draw the words on paper. ☐
5 The students listen to music while they study. ☑

• Does this seem a good way of learning to you?
• How do you remember new words?

LANGUAGE STUDY

Revision of adverbs

1 Complete the second sentence with an adverb so that it means the same as the first.

1 He is a bad player.   – He plays ....
2 He is a slow learner.   – He learns ....
3 He was a hard worker.   – He worked ....
4 She has got a beautiful voice. – She sings ....
5 He is a fast walker.   – He walks ....
6 She is a quick thinker.   – She thinks ....
7 She is a good writer.   – She writes ....

2 Important differences

Study the three pairs of sentences. Note the difference between the words in **bold**.

1a She is studying **hard**. 1b She is **hardly** studying.
2a She never comes **late** to school. 2b She hasn't been to school **lately**.
3a Exam time is getting **near**. 3b She **nearly** failed her exams.

3 Which of these comments could you add to which sentence above?

a Perhaps she's sick. *(2b)* d She's always on time. *(2a)*
b What a lazy girl! *(1b)* e She had a lucky escape. *(3b)*
c Just another two weeks! *(3a)* f She does two hours' homework every morning. *(1a)*

4 Which words in bold mean: *not on time, not much, close, almost, recently, a lot?*

WRITING

Learning to swim

1 What is going on in the picture? How do you think the child feels? Do you remember learning to swim? How did you feel?

2 Quickly read through the text and find out the different stages the writer went through when she was learning how to swim.

- What did you think of the teacher's method?
- Could it be applied to other kinds of learning?

3 Punctuate the text and arrange it into three paragraphs.

I shall never forget how I learned to swim I was nine years old and like many other children I was terrified of the water However my teacher Miss Townsend had a wonderful system for teaching swimming it worked with nine children out of ten Once a week we all went to the swimming pool The first couple of times we got used to the water and splashed about in the shallow end After that we had a kind of board which helped us to float when we moved up and down the pool by kicking our legs By now most of us knew how to float but we did not have the confidence to swim on our own Our teacher had a brilliant idea She took two ordinary cotton reels and tied a long piece of string between them I held one of them and Miss Townsend held the other and I swam for the very first time supported by my belief in the power of the tiny cotton reel

4 Now write a story about how you were taught to do something.

8 City Life

SPEAKING

Look at these photographs.
Which cities do you associate with them?

A *A big city* 2→

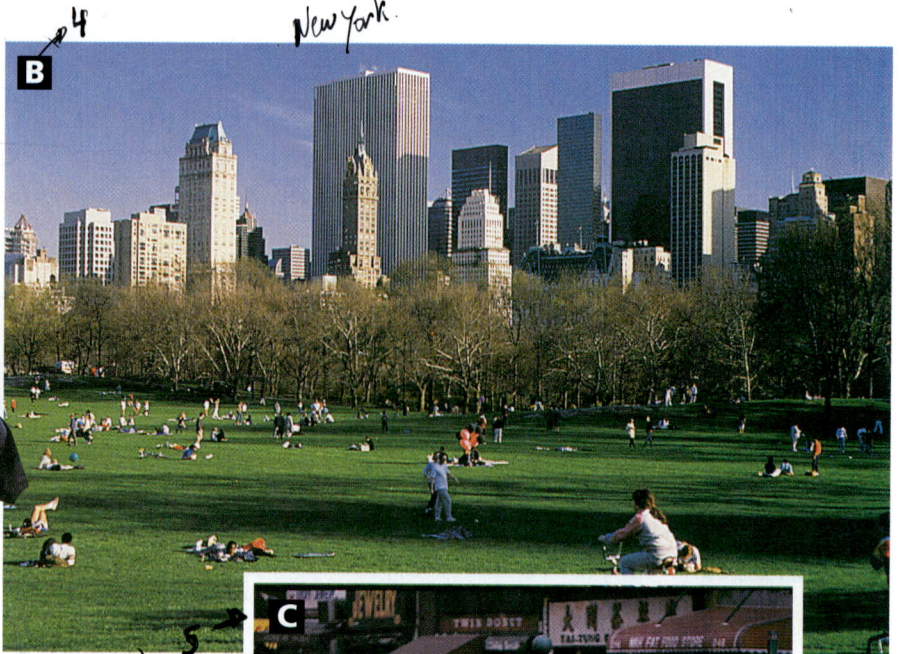

B 4 New York

oriental city (Singapore) 5 →

3 → D

C *American city*

American city (subway). 1.

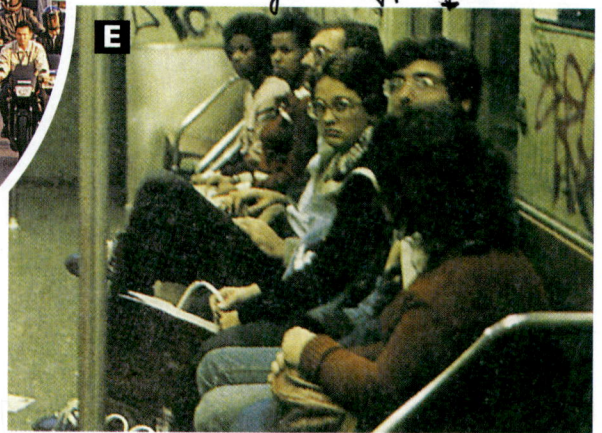

E

LISTENING

City thoughts

Listen to the thoughts of people in some of the photographs. Who do the thoughts belong to?
How do you know?

70

VOCABULARY

City Life

Read this passage about life in London to get a general idea of what it is about, then choose the most appropriate word (**A**, **B**, or **C**) below to fill each of the gaps.

There was a time when you could cross London on a leisurely morning walk. Nowadays the city has become so (1) .... by exhaust fumes that much of the pleasure has been taken out of walking. The problem has been made worse by the terrible traffic (2) .... which block the main roads. Fortunately, one of its magnificent parks is never too far away. There are still a hundred and one things to do and see which is why (3) .... is one of London's most important industries. All year round tourists flock to visit its (4) .... museums and sights and witness (5) .... like the changing of the guard at Buckingham Palace. Hotels can be dear, so I would advise visitors to rent a room with a (6) .... as it will give them the opportunity to experience everyday family life at first hand. Getting around London is easy using its (7) .... transport service. Avoid blocked streets by using the (8) .... network. Although it can appear complicated at first sight, it is a lot more comfortable and much safer than say the New York (9) .... You should buy a Travelcard – a kind of season ticket – which means you don't have to pay a (10) .... each time you get on a bus or train! A guide book too is also a(n) (11) .... companion.

Unfortunately, in recent years residential areas close to the (12) .... have started to suffer from (13) .... problems. You can often see (14) .... people sleeping in parks or begging and it is not always safe to walk alone at night. So even though for most people the (15) .... of living has risen, the quality of life has declined. This is why so many people, the famous London (16) .... , prefer a long train journey to work rather than live in the city. They would rather live in one of its leafy (17) .... or in the country. Even though they have to stand all the way in the (18) .... hour they may feel that the sacrifice of a long (19) .... to work is worthwhile for the sake of their families. When there are transport problems it often (20) .... them a long time to get home.

	A	B	C
1	stained	polluted	gassed
2	lights	crowds	jams
3	sightseeing	tourism	visiting
4	history	ancient	historic
5	heritage	traditions	customs
6	hostel	landlady	hotel
7	civil	private	public
8	coach	metro	underground
9	motorway	subway	tram
10	fee	fare	tip
11	invaluable	worthless	priceless
12	centre	downtown	suburban
13	social	sociable	society
14	drug-addict	homeless	tramps
15	level	standard	cost
16	computers	trainers	commuters
17	outskirts	suburbs	suburban
18	point	busy	rush
19	voyage	trip	journey
20	needs	wants	takes

SPEAKING

1 Try to describe the scenes in the photographs using as much of the vocabulary as you can from the previous exercise.

2 How do you think the people feel in each of the situations you can see?

READING

Poppy is a Greek student who is going to do an intensive English course in London. She has received a letter from a friend of her father's, who has arranged her accommodation for her.

1 Read the letter and put the paragraphs in the right order.

2 Look at the underground map on page 77 and follow the route suggested by Martin.

1

Dear Poppy

2 Turn left just as you come out of the station and go straight on. Brooksville Avenue is the fifth road on the left. It's a ten minute walk. If you've got a lot of luggage, then you could always get off the Underground at Hyde Park Corner and take a taxi.

3 She is an extremely nice woman in her fifties and has been a family friend for years. Her husband died two years ago so she lives alone. I have arranged for you to have bed and breakfast there, which will cost you £55 a week. You'll also be able to have limited use of the kitchen for basic cooking.

4 I am writing to confirm the arrangements for your accommodation while you are in London. Your father told me that you'll be arriving at Heathrow Airport on 20th September. I'll do my best to make sure someone from my office is there to meet you.

5 As I said, I am 99% certain you'll be met but, in case something goes wrong, this is how you get there. The best way of getting to the centre of London from Heathrow is by Underground. Take the Underground to Piccadilly Circus then change to a northbound Bakerloo train and get off at Queen's Park station. This part of the journey will take about fifty minutes.

6 All the same, I'd better give you the full name and address of your landlady just in case there are any problems :

Mrs Angela Hallam
98 Brooksville Avenue
London NW13
Tel: 0181-623-8990

7 I look forward to seeing you soon.
Best wishes,
Martin Smith

3 Question making

Poppy is phoning an American friend who wants to visit her in London.
What are her friend's questions?

1 .... ?
   She's in her fifties.

2 .... ?
   She was, but now she's a widow.

3 .... ?
   £55 a week.

4 .... ?
   Just light meals.

5 .... ?
   Heathrow.

6 .... ?
   No, you have to change at Piccadilly Circus.

7 .... ?
   About fifty minutes.

8 .... ?
   About a kilometre.

9 .... ?
   No, the fifth.

WRITING

Imagine someone is coming to visit you from abroad. Write a letter explaining how to reach you by public transport.

LISTENING

Two cities

Poppy has arrived at Mrs Hallam's in London.
Listen to their conversation. **Part A** is about London and **Part B** is about Athens.

1 Part A Listen once and answer these general questions.

1 How does Mrs Hallam feel about London?
2 How does Poppy react to what she hears?
3 What sort of person is Mrs Hallam?

2 Part A Listen again and find answers to these more specific questions.

1 When was Mrs Hallam's house built?
2 Why is London so spread out?
3 Why have people left the city for the countryside?
4 What does Mrs Hallam say about her own area?
5 What social problems does she mention?
6 Why did she move back to London?

3 Part B Listen once and answer these general questions.

1 Has Mrs Hallam ever been to Athens?
2 What big problem does Poppy mention?

4 Part B Listen once again. What solution has been tried?

WRITING

Summary writing

You are going to write a summary of the advantages and disadvantages of London and Athens.

1 Complete the grid with the main points from the conversation between Mrs Hallam and Poppy.

CITY	ADVANTAGES	DISADVANTAGES
London		
Athens		

2 Compare your grid with a partner and decide on the major points you will mention in your summary.

3 In your own words, write a paragraph summarizing the advantages and disadvantages of the two cities.

READING

Rome the transformer

1 In the 1970s, Denise Lawrence spent four years in Rome. Read the text and answer these key questions.

1 What was Denise like before she lived in Rome?
2 What effect did living in Rome have on her?
3 What's Denise's theory about becoming a Roman?

2 Match the headings (**A–F**) with paragraphs (**1–6**).

> A Skills and customs. *4*
> B A sad case. *2*
> C The final exam. *6*
> D One of the crowd. *3*
> E It could happen to you. *5*
> F The transformer. *1*

3 Decide if these statements are **true** or **false**.

1 Southern Europe has helped to civilize the north. *T*
2 Denise used to carefully control her behaviour. *T*
3 It is easy to become a Roman. *T*
4 Denise believes it can be good to disobey rules. *F*
5 It can be very dangerous to have a discussion in Rome. *F*
6 The best way of crossing the road in Rome is to run. *F*

4 Word search

Find the nouns that can be made from these adjectives and verbs, e.g. **behave** →**behaviour**:

grateful ....*Gratitude (1)*.... frustrated ....*frustration*.... ;
proud ....*Pride*....; appear ....*appearance (3)*....
violent ....*Violence*....; speak ....*Speech (5)*....
embarrasses ....*Embarrasment (5)*.... please ....*pleasure (6)*....;
recognise ....*recognition (4)*.... confident ....*confidence (6)*....

nice/elegant

1 **F** The years I spent in Rome changed me. The city and its people civilized me. This is hardly surprising because Mediterranean cultures have been doing this to barbarians for centuries. It helps to explain the affection and gratitude the English feel for Italy, a country which has taught many of us how to live, feel and 'be'.

2 **B** Before I lived in Rome, I was happy to own two scruffy pairs of jeans and have wild and unruly hair. I always waited for the green man at pedestrian crossings. I ate in order to exist. I queued obsessively (the *true* national sport in England), and never sounded the horn of a car in warning or frustration. I had probably never *really* enjoyed myself or lost my inhibitions.

3 **D** Yet within a year of living in Rome, I had found a new pride in my appearance with my smart clothes and hairstyle. I could fight my way onto a bus and play 'La Cucaracha' on my car horn from absolute joy. I no longer felt like a stranger – I felt I belonged there. I'm convinced that this could happen to anyone. Nor is there anything genetic about it: I've seen repressed English people and retiring Swedes and Germans totally adopt the behaviour of their hosts. If you went to live in Rome, you'd become a Roman, too.

4 **A** Pretty quickly, you'd take more care of how you looked. You'd drink your coffee strong and black – not long and milky. You'd learn a healthy disrespect for petty rules and regulations. You'd develop the skills of a Grand Prix racing driver – and be able to squeeze your car into a space with no room left for even a pack of cigarettes.

5 **E** And how would you feel about your magnificent surroundings?

Well, you'd no longer walk past famous buildings with your mouth open like a Venus fly-trap – you'd take the Trevi Fountain and the Colosseum and Forum for granted. The changes inside would be even greater. You'd be incapable of speech without moving your hands, yet be able to argue passionately without a hint of physical violence. You'd find pleasure in perfect food and drink and evenings spent in atmospheric cafés overlooking delightful squares. You would *belong* there. When pink and puffy northerners in their awful clothes crossed your path you would look away in embarrassment. Their eyes would pass over you without recognition.

6 **C** However, the real test is this: while deep in conversation, step into the road and stroll casually across six lanes of speeding traffic full of confidence that the cars will miss you. If you can do this, then you'll be a Roman.

[handwritten top:] 1st type → present simple → future simple → probable ans occurs. 2nd type → past simple → conditional simple → improbable. 3rd type → past perfect → perfect conditional → very improbable.

SET A B C D **8**

LANGUAGE STUDY

The first and second conditional

[handwritten: Type I → Imperative form. Eat it if you want to go out!]

1 Look at these two sentences.

a *If you move to Rome, **you'll become** a Roman too.*
b *If you moved to Rome, **you'd become** a Roman too.*

[handwritten: Don't smoke if you want to live longer!]

In which sentence does the speaker believe you may possibly move to Rome? *[handwritten: a]*
In which one does the speaker believe that this is unlikely (or even impossible)? *[handwritten: b]*

2 Whether we use the first or second conditional often depends on how likely we think something is. We often use the second conditional when we are imagining or day-dreaming.

*If I **had** £1,000,000, I **would buy** a yacht. (But I'm quite ordinary; I'll never have £1,000,000.)* *[handwritten: Normal]*

3 Study the 'probability meter' and the example, then expand the other words to make complete sentences using either the first or second conditional.

[handwritten: carpet → Alfombras (Moquets). Rug/Mat → Alfombras.]

SPEAKING

Cultural exchanges

Denise says she learnt a lot from living in Rome. What lessons could people from your country teach or learn from other cultures? Think about:

- driving
- working hard
- honesty
- enjoying food and drink
- music and fashion
- personal relationships

WRITING

Just like you!

A foreigner really wants to become exactly like someone from your country. Write down the advice you would give. Cover the categories you discussed in the speaking exercise.

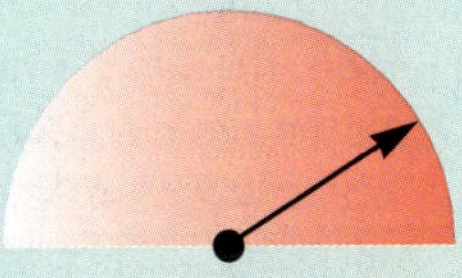

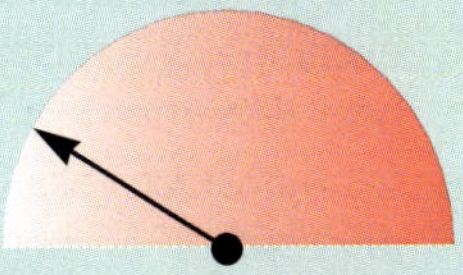

Example

[handwritten: Type 0 → present simple → present simple → universal truth.]

possible but unlikely — quite possible
impossible — definite

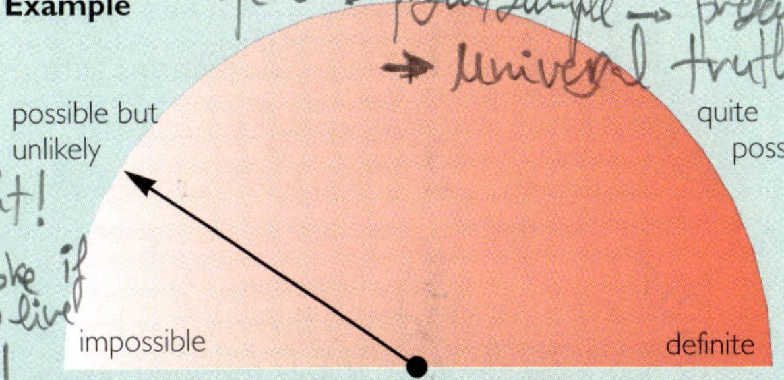

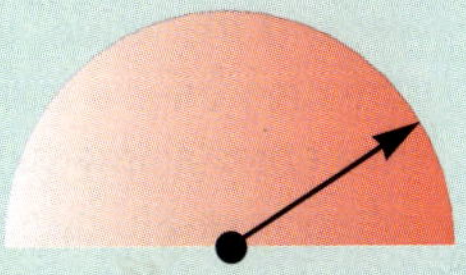

If/fewer tourists/go to Rome/it be less crowded.
If fewer tourists went to Rome, it would be less crowded.

1 If I/eat less pasta/I/lose a lot of weight.
[handwritten: Type I. If I eat less pasta I'll lose a lot of weight.]

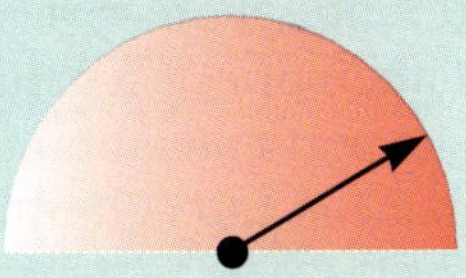

2 If Rome/less polluted/life/be much more pleasant.
[handwritten: Type II → If Rome were less polluted life would be much more pleasant. → more hypothetical.]

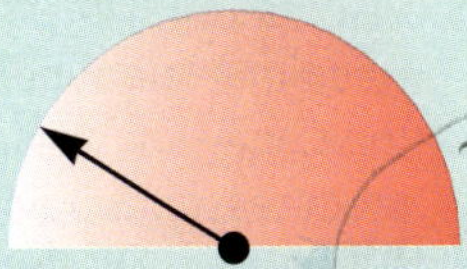

3 If you/cross road now/you/get run over.
[handwritten: If you cross the road you'll get run over.]

4 If you/cross road now/you/get run over.
[handwritten: If you crossed road you would get run over.]

5 If underground/be/more efficient/I/use it more often.
[handwritten: If the underground were more efficient I would use it more often.]

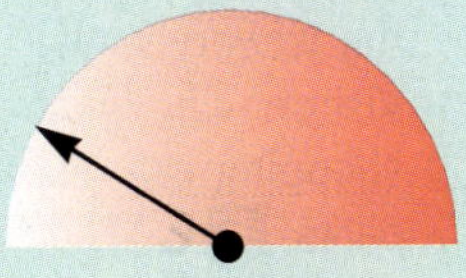

6 If you/enjoy/ice cream/you/be/in heaven in Rome.
[handwritten: If you enjoy ice cream you'll be in heaven in Rome.]

7 What/you do/if/I give you a plane ticket?
[handwritten: What would you do if I gave you a plane ticket.]

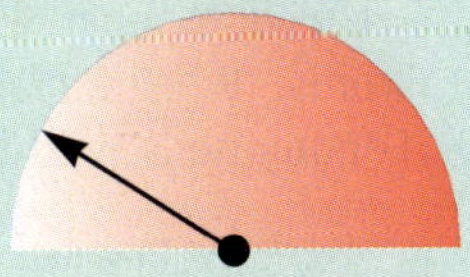

75

READING

London then and now

1 Match the pictures with the pieces of text to which they refer.

2 Choose which of the following sentences (**A–F**) fits each gap (**1–6**).

A	However, the city has not seen only royalty and glamour.
B	By this time, it had already expanded well beyond its medieval boundaries.
C	It was founded on the river's north bank by the Romans in AD 43 at the river's lowest convenient crossing point.
D	In fact, it is now difficult to tell where London begins and ends!
E	Its cultural life is rich and varied; during the day, you can visit its museums which contain priceless exhibits.
F	The port and empire have now gone and nowadays it owes its existence to being a financial and cultural centre.

London is on the River Thames about 40 miles from the coast. **1** It became a successful and important city which was never left empty even after the departure of the legions. The Danes sacked and burnt the city which was re-fortified by King Alfred (871-899). Following the Norman conquest in 1066 one of its most famous landmarks, the Tower of London, was constructed by William the Conqueror. Over the next centuries London continued to prosper and grow. In 1500 it had a population of about 50,000 which had mushroomed to around half a million in 1700. **2** Shakespeare's theatre had been constructed beyond the city limits on the south bank a century earlier but was now part of the city. London's period of most dramatic growth was in the 1800s. In 1800 the population was just under a million but at the time of Queen Victoria's diamond jubilee in 1897 it was over five million and was the largest city in the world. These days it has around 7,000,000 inhabitants and is spread over a vast area. **3** Its fortunes have changed along with Britain's as a whole. It was once the world's greatest port and the hub of an enormous overseas' empire. **4** Perhaps it is most famous as the home of the British monarchy.

Visitors can witness the timeless traditions surrounding it. Since Edward the Confessor, William the Conqueror's predecessor, Britain has had 47 rulers. **5** In 1348, the Black Death killed half its population. In 1665, it struck again and killed over 1,000 a week. In 1666, the Great Fire destroyed nearly all the old city. During the Second World War, bombs destroyed the docklands. Since then, they have been rebuilt as smart residential areas. Today, the capital has something for everyone. It has some of the world's best department stores. The most famous store of all is Harrods which prides itself on being able to obtain anything from a pin to an elephant. There are real bargains to be found in the January sales.

Visitors who want a break from shopping can relax in its beautiful parks. **6** The most visited destination is the British Museum which houses treasures from all around the world. In the evening its theatres offer a marvellous range of live entertainment. Overseas visitors often take the opportunity to go to at least one of the musicals which are always playing. With so much on offer, we have to agree with Dr Johnson's words: 'When a man is tired of London he is tired of life.'

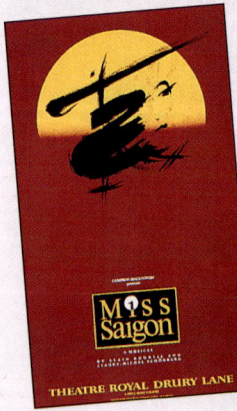

WRITING

Answer these questions about London. Then use the same questions to make notes about your own town or capital city, and write about it.

1 Where is it and what is its population? *7 000 000 inhabitant*
2 What are its origins and what is it known for today? *Romans AD 43*
3 What are its history and traditions (good and bad things)? *theatre* *Not famous for food (restaurants) museums, ...*
4 What can visitors do?

LISTENING

Finding the way

1 Poppy needs help to find a restaurant in Covent Garden. Listen and fill in the gaps in the dialogue.

POPPY: I was (1) ...Wondering if you could... help me, Mrs Hallam. I want to get to Covent Garden.

MRS HALLAM: Oh yes. That's easy. Let's look at the Underground map. Right, we're in West London, so you (2) ...Take the....... – that's the Bakerloo line – to Piccadilly Circus. Then (3) ...change..... to the Piccadilly line, and (4) ...take the..... eastbound tube to Covent Garden. *imperative*

POPPY: Thank you. How (5) ...long do you think it will.. ?

MRS HALLAM: About half an hour.

Poppy is at Covent Garden but can't find the restaurant.

POPPY: Excuse me. (6) ...Could you.. tell me (7) ...the way to.. Garrick Street?

PASSER-BY 1: Sorry, (8) ...I'm a stranger here myself..

POPPY: Oh dear. Excuse me (9) ...Can you tell me where.. Garrick Street is?

PASSER-BY 2: Yes, but you're walking the wrong way. (10) ...Go down.... the tube station, *this road past the tube station* (11) ...Take the 3... fourth turning (12) ...on the left... and cut through into Garrick Street. It's only a couple of minutes' walk. *imperative*

POPPY: Thanks a lot. (13) ...Do you happen.. time, please? *Do you happen to know the time please?* *to par casualidad tiene la hora.*

PASSER-BY 2: Yes, it's 8.15.

2 Look at the completed texts and study the ways in which Poppy makes requests. How do Mrs Hallam and Passer-by 2 give Poppy directions? *asking.* *- Poppy makes direct questions.*

SPEAKING

Giving directions

In pairs, using the Underground map, ask for and give each other directions from:

• Notting Hill Gate to Charing Cross.
• Knightsbridge to Covent Garden.
• Elephant and Castle to Euston.
• Piccadilly Circus to High Street Kensington.

READING

A case of prejudice?

1 Before you read the article, study these dictionary definitions.

> **prejudice** – (an example of) unfair and often unfavourable feeling or opinion not based on reason or enough knowledge: *a new law to discourage racial prejudice (prejudice against members of other races); a prejudice against women drivers*

> **discrimination – -nated, -nating**
> 1 (between) to see or make a difference (between two or more things or people): *You must try to discriminate between facts and opinions.* 2 (against/in favour of) usu. derog. to treat (a person or group) as worse/better than others: *This law discriminates against lower paid workers.*

2 Read the article and find out:

- who Nigel Benn is.
- what happened to him on the motorway.
- why the police apologized to Benn last year.

Stopped because I was a black in a white Porsche

BOXING CHAMP NIGEL BENN claimed last night he was stopped by cops because he was a BLACK man driving a flashy WHITE sports car.

Benn, nicknamed 'the Dark Destroyer', said one officer alleged his £140,000 Porsche 911 Turbo was stolen.

The twenty-six-year-old world middleweight champ said: 'The policeman tried to humiliate me because I was a black man driving an expensive car.'

It happened as Benn and his black manager, Ambrose Mendy, were driving in the slow moving traffic on the M25. The boxer was changing lanes when a policeman jumped out from a parked patrol car. Benn said: 'He hit the roof of my car and said, "I believe this car is stolen." He was going crazy and kept swearing. I said I was Nigel Benn, but he still gave me a ticket.'

Thames Valley Police said: 'Any complaint will be investigated.' Last January,

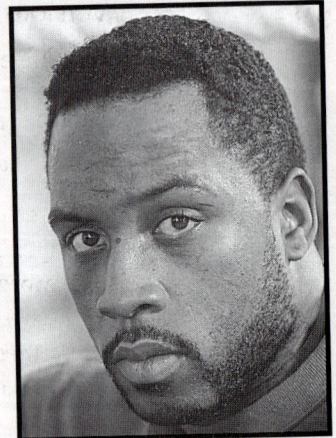

police apologised to Benn after his picture was used as a 'wanted' photo in a hunt for a lookalike gunman.

3 Discussion

In pairs or groups, discuss these questions.

1 How far do you agree with the headline?
2 Do you think the police had a good reason for stopping Benn?
3 Do you agree that this is an example of racial prejudice?
4 What would have happened in your country?
5 In your experience, which groups are often the victims of prejudice?

VOCABULARY

Expressions associated with colours

Fill each gap with the name of a common colour to make idioms.

1 His arrival took everybody by surprise; it was completely out of the ....~~BLUE~~........ . *→ unexpectively*
2 She made me so angry, I saw ....~~RED~~........ *angry: alem*
3 When he saw his neighbour's new car, he was ....~~GREEN~~........ with envy.
4 Draw your gun, sheriff! Or are you too ....~~YELLOW!~~........ ? *→ finito (stain) → forgotten/scar*
5 People in songs say they feel ....~~BLUE~~........ when they're unhappy.
6 The political situation looks ....~~BLACK~~........ . I think there's going to be war.
7 Why do you always see things in ....~~BLACK~~........ and ....~~WHITE~~........ ? Life isn't like that, most things are grey.
8 She is so ....~~GREEN~~........ ; she'll believe anything anyone tells her. *To BE NAIVE : Ser ingenuo.*
9 It's better to tell a ....~~WHITE~~........ lie than tell the truth and hurt someone.
10 Last month, our bank account was in the ....~~BLACK~~........ but since that expensive holiday, it's been in the ....~~RED~~........ .

SPEAKING

Versions of the truth

The Nigel Benn case has caused bad publicity for the police. Chief Inspector Hunter is investigating what really happened.
The Chief Inspector has called a meeting of the people involved in the case. When your teacher has given you roles, think about what you will say, and then act out the meeting:

- Chief Inspector Hunter
- Nigel Benn
- Ambrose Mendy
- The policeman in the patrol car
- Witness 1: a lorry driver
- Witness 2: a motorist

Try to use as many of the colour idioms as possible from the Vocabulary exercise above.

VOCABULARY

Adjectives of personality

1 Join these split sentences so they make sense.

1 She is incredibly mean; (K)
2 It isn't fair (J)
3 She wasn't sympathetic; (G)
4 You have to be sensitive (C)
5 It is extremely cruel (i)
6 Anna is really bright; (a)
7 Don't be so greedy; (B)
8 Suspicious people (L)
9 Try to be brave Simon; (D)
10 He is so dull (E)
11 She's a shy person (F)
12 Cathy is so arrogant; (H)

a she can read and she's only three years old.
b you've already eaten enough.
c to write poetry.
d this is going to hurt a little.
e he sends everyone to sleep.
f so she avoids going to parties.
g she just laughed when I told her my problem.
h she has no respect for other people.
i to kick the cat.
j to jump the queue like that.
k she never buys anyone a coffee.
l never believe what you say.

2 Look at the adjectives in the sentences

• Which adjective is the opposite of:
  a generous?
  b trusting?
• Which adjective means:
  c courageous, unafraid of pain or danger
  d intelligent and lively?
  e nervous in the company of others?
  f extremely unkind?
  g boring?
  h proud and self-important?
• Which adjective is often confused with:
  i sensible?
  j nice?

SPEAKING

Who are you?

1 We can analyse someone's personality by finding out which colours they like.

Study the five coloured circles carefully. Think about how each of the colours makes you feel. Now put them in order of preference. For example, if you like the colour yellow the best, then put a 1 by it. If red is your least favourite, then put a 5 by it, and so on. Try to think of the colours simply as colours, not whether they would suit you to wear or whether they are fashionable.

2 Now look at page 81 and see what your order tells you about your personality!

(handwritten note top:) TO RECOVER = TO BE ON THE MEND = = recuperarse = getting better

LANGUAGE STUDY

Different types of description

1 Match the answers (a–d) with the questions (1–4).

1 What's she like? *(c y d)* → a Much better. → *The health.*
2 How is she? → b Reading and playing tennis.
3 What does she like? → c Tall and slim.
4 What does she look like? → d Kind. → *character and physical appearance.*

(handwritten left:) ¿Como estás? (d) → ¿Como estás de salud? (a)

(handwritten right:)
– SKINNY → flacucho.
– THIN → delgad (normal)
– SLIM → (favorable).

2 Which question asks about:

a appearance? b preferences? c character? d health?
   1 y 4   3   1   2

LISTENING

1 Carmen works in a travel agent's in London. Her aunt is coming to visit her from Spain. Unfortunately, Carmen can't go to the airport to meet her aunt, so she rings her fiancé, Roger, who agrees to go instead.

You are going to hear Carmen's side of the telephone conversation. What five things do you think Roger wants to know? Make notes.

(handwritten:) MAIDEN NAME: Apellidos de soltera. SURNAME: Apellidos and plump/ chubby = little bit fat ... about ...

NOTES

1 ....
2 ....
3 ....
4 ....
5 ....

(handwritten in notes:)
1 quite short of 55 years old curly brain She ...
2 She doesn't speak english (a word).
3 She wants to go shopping. Went to theatre.

(handwritten right:)
1.— What does she look like?
2.— Very nice very ... lucky ... if she likes!

2 This time, listen to both sides of the conversation. Were you right?

(handwritten:)
5.— What does she like doing?
3.— How is she?
4.— What is her english like?

(handwritten left:) coun = gênau.

SPEAKING

In pairs, take it in turns to imagine that you are in a situation like Carmen's. Your partner has agreed to meet one of your friends or relatives that he/she has never seen before, and to look after your friend/relative for the day.
Remember to ask about appearance, character, likes and dislikes.

(handwritten bottom left:)
– A FELT–TIP PEN → rotulador
– DRAB → old fashioned not life.
→ TO EAT JUST FOR THE SAKE OF IT
– TO STUFF YOURSELF → comer por hábito.

	1st	2nd	3rd	4th	5th	
BLACK ●	cruel	bad-tempered	mean	easy-going	cheerful	
YELLOW ○	sociable	romantic	sympathetic	dull	hard-working	
GREEN ●	bright	arrogant	suspicious	practical	greedy (avaricioso)	
RED ●	aggressive	brave	efficient	fair	shy	
BLUE ○	calm	sensitive	generous	lazy	dishonest	

DO YOU AGREE WITH THE INTERPRETATION/FIND OUT WHAT YOUR CLASSMATES THINK ALSO.

WRITING

The nanny hunt

1 Look at this advertisement which appeared in the *Nanny* magazine.

- Who are the couple looking for?
- What qualities would the ideal person have?

> **Psychologist wife and writer husband** (working at home) desperately seek live-in nanny to take care of three young children aged 6, 5 and nine months. Apply by sending letter and photo. Also put these colours in order of preference – blue, red, green, yellow and black. Send letter and photo to: **Professor and Mr Wallace, 265 Queen Elizabeth Way, London SW15**

2 Before you read the letters, look at the photographs of the three girls and describe them. What do you think they are like as people? Which one looks the most suitable from her photograph?

3 Look at letter **A** carefully. There are over fifteen common mistakes in it. Do your best to correct the letter.

4 Compare letters **B** and **C**.

- Which of the two letters is more appropriate?
- What advice would you give to Sally Fairclough if she showed you her letter before she posted it?
- Make a list of any formal/informal language you can find in the two letters.

5 Look at the colour choices made by each applicant, and at their letters, and decide who Professor Wallace might give the job to.

6 Imagine that you want to apply for a job as a nanny, au pair or butler. Write a letter of application which is friendly but not too informal, telling your potential employers something about yourself.

Remember to add your colour preferences!

A

Richmount St 57
Churchington

Dear Mr and Mrs Wallace,

I am writing for to apply the job which has been advertised in the 'Nanny' magazine of last week. I have twenty three years and am coming from Andorra. I am in England since six months and I am here for to improve my English. I am working like an au pair by an english family. They are very sympathetic but the husband has a work in Germany so the family will go there. The order of my colours favourite are blue, yellow, red, black, green.

(I salute you attentively.)

Yours faithfully,

Nadia Ivanovic

B

Dear Mr and Mrs Wallace,

Hello there. I saw your ad in a magazine and really thought I'd like to apply. I am 19 years old and left school last year. I am working in a clothes shop at the moment, just to fill in. I haven't had any training as a nanny but I love kids and I come from a big family. What's more, I really could really do with a job! I can start straight away if you like. Here is a photo of me. It would be great if we could have a chat next Friday because I am going to a party in London on Friday evening. I hope to hear from you soon.

Bye for now!

All the best,
Sally Fairclough

PS My favourite colours are yellow, green, red, blue and black.

C

Dear Professor and Mr Wallace,

I am writing in reply to your advertisement in last week's Nanny magazine.

I am a twenty-six-year-old fully qualified children's nanny and nurse with five years' experience. I have worked for a number of British families and those of the foreign diplomatic community. I can supply you with references if you should require them. I am currently employed as a nanny to two American children but my contract is coming to an end and I am available for interview at your convenience. I could commence a new position almost immediately. I have enclosed a recent photograph.

As requested, my order of preference for the colours you mentioned is black, yellow, red, green and blue.

I look forward to your reply.

Yours sincerely,

Lucy Clinton-Rogers

Lucy Clinton-Rogers

Hasta qué punto.

SPEAKING

- How far does the picture below match your idea of the typical Englishman?
- How does he feel, and why?

READING

The typical Englishman

Read the paragraph and see if it agrees with your stereotype of the typical Englishman.

The typical Englishman works in a London bank but lives in the countryside, in a house with a lovely garden. Every day he reads *The Times* newspaper and does the crossword on the way to work. He never speaks to anybody on the train, but will talk to you about the weather or cricket if you meet him in the pub at lunchtime. He always wears a dark suit to work and always carries an umbrella. He gave up smoking his pipe and wearing a bowler hat some years ago. At the weekend, he wears an old tweed jacket and a pair of gardening trousers. He likes plain, simple food and drinks tea at every opportunity. In his free time, he works in his garden, plays golf or takes his dog for a walk. He is suspicious of all foreigners. He is kind and polite to his wife but does not show her a lot of affection. His wife is a snob who dresses rather badly. They both admire members of the Royal Family and copy their accents. He is proud of his son, who is at Cambridge University, (but would rather die than tell him). He is rather worried about his daughter, who is currently living with a punk, but hopes that she will eventually marry a doctor or an accountant.

WRITING

National stereotypes

Write a similar paragraph with a stereotypical view of someone from your own country. Then swap them and compare them!

Think about:
- his/her clothes;
- the newspaper he/she reads;
- his/her typical job;
- how he/she spends the weekend;
- his/her role models;
- how he/she shows affection.

LISTENING

Agreeing and disagreeing

Shirley and Simon are talking about the 'typical Englishman' who has been described in the first paragraph.

1 Listen and answer these questions.

[handwritten: ya no existe]

1 Who believes the 'typical Englishman' of the article no longer exists?
2 Why was Simon surprised in the post office?
3 What do they think about the typical English family?
4 Why do they think the British have a poor reputation abroad?

2 Listen again and put the following expressions in the order in which you hear them. Which ones show: full agreement, partial agreement, disagreement?

a Absolutely, ... *[handwritten: Full agreement]*
b Alright, but ... *[handwritten: Partial "]*
c That's right, ... *[handwritten: Full agreement]*
d That's just not true. *[handwritten: disagreement]*
e You're right. *[handwritten: Full agreement]*

SPEAKING

We're all different!

[handwritten: trans]

1 Draw a map of your country and its main cities. If people from a particular area or city have a reputation for being mean, write 'mean' beside it. Try to use some of the adjectives you looked at in Set B of this Unit.

2 When you have finished, talk about your map with a partner. Your partner must agree or disagree with you!

CHAUVINISM ⇒ Machismo.

READING

1 Look at the photo and headline for the newspaper article. What do you think the article will be about? It's about the right of the (womans) (men) at work. Read the article quickly and check your predictions. (people)

→ Género (masculino/femenino)

The Gender Trap → Trampa

ARE YOU FOREIGN, AGED BETWEEN 17 AND 27 AND UNMARRIED? If so, have you thought of getting a job as an au pair? **1** D You stay with an English family and, in return for housework and babysitting, you get food and accommodation and a little pocket money. You can also pick up a lot of English. **2** F It doesn't really matter where you're from, but you have to be female, as several male au pairs have found out, the hard way.

25-year-old Arnie, from Iceland, was taken on to look after four-year-old Sam. Arnie is ideal; he's great with Sam – he bathes him and picks him up from nursery and has even helped with painting and decorating. Nevertheless, the authorities want to kick him out because he's a man. **3** B This isn't the first case of sex discrimination. **4** A Of course, if he had had an EC passport, probably nothing would have happened. In theory, he still wouldn't have been able to work, but nobody would have checked. **5** C Understandably, Hoken was furious: 'What do they want me to do.' he asked angrily, 'put on a skirt and wear a wig? It's ridiculous!' He wished he had known about these regulations before

coming all the way to England. **6** E 'How could a boy be an au pair? A girl can take far better care of a two-year-old baby than a boy – he has different instincts about feeding; she's better equipped to do the housework.'

2 Read the text carefully and decide which sentence (**A**–**E**) belongs in which gap (**1**–**6**).

> **A** Two years ago, Hoken Larsson from Sweden was turned away at immigration despite being the ideal man for the job.
> **B** English law says that only girls are allowed to be au pairs.
> **C** The divorcee who had wanted to employ him said that her eight-year-old son needed a male presence about the house.
> **D** It's a great way of spending a year in England.
> **E** Maria Mirkova, who heads an au-pair agency, would disagree with Hoken.
> **F** However, there's a catch!

Trap = Trampa

3 Decide whether these statements are **true** or **false**.

1 English girls can work as au pairs in England. *F*
2 Arnie is still in England. *T*
3 Hoken never started his job. *T*
4 Hoken knew about the regulations for au pairs before coming to England. *F*
5 Maria Mirkova believes that boys can be good au pairs. *F*

4 How far do you agree with Maria Mirkova? *I am completely disagreeing with Maria because a qualified man can do this ~~task~~ as better as a woman, and I think that a man can have instinct about feeding, although womans have more developed this instinct.*

LANGUAGE STUDY

The third conditional and **wish**

1 Look at this sentence from the text.

*If he **had had** an EC passport, probably nothing **would have** happened.*
If + had + PAST PARTICIPLE + WOULD HAVE + PAST PARTICIPLE

The time is past and nothing can you do about.

This construction is usually called the THIRD CONDITIONAL.
Now study this way of expressing regret about the past.

if
*He **wished** he **had known** about these regulations...* *because now he ~~~~ has to leave the country.*

| **Wished + had + PAST PARTICIPLE** | *not consequence.*
NO ~~se~~ UA EL WOULD ~~SERVE~~.

A/to REGRET = = arrepentimiento/ arrepentirse.

What similarities do you notice between this construction and the third conditional?

2 Practice

Make two sentences around each of these mini-situations, one using the third conditional and one using **wished**.

He wished he hadn't lazy at school.
1 Alan was lazy at school. He didn't pass his exams. → *IF ALAN HADN'T BEEN LAZY AT school HE WOULD HAVE PAST HIS EXAMS*

If she had drunk less champagne last night she wouldn't have a terrible headache now.
2 Caroline drank too much champagne last night. Now she has a terrible headache.
3 The policemen who stopped Nigel Benn got into trouble with their inspector.

→ CAROLINE WISHED ~~HE~~ HAD ~~to~~ ~~~~ DRUNK to much CHAMPAGNE LAST NIGHT BECAUSE NOW SHE HAS A TERRIBLE HEADACHE.
→ The policemen wished They hadn't stop Nigel Benn because they got into trouble with their inspector.

SPEAKING

A woman's place

1 Look at this list of jobs. In pairs, decide which ones are usually done by men and which are usually done by women. Which ones could be done by both?

soldier   secretary   teacher   doctor   taxi-driver
mechanic   carpenter   flight attendant
lorry driver   nurse   coal miner   bullfighter
shop assistant   au pair   boxer   accountant
cook   hairdresser

2 In your country, which of these jobs would only be done by men?

3 People used to say: 'A woman's place is in the home.'
How popular do you think this view was or is in your country?

Could you eat it?

Going to different countries often means getting used to food which is very different from your own.

Look at these dishes. Which countries do they come from?

sheep's eyes   snails   snake   veal cooked in milk   dog   birds' nests
toad-in-the-hole   tripe and onions   brains   raw fish   horse   turtle

Which ones could you never eat, even if you were starving?
Are there any dishes in your country which you know most foreigners wouldn't try?

Toad-in-the-hole!

Poppy is meeting Martin Smith, her father's friend, and Martin's wife, Moira, at a traditional English restaurant in Covent Garden.

1 Look at the menu. (Your teacher will explain any items you don't understand.) Then listen and make a note of what each person decides to order.

2 Listen again and write down the exact words Moira uses when she:

- decides what to eat.
- tells Poppy what she has decided to order.

The Hot Pot Traditional English Restaurant

Starters · all at £4.50
Smoked salmon
Avocado pear & prawns
Watercress soup
Cheese & onion tart

Main Courses · all at £7.00
Meat
Grilled lamb chops in a mint sauce
Roast Beef & Yorkshire pudding
Duck in orange sauce
Toad-in-the-hole

Fish
Grilled sole
Salmon fillet baked in pastry

All main courses served with vegetables

Desserts · all at £3.50
Apple pie & cream
Bread-and-butter pudding
Luxury ice-creams

Cheese selection · £3.50

All prices include VAT
12½% service charge

to go dutch: to pay half each (pgan a medise)

LANGUAGE STUDY

Going to or will?

1 **Going to** has two main uses:

- to talk about future plans and events which have already been decided: *I'm going to be a policeman when I grow up.* (I decided this years ago.)

- as a way of predicting something you can actually see is going to happen:
  '*Look at that fat lady, Mummy.*'
  '*She's not fat, darling, she's **going to have** a baby.*'

2 Match the examples using **will** with the definitions of their use.

1 Will you open the door for me? (f)
2 If you do that again, I'll be very angry. (d)
3 I will go to the disco if I want to, Dad. (a)
4 Don't worry, I'll give you a lift. (b)
5 You will marry a tall stranger. (c)
6 I hope she'll believe me. (e)

a An expression of determination.
b A spontaneous decision/offer.
c A prediction. *(a general prediction).*
d A condition, threat or promise.
e After verbs like *think, hope, doubt*.
f An order/request.

3 Now look at the tapescript for the conversation in the listening exercise. Can you explain the use of **will** and **going to**?

4 Look at the following situations and decide what you would say in each. There may be more than one possible answer.

1 It is 3 a.m. Some people are making a lot of noise in front of your house. What do you say to them as a warning before you call the police? → *Could/Would you please make less noise?*
2 The sky is full of dark clouds. Your friend suggests a game of tennis. What do you reply? *It's going to rain*
3 You see an older person trying to lift a heavy suitcase onto a train. What do you say when you want to help? → *Don't worry I'll take your suitcase. I'll put it onto the train*
4 You are determined to lose three kilos before your next summer holiday. What do you say to yourself? *I will lose three kilos before next summer (con conviccion)*
5 You don't know what to buy your father for his birthday. Suddenly you have a brilliant idea! What do you say to yourself? And then… *I think I'll buy him a tie.*
6 what do you tell your mother? *I'm going to buy him a tie.*

SPEAKING

Role play

Imagine you are on holiday in England and you go to the Hot Pot Restaurant. In groups of four, act out a situation where three of you are customers and the fourth is the waiter.

WRITING

Making a menu

Make up a typical menu from your country. Decide how you will explain the dishes to your customers. Perhaps you could write the explanations on the menu itself.

LISTENING

1 What reputation, if any, does English food have in your country?

2 You are going to hear five people talking about English food. Decide who says what by writing the number of a speaker (**1–5**) in the boxes.

Which speaker (**1–5**)

A believes English cooking can be as good as any other? ☐5
B was unimpressed by the choice of food when they were on holiday? ☐4
C talks about the international nature of restaurants in England? ☐1
D has changed their mind about English food? ☐2
E has discovered that the awful stories are true? ☐3

VOCABULARY ✗ **Cooking**

[handwritten: (1) TO SHAKE = AGITAR · TO MINCE (MEAT) = PICAR (CARNE) · TO CARVE = TRINCHAR · TO CUT UP = TROCEAR]

1 Match the words in the box with the pictures in the word map opposite.

to mix   to boil   a frying pan   to roast   to bake   to slice   to fry   to stir   a pot
a bowl   to spread   a dish   to chop   a saucepan   to sprinkle   to beat   to grill

[handwritten: TO POACH = ESCALFAR (HUEVO) · TO BROWN = GRATINAR]

2 Can you add any more words?

[handwritten: TO TOAST = TOSTAR. TO SIEVE = COLAR · TO BLEND = MEZCLAR (LIQUIDS) · TO WHISK = MEZCLAR]

3 What is the difference between these three things: *receipt, prescription, recipe?*

[handwritten: SCRAMBLED EGGS = HUEVOS REVUELTOS. · recibo · prescripción (médica) · receta (cocina)]

LISTENING

You are going to hear how to make a famous traditional English dish: 'Bread-and-Butter Pudding'.

1 Listen carefully and make notes under these headings:

Ingredients	Utensils	Method
– THREE QUARTS OF WHITE MILK		
– 200 grams BUTTER		
– 4 LARGE or 6 SMALL EGGS.		
– 250 grams SUGAR.		
– SOME DRIED SULTANAS (NO GRAMES)		
– OR A LITTLE RAISINS		
– HALF A DOZEN OF SLICES OF WHITE BREAD		

2 Look at the tapescript on page 162 and check if you missed anything.

WRITING

Using the tapescript as a guide, write a simple recipe for a dish from your country.

COOKERY

ACTIONS

CUTTING

A

B

PREPARING

C

D

E

F

COOKING

G

H

I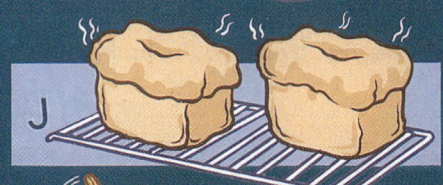

J

K

L

EQUIPMENT

M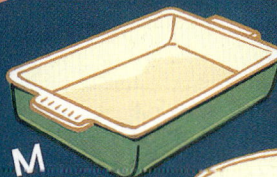

N

O

P

Q

LISTENING

Watch your body language

Dr Ian Williams is being interviewed about the different meanings gestures can have. Listen and complete the notes.

Dr Williams was involved in a misunderstanding when he was in (1) ......INDIA..... . He thought that when the person was (2) ..SHAKING.. their head they meant 'no'. In fact, this movement meant (3) ..CARRY ON TALKING BECAUSE I'M INTERESTING

Thumbing your nose.

This is a (4) .....UNIVERSAL.. European gesture. It means the same in (5) ...FROM OSLO...... as in (6) ....MADRID.... .

Thumbs up.

In Britain and Northern Europe it means (7) .....OK......... .
In Greece and Italy people (8) ..WON'T UNDERSTAND IT....

The 'hand purse'.

This is the most (9) ....CONFUSING... gesture of all.
In Italy it means (10) ...I DON'T UNDERSTAND / WHAT ARE YOU GETTING AT?
In Greece it means (11) ...SOMETHING IS GOOD.
In Spain it means (12) ...A...LOT..... .

Dr Williams has two pieces of advice for travellers.
i) Don't copy local gestures because it (13) ~~BAD REFLECTS~~ CAN CAUSE OFFENCE / CAN SEEM JOKEY
ii) Never copy (14) ...LOCAL TABOO GESTURES
Carol Jones thinks the best thing to do is simply to (15) ..KEEP YOUR HANDS IN YOUR POCKETS

LANGUAGE STUDY

Remember, forget and remind

1 Remember and forget

What is the difference between the uses of **remember** in these two sentences taken from the conversation?

a *I **remember** going to India.* (Things that happened)
b *...**remember** to keep your hands in your pockets.* (to do something in the future)

Notice that **(not) forget to** can be used in the same way as **remember to**.
*... **don't forget to** keep your hands in your pockets.*

2 Remind

If you **remind someone to do something**, you are helping them to remember.

3 Complete the sentences using an appropriate form of **remember, remind** or **forget**.

1 Can you ....REMIND.. me to post this letter?
2 I can't find my car keys, but I ...REMEMBER... seeing them here earlier.
3 Oh, dear! It's his birthday and I've ...FORGOTTEN.. to buy him a present.
4 Do you think you could ...REMIND... me how to use the photocopier?
5 Don't ....FORGET.. to ask for a receipt. → continuous
DON'T FORGET 6 ...REMEMBER.... to be back by 11.00 otherwise there will be trouble!
7 I ..REMEMBER.. overtaking the lorry, but everything afterwards is a blank.
8 Always ...REMEMBER.. to get good travel insurance when you go abroad.

with always you can't use Don't Forget → don't ever Forget (yo

READING

Keep your hands in your pockets!

This is an extract from a humorous advertisement for Heathrow, London's most important airport, where people of all nationalities and cultures meet. In it, Desmond Morris talks about the problems associated with different nationalities' body language. Here, he looks at a few misunderstandings which could occur.

Choose the best answer (**A, B** or **C**) for questions 1–6.

1 Who thinks he will have to pay for the trolley service?
  A The Japanese.
  B The Frenchman.
  C The American.

2 Who thinks he is going to see a murder?
  A The American.
  B The Japanese.
  C The Tunisian.

3 How does the Frenchman insult the Colombian?
  A On purpose.
  B By mistake .
  C By what he says.

4 Why does the Syrian get angry?
  A Because of what the Colombian says.
  B Because the Greek wants to hit the Colombian.
  C Because of something he sees.

5 Who insults the Greek?
  A The waiter.
  B The Syrian.
  C The Colombian.

6 Who does the Greek insult?
  A The Syrian.
  B The waiter.
  C Nobody.

Is there at least one truly international gesture? Don't bet on it!

A Japanese asks an American passenger whether Heathrow has a luggage trolley service. It has. And as it happens, this service is not only first class, but FREE! So the Yank replies with the famous 'A-OK' ring gesture. But to the Japanese this signifies 'money' and he concludes there is a charge for the service. Meanwhile, a Tunisian on-looker thinks the American is telling the Japanese that he is a worthless rogue and he is going to kill him.

The ring gesture can have further meanings ...
A Frenchman has just read a British Airport Authorities advertisement. Glancing round the restaurant in Terminal 4, he remarks wonderingly to his wife, 'You know how much zis airport cost the British taxpayer? Not a sou.' And he makes the finger-and-thumb ring, which to him means 'zero'. Unfortunately, at the same time, he is glancing at a Colombian who is enjoying a fine Burgundy with his steak Béarnaise. The Colombian, enraged by the deadly obscenity which he assumes is directed at him, chokes on his wine and catches his nose with finger and thumb. This appalls a Syrian opposite, who thinks the Colombian is telling him to 'go to hell'. The Syrian is restrained with difficulty by his Greek colleague from getting up and punching the Colombian on the nose. Meanwhile the *maitre d'* hurries over and attempts to calm the situation with two out-thrust palms. This, of course, is taken by the Greek to be a double 'moutza' and, in his rage, he promptly skewers the unfortunate man with his fish-knife.

SPEAKING

Just good manners (Buenos Modales)

Below is some advice for travellers to Japan and to Arab countries.

1 Work in pairs. One of you should read about Japan while the other reads about Arab countries.

2 When you have finished, look at the pictures and explain to each other the social rules which have been broken in each one.

3 Now read the article you haven't yet looked at. Is there anything your partner forgot to tell you?

4 Go through the texts and underline all the useful words and expressions which are used to express what you **must** and **mustn't** do.

LANGUAGE STUDY

In case

1 In the text about Japan, it says:

*You shouldn't sit on tables **in case** you offend someone.*
= You should avoid sitting on a table because you might offend someone if you do.

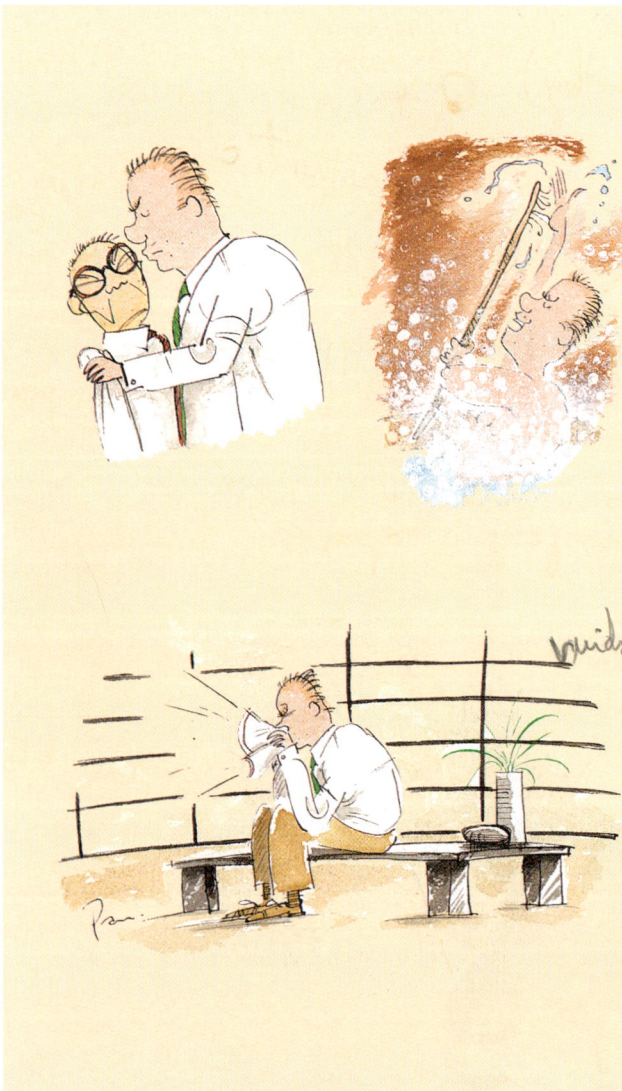

Never kiss people as a greeting; shake hands or bow instead. Always take off your shoes when you go into someone's flat. Never blow your nose in public – the Japanese find this quite shocking.

You shouldn't sit on tables in case you offend someone. When you take a bath, make sure that you wash with soap *before* you get into the bath. Whatever you do never use soap *in* the bath itself; the bath is just for relaxation.

Don't expect to be invited to Japanese homes. Most entertaining is done in restaurants and clubs. Be prepared to drink a lot! Don't be shocked if Japanese people drink soup noisily; this is perfectly acceptable in Japan and is not considered bad manners.

Traditionally, the Japanese are great gift-givers and it is common, and a sign of respect, to exchange presents, so make sure you have a selection of typical gifts from your country in case you need them.

22

We use **in case** + PRESENT SIMPLE to talk about things we do now in order to prevent problems later.

I'll take a map **in case** *I get lost.* (Because if I *do* get lost, I won't be able to find my way without a map.)

2 Now rewrite these sentences using **in case** where possible.

[handwritten: I'll take my coat in case the weather changes]

1 I'll take my coat because the weather may change.
2 I think I'll buy a thick paperback. I may have to wait a long time at the airport.
3 Cash often gets stolen, so I'll take some traveller's cheques.
4 I'd better take some tablets because I often get seasick.
5 I'll travel to Majorca if I can get a flight.

[handwritten notes]

Customs do vary, but on the whole these rules are true for all Arab countries. Travellers should always dress modestly. Don't wear shorts. Men should always wear shirts. Women should cover their arms and never walk around in sun dresses. It is wise to carry a scarf with you in case you need to cover your hair.

Arabs are hospitable and may invite you home. Take off your shoes when you enter the home. Even if alcohol is offered stick to tea or soft drinks. In some countries men and women eat in separate rooms.

Men shouldn't expect to meet the female members of the host's family and don't take them flowers. People usually sit on cushions or mattresses on the ground. It is bad manners to stretch out your legs and show the soles of your feet.

Traditionally, meals are eaten from a communal dish using the fingers. Never pick up food with your left hand as this is considered disgusting.

23

WRITING

An advice sheet for foreigners

1 Imagine that you are preparing an advice sheet for visitors to your country.

Make a list of things that visitors to your country
• **should/must** do.
• **shouldn't/mustn't** do.

2 Now decide which ones are the most/least important.

3 Using the texts you have read as a model, write an advice sheet for visitors to your country.

WIDESPREAD = Expandidos.

New Found Land

1 A large island has been discovered. An international community of 10,000 men and women are going to start a new country there. Imagine that you have to decide the laws of the new country. Discuss the following questions.

New Found Land Laws

1 What will the island's official language be? *English/Spanish.*

2 Will you have the death penalty? *Yes/no.*

3 Will you have a king or queen, or a president? *A Republic system.*

4 Who will be able to vote and from what age? *18 is the most reasonable age.*

5 Will citizens be allowed to carry guns? *Yes but with caution.*

6 What will the speed limit be? Will drivers have to wear seat belts? *120/yes obligatory*

7 Will you have censorship? *A limit but with a free of speech.*

8 Will you have a state religion? *No/The people should choose.*

9 Will young people do some kind of military or national service? *Professional army.*

10 At what age will compulsory education end? *16 years old. obligatory*

11 What will your immigration policy be? *No/free of movement.*

12 Which other two questions would you add to this list? *—Health system. —Tax system.*

2 Speakers' Corner

Speakers' Corner is a part of Hyde Park, in London, where people are free to say whatever they like.

Two or three people in your class should choose the question from the list above that they feel most strongly about. They should stand in separate parts of the class and start talking about their point of view. The rest of the class can move from person to person. Feel free to disagree and interrupt!

VOCABULARY

Geography

Study the words in the box and look up any meanings you are unsure of. Make as many connections as you can between the various words.

Example: A *stream* is a small river.
You would probably find a *swamp* in the jungle.

sea	jungle	harbour	desert	waterfall	forest	hill	coral	coast	pool
spring	mountain	oasis	river	plain	swamp	beach	wave	bay	stream
port	valley	lake	tide	wood	island	plateau

READING

Describing a country's geography

1 Which two countries are described below? Can you guess?

A

A country in E. Asia covering vast areas of land, ranging from the low-lying and densely populated plains of the NE to the high peaks of the Tibetan Plateau in the W, rising well over 5000 m (16,500 ft). In the far NW, much of the land is desert or semi-desert. The country falls into three regions around its three main rivers: the Yellow River in the N, the Yangtze in the centre and the Xi Jiang in the S.

B

A country in NW South America, lying on the Equator, from which it takes its name. It includes the Galapagos Islands 1000 km (600 miles) out in the Pacific. It consists chiefly of a coastal plain in the W, separated from the tropical jungles and rivers of the Amazon Basin (Oriente) by the ranges and plateaux of the Andes (containing several active volcanoes, including Cotopaxi). There are frequent disastrous earthquakes.

2 Make notes on the countries under these headings:

NAME	LOCATION	GEOGRAPHICAL FEATURES
....	....	....
....	....	....
....	....	....

SPEAKING

The newest continent

Work in pairs to complete the maps of the main sights of Australia.

STUDENT A look at the map on page 140. STUDENT B look at the map on page 144.

WRITING

My own country

Use the headings from exercise **2** above and make notes about your country. Then write a short description of it.

READING

Discover Australia

Read the advertisement in the brochure and decide if the following statements are **true** or **false**.

1 Someone will meet you when you arrive in Sydney. F
2 You will spend a whole day touring Sydney. T
3 The Featherdale Wildlife Park is in Alice Springs. F
4 You will fly from Alice Springs to Palm Valley. F
5 You will be able to ride a camel at the Virginia Camel Farm. T
6 The Olgas are valleys. F
7 You will see the sunset over the Olgas. F
8 You can see crocodiles in the Kakadu National Park. T
9 The Wangi Falls are above the rainforest. T
10 You'll see tropical fish from the catamaran. F

Discover
Australia in 14 days

Day 1

Arrive in **Sydney**. Make your own way to the **Central Plaza Hotel**.

Day 2

A full day touring **Sydney**, including a cruise around the m a g n i f i c e n t harbour. Your tour includes the Opera House, colourful King's Cross, famous Bondi Beach, Double Bay and the Harbour Bridge.

Day 3

Tour through the picturesque **Blue Mountains**. Visit the Featherdale Wildlife Park where kangaroos and koalas (you can cuddle one!) can be seen.

Day 4

Fly to **Alice Springs**. Tour of Alice in the afternoon.

Day 5

Travel by special 4WD vehicle through the colourful mountain ranges in **Palm Valley** where unique plants of a species thousands of years old still survive. Superb oasis scenery.

Day 6

On the way to **Ayer's Rock**, call at the Virginia Camel Farm. There's time for a camel ride. In the afternoon see the nearby Olgas (twenty-eight domes of rock that dominate the western skyline) returning in time to see the sunset over Ayer's Rock.

Day 7

View sunrise on **Ayer's Rock**. 7.15 start for those wishing to climb. In the caves beneath the rock, find out about the aboriginals' 'dream time' mythology, or simply tour around the base of this monolith. Return to **Alice Springs**.

Day 8

Fly to **Darwin** where you will transfer to your hotel.

Day 9

Travel to **Kakadu National Park**. Watch out for wildlife as we make our way to Cooinda and Yellow Waters Billabong. Enjoy an exciting boat cruise to observe the crocodiles and birdlife.

Day 10

Visit **Ubirr Rock** and see many aboriginal rock drawings and paintings.

Day 11

A sandstone plateau forms the Tabletop Range. Close to its edge, springs and streams form rock pools which tumble as the **Wangi Falls** into the rainforest below.

Day 12

Fly to **Cairns** today. Transfer to your hotel.

Day 13

Cruise to the **Great Barrier Reef**, including the outer reef. Travel by air-conditioned catamaran. There's time for swimming, snorkelling and coral viewing. See shoals of tropical fish from a sub-sea vessel. Lunch, glass-bottom boat ride included.

Day 14

Depart from **Cairns**. End of tour.

(handwritten notes at top)
"THE BUSH"
"THE OUTBACK"
ZONA SELVADERTICA (jólo en AUSTRALIA).
A BEAK / BILL = Pico
BIRD   DUCK
A DWELLER (person leaving in a house)
TO DWELL (TO LIVE / VERY FORMAL)
A DWELLING (HABITAT)
TO BE DECEAED = ETAR PALLECIDO.
TO BE DISEASED = ETAR ENFERMO.

LANGUAGE STUDY

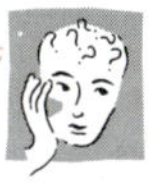

Uses of **a/an**, **the** and **some**

1 a/an

We use **a/an** (the indefinite article)

- before singular countable nouns when we are talking about *one* of something in a general, non-specific way. *We saw a kangaroo from our landrover.*
- for somebody's job or profession. *She's a travel agent.*

We do not use **a**

- before plural nouns (e.g. *kangaroos*)
- before uncountable nouns (e.g. *oil, sugar* and *water*)
- before abstract nouns or nouns expressing concepts (e.g. *love, art, weather*)

the

We use **the** (the definite article)

- before uncountable nouns and singular and plural countable nouns when we move from the general to the specific. *We saw a kangaroo from our landrover. **The** kangaroo was running. All **the** animals were running. I'm thirsty – where's **the** water?*
- before some place names (but not usually towns, cities or countries) and geographical/environmental features. *We saw **the** Olgas/**the** coast.*
- when we are talking about a species or a class. ***The** kangaroo is an interesting creature.*
- before superlatives. ***The** best, **the** most interesting …*

We do not use **the**

- before plural countable nouns if we are talking about something in general. *I like koalas.*

some

We use **some**

- before uncountable and plural countable nouns if we are describing something that we can see or that exists. *There are **some** koalas over there.*

2 Study the sentences and identify any extra and unnecessary articles (**a/the**).

1 Although I like the wildlife, I hate the dingoes.
2 The Ayres Rock is a most fascinating place.
3 The baby kangaroos are called 'joeys'.
4 Have you ever eaten the kangaroo meat?
5 We travelled by a landrover and I rode on a camel.
6 We took a boat to the Great Barrier Reef.
7 There's a postcard from the Sydney for you.
8 Kakadu is the most amazing place I have ever visited.
9 She's doing the research into the koala for her degree. *(handwritten: investigation)*

10 It loves the leaves, especially the leaves of the eucalyptus tree.
11 The water there is so beautifully clear that you can see the coral.
12 There were a millions of sheep on the farm.

LISTENING

(handwritten: dedo de los pies. pied de los animales (...))

The world's favourite Australians

1 Listen to the talk about Australian wildlife. Tick what is special about the duck-billed platypus.

a It has toes. ☑
b It has fur. ☑ *(handwritten: webbed feet)*
c It has feathers. ☐
d It gives birth to its young. ☐
e It is cold-blooded, like a snake. ☐ *(handwritten: sangre fría.)*

2 Complete these notes about the koala.

Koalas are unusual for three main reasons:

- They are active (1) ...AT NIGHT... so they spend most of the day (2) ...ASLEEP... in trees. *(handwritten: asleep (pyjamas, etc))*
- They don't have (3) ...TAILS... which is strange for tree dwellers.
- They have (4) ...POUCHES... like kangaroos, but theirs open (5) ...DOWNWARDS... ! *(handwritten: hacia abajo)*

The koala and its enemies.
Two hundred years ago the koala's main enemies were (6) ...DINGOES... (wild dogs) and (7) ...ABORIGINES... (native Australians). When the European settlers came the koala population grew because the settlers (8) ...SHOT THE DINGOES... However, about seventy years ago the koalas were (9) ...HUNTED... for their (10) ...FUR... In 1924 (11) ...2 million koala... skins were exported. Nowadays the koala faces other dangers, koalas eat (12) ...ENORMOUS amounts of leaves... from (13) ...GUM... trees and the forests are being cut down. Also (14) ...DISEASE... and (15) ...CARS... are two further dangers. *(handwritten: ILLNESS = ENFERMEDAD)*

Other points
If you see a koala it isn't a good idea to (16) ...PICK IT UP... *(handwritten: = coger)*
It could (17) ...SCRATCH... with its claws. Incidentally the word koala means '(18) ...I DON'T DRINK...'

3 Look at the tapescript on page 163 and notice when the definite and indefinite articles are used. Some are in bold type. Can you explain their use?

READING

1 Read the text and find out why this story is different from the ones we usually hear about the environment.

2 Now complete the text using just one word to fill each of the gaps. Here are four of the words to help you: experiment, given, further, each

The North Pole is an inhospitable place. Yet, in the distant parts of Alaska there is a tribe of Inuit who sustain their traditional (1) .... of life by hunting and fishing and killing a few whales (2) .... year. Men do not leave their houses (3) .... a rifle as there have been cases of people being (4) .... by polar bears. When oil was discovered in the late 1960s, the Inuit rights were not respected and they lost (5) .... of their land. It has to be said they were (6) .... a large area which is their own. Now, the native Alaskans want to (7) .... advantage of the oil reserves on their land and exploit them for their (8) .... benefit. They are (9) .... opposed by environmentalists who believe (10) .... exploitation could damage the environment. In the (11) .... the Inuit have been badly treated and have no reason to trust the white man. In the 1950s they were given radioactive iodine to drink as part of an (12) .... to see how they coped so (13) .... with the cold. Needless to say, (14) .... but one of the people (15) .... was killed as a direct result.

READING

Xingu, the forbidden area

1 The singer Sting visited the Brazilian rainforest with the writer J.P. Dutilleux. Here is an extract from the book they wrote. Look at the picture of Sting with the Indian chief Raoni and describe them. What do you think the rainforest is like? How dangerous do you think it would be in the rainforest?

Now that we are out of the clouds, we can see the land below us stretching to the horizon. It's a desert of red dust. J.P. looks sad.

'All of this was rainforest ten years ago,' says J.P. 'A few isolated tree stumps are left to remind us of what used to be there. This is the kind of devastation only men can cause. I feel angry for my children and their children, being robbed of the earth's beauty for the sake of dirty money.'

'We lose 100 species of plant and animal every day,' says our guide. 'Who knows, a cure for AIDS or cancer could have existed down there just waiting to be discovered, it's a living laboratory. But what do we do? We burn it all down. It's criminal.'

'So why doesn't someone do something about it?'

'Look, Sting, this is the last frontier. You are visiting a place that very few white people have ever seen. No president of Brazil has ever visited this area. We can't depend on anyone else. Each person that comes here has to take responsibility. Look, there's the Indian border.'

The sight below us is remarkable. The wasteland suddenly ends in a wall of gigantic forest. Two planets have been put side by side. A dead and devastated world, cheek-to-cheek with a world of green beauty and life, the Xingu.

'Where the Indians are, the forest is protected, and where they aren't, it is not. That's why the Indians are systematically being wiped out.' There used to be six million Indians in the Amazon Basin. Now there are only two hundred thousand. They've been killed, sometimes by guns, sometimes by blankets carrying disease dropped on villages, destroyed by alcohol and the demoralization of their culture.

'How big is the protected area of the Xingu?'

'It's about the size of Belgium. It's a showpiece. The tribe we're visiting are a peaceful tribe, but they are protected by the hostile tribes of the Lower Xingu of which Raoni is the chief.'

'How hostile?' J.P. doesn't answer.

A straight highway from north to south has been cut through the thick forest ... the Trans-Amazonian highway. Traffic is not allowed to stop. Anyone who entered the forest would be killed by Indian patrols. We all suddenly realize we're not entering Disneyland. J.P. just smiles.

2 Read the text carefully and answer the multiple choice questions.

1 What do they see down below when they come out of the clouds?
A A few live trees.
B The rainforest.
C A dead landscape.

2 What has been lost in the rainforest?
A Potential answers to disease. → *enfermedad.*
B An experiment.
C A few examples of wildlife and plants.

3 According to J.P. who has ultimate responsibility for what is happening?
A The president.
B White men.
C Everyone.

4 How does the landscape change from desert to rainforest?
A Mysteriously.
B Dramatically.
C Slowly.

5 Why are the Indians important for the forest?
A Because the forest is being wiped out.
B Because there are only 200,000 Indians left.
C Because it cannot be harmed if they are there.

6 How were the Indians killed?
A In a tribal war.
B With bombs.
C By various methods.

7 Who is Raoni?
A The ruler of the Xingu.
B A warrior chief.
C A harmless chieftain from the Lower Xingu.

8 What would you say to a driver on the Amazonian highway?
A Take the opportunity to meet the Indians.
B Keep going.
C It's more fun than Disneyland.

LANGUAGE STUDY

The passive

'They **are protected** by the hostile tribes of the Lower Xingu.'

1 Study these two sentences and how they are both formed.

a ACTIVE *A crocodile ate the explorer.*
    SUBJECT + VERB + OBJECT
b PASSIVE *The explorer was eaten by a crocodile.*
    SUBJECT + to be + PAST + AGENT
                    PARTICIPLE

1 What happens to the verb when you change the sentence from active to passive?
2 What happens to the object of sentence **a** in sentence **b**?
3 What happens to the subject of sentence **a** in sentence **b**?

Note: If the subject of the active sentence is not important because the emphasis is on the verb (the action) or the object (who/what the action is happening to), the passive sentence does not contain an agent.

2 Rewrite the following sentences, converting the verbs from **active** to *passive* or *passive* to **active**. Identify the tense in each case.

1 The Indians **protect** the forests.
2 The Indians *are being wiped out* by guns and disease.
3 Children *will be robbed* of the earth's beauty by human greed.
4 Very few white people **have seen** this place.
5 Alcohol **destroyed** thousands of Indians.

3 In other words.

Rephrase these sentences beginning with the words in **bold**.
1 Factories pollute **rivers and lakes**.
2 Fire destroyed **the forest**.
3 Many countries were affected by **the nuclear explosion**.
4 Thousands of sea birds are killed by **oil from tankers**.
5 Gases have damaged **the ozone layer** ...
6 ...so more people will probably be killed by **skin cancer**.
7 Some countries have been affected by **changes in the weather**.

(handwritten notes at top) TO BE NAIVE = INOCENT = INGENUO. WALKNUTS = Nueces. COBNUT = Avellana. ALMOND = Almendras. BRAZILNUT = Coquito. jungle (amazon jungle).

LISTENING

Don't be so green!

Maria, from Brazil, is a postgraduate student in England. She is discussing practical ways to save the rainforest.

1 Listen and complete the notes.

Maria feels that rich countries are (1) .... responsible for damage to the forest because of the (2) .... their banks made. Poor countries are desperate for dollars to pay the banks back and so have to clear (3) .... Coffee is not as good to export as beef because the coffee-producing country only gets about (4) .... a jar. The importing country adds value to the coffee by (5) .... and (6) .... it. Producing countries can't process the coffee themselves because they aren't (7) .... enough. Maria thinks that the best way of preserving the forests is by giving people alternative employment and encouraging them to buy products like (8) .... and (9) .... which are natural products of the forest. There is no morality just (10) ....

(handwritten answers: (1) INDIRECTLY YOUR; (2) MAKE LOAN; (3) THE LAND TO PROVIDE LAND FOR CATTLE; (4) TO PENS; (5) ROASTING; (6) GRINDING; (7) POWERFUL; (8) NUTS; (9) RUBBER; (10) ECONOMICS. Side notes: Meat (of a cow); Molen; fruit or seed; BARK = corteza del árbol; SAP = savia del árbol; CAUCHO.)

2 How far do you agree with what Maria says? How far does Frank accept the responsibility which developed countries have? Who wins their discussion?

VOCABULARY

Verbs with prepositions

1 Match the halves to form complete sentences.

1 You blame someone **for** doing something — a when you think something is a bad idea.
2 You thank someone **for** doing something — b when he/she has done something wrong.
3 You congratulate someone **on** doing something — c when you think it's his/her fault.
4 You accuse someone **of** doing something — d when you're grateful.
5 You prevent someone **from** doing something — e when he/she has done something well.

(handwritten matches: 1–b, 2–d, 3–e, 4–c, 5–a)

2 Now use the correct combination of verb and preposition to expand the following sentences. *He blames the government for cutting down trees.*

1 He/blame/government/cut down/trees.
2 He/thank/Indians/welcome/him/to their village. → *He thanks the Indians for welcoming him*
3 He/congratulate/local people/protect/their forests. → *He congratulated for protecting their forests to their village / the local people*
4 He accuse/politicians/not understand/problem. → *He accuse politicians for not understanding the problem*
5 The politicians/prevent/Indians/live/traditional way. → *The politicians prevent to Indians for living in a traditional way*

WRITING

Describing a process

1 Put the verbs in brackets into the passive and put sentences a–h in the right order to describe how instant coffee is made. Use the pictures to help you.

Coffee is grown in a warm climate but the beans are exported to make instant coffee.

a This coffee (spray) into hot air. *is sprayed*
b When they arrive at their destination, the beans (buy) by a coffee dealer and (sell) to a coffee processor. *is bought   is sold*
c The hot air evaporates the water and coffee powder (leave) and freeze-dried. *is left*
d The 'cherries', each containing two coffee beans, (pick) and (dry) in the sun. *is picked   is dried*
e These imported coffee beans (roast) and (grind). → *is roasted   is ground*
f When dry, the beans (separate) from their shells, (put) into sacks and (export). *is separated   is put   is exported*
g When trees are several years old, they flower and (produce) green berries which ripen into 'cherries'. *is produced*
h In order to produce instant coffee powder, huge pots of fresh coffee (make). *is made*

2 Think of a product from your country. Write a short text describing how it is made.

VOCABULARY

Newspapers

Complete the words in the following sentences.

1 The E. *ditor* .... is the person in charge of a newspaper.
2 J*ournalists* .... are people who write and report for newspapers.
3 The h. *eadline* .... of the main story are always on the front page of the newspaper in big letters.
4 A newspaper contains lots of stories or ar. *ticles* ....
5 A 'scoop' is an ex. *clusive* .... story which one paper reports before any of the others.
6 In Britain, there are two main types of newspapers: the '*popular* .... papers' often make news stories more sensational; the 'qu. *ality* .... papers' are more serious.
7 In some countries, c. *ensorship* .. exists; this means that the government decides what the newspapers contain.

LISTENING

Jackie Green is answering some questions about the British press from a German student called Hans. Listen to what she has to say and complete the tasks and the notes. You will need to listen to their conversation at least twice.

1 Write **DMi** for the *Daily Mirror*, **DMa** for the *Daily Mail*, **DT** for the *Daily Telegraph*, **Ti** for the *Times*, **G** for the *Guardian*, **I** for the *Independent* and **S** for the *Sun* in the boxes **1–7**.

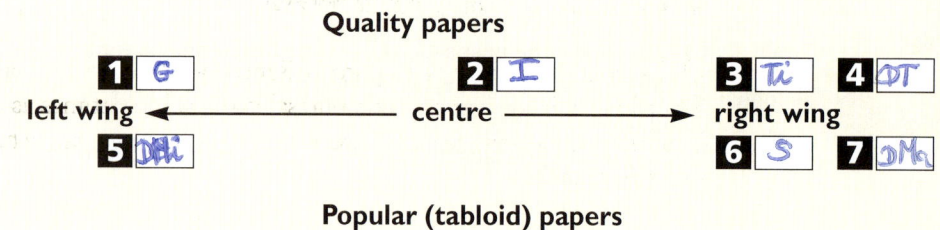

Quality papers

| 1 G | | 2 I | | 3 Ti | 4 DT |

left wing ⟵ centre ⟶ right wing

| 5 DMi | | | | 6 S | 7 DMa |

Popular (tabloid) papers

2 Now complete these sentences.

1 Tabloids are mostly read by (8) .... although the Daily Mail is a (9) .... tabloid.
2 People tend to choose papers on the basis of (10) .... , (11) .... and (12) ....
3 Most papers are owned by (13) ....
4 The Sun sells (14) .... and the Daily Mirror (15) .... copies each day.
5 The (16) .... newspaper claimed it won an election for the (17) .... Party.
6 There is no (18) .... because there is a tradition of freedom of the press.

3 Answer the following question.

What does Jackie think about the story about the TV presenter?
(19) ....

4 Imagine you are telling a foreigner about the kinds of newspapers you have in your country. What would you say?

LISTENING

How to get an interview

1 Listen to the conversation and work out who the people in the photographs are.

[handwritten: journalist →]

[handwritten: Minder = = bodyguard. → Oliver Reed. → film actor]

2 Listen again and think about these questions.

1 Why did the journalist go to the West Indies? *[handwritten: He wanted to obtain a good story about Oliver Reed (his funeral wedding)]*
2 What was the journalist's big problem? *[handwritten: He refuse to speak with anybody. And he is protected by a minder]*
3 How did he get round it? *[handwritten: He get the information from the minder and schoolgirl]*
4 Was it a fair way of getting an interview? *[handwritten: It isn't fair this way to obtain the information justo.]*

3 Look at the tapescript on page 164 and find the different ways in which **get** is used. Sometimes it is used as part of a phrasal verb and sometimes as a substitute for another verb. Find the uses which mean: *to encourage/persuade, to escape, to be in the act of doing something, to catch, to take*

4 🔲 Stress and intonation *[handwritten: emphasys]*

Listen to this extract. How and why is the stress of the third sentence different?

ANNABEL: You know Oliver Reed?
JULIAN: The film director?
ANNABEL: That's Oliver Stone. Oliver Reed, the actor.

Now listen to this extract. Mark the stress showing where Annabel contradicts and corrects Julian.

ANNABEL: … he married a schoolgirl.
JULIAN: Who, this reporter? *[handwritten: wearing, what's his name?]*
ANNABEL: No, Oliver Reed.
JULIAN: What! He must have been twice her age!
ANNABEL: Three times, actually.

In pairs, practise saying the two extracts.

SPEAKING

Getting the facts straight *[handwritten: → obtener la información correcta.]*

There is a revolution in the capital of Moronia. Journalist Kit Lucas is there for the *Daily Planet* newspaper and is on the phone to the Editor in London. Work in pairs.

STUDENT A You are Kit Lucas. Turn to page 141.
STUDENT B You are the Editor of the *Daily Planet*. Turn to page 144.

VOCABULARY

Understanding the headlines

1 The words used in newspaper headlines are often short and dramatic. Match each headline word with its synonym on the right.

8 a ROW   1 leave/resign *i*
3 b AXE   2 get married *e*
4 c RIFT   3 cut *b*
6 d DRAMA   4 break/division *c*
2 e WED   5 question/interrogate *g*
9 f BLAZE   6 exciting event *d*
5 g QUIZ   7 anger *h*
7 h FURY   8 argue/argument *a*
1 i QUIT   9 fire *f*

2 Headlines use a characteristic 'grammar', too. Look at these two examples.

Princess to wed pop idol

infinitive to indicate the future

= The princess is going to marry a pop star.
The INFINITIVE is used to talk about the future.

Boss axes 1,000 jobs

present simple for a past action ✗

= The owner has cut 1,000 jobs at his business.
The PRESENT SIMPLE is used to talk about the past.

3 Study these headlines and put them into ordinary English. Think of stories behind the headlines.

1 MINISTER TO AXE HOSPITALS *MINISTER AXES HOSPITALS*
2 ROYAL COUPLE SAYS NO TO RIFT RUMOUR *ROYAL COUPLE NO TO RIFT RUMOUR.*
3 FIRE CHIEF TO QUIT AFTER BLAZE DRAMA *FIRE CHIEF QUITS AFTER BLAZE DRAMA.*
4 POLICE QUIZ TEACHER IN EXAM ROW
5 FURY AS GOVERNMENT RIFT WIDENS
6 PRINCESS WEDS IN PALACE DRAMA
PRINCESS TO WED IN PALACE DRAMA.
FIRE CHIEF QUIT AFTER BLAZE DRAMA.

4 Invent a headline of your own and tell the story behind it.

POLICE QUIZS TEACHER IN EXAM ROW.

READING

The scoop!

Wensley Clarkson waited outside Paul and Linda McCartney's deserted country house for an interview.

1 Read the text and discuss which title would best describe the story:

a How to make the truth interesting.
b Anything for a story.
c Journalists are liars.

Perhaps you can invent a better title of your own.

2 Match what actually happened (1–5) with the journalist's account (a–e). Example: 1–e

e 1 The journalist said: 'I can see from both of you that these marriage rift stories are untrue.'
a 2 Paul said: 'Load of nonsense.'
d 3 The journalist said: 'I suppose you wish these gossips would stop.'
c 4 The journalist asked: 'Would you call them muckspreaders?'
b 5 The journalist did not ask Paul about the court case in Germany.

2 a Paul angrily denied rumours of a rift in their fourteen-year marriage.
5 b Paul was tight-lipped about the court case.
4 c Paul said: 'We are targets again for these malicious muckspreaders.'
3 d Paul said: 'I just wish these gossips would go away and stop talking rubbish.'
1 e Paul insisted: 'I want the world to know that Linda and I are as happy as ever.'

The electric window slid down and with that inimitable smile known to millions, he asked me: 'Yes, what can I do for you?' It was a very relaxed approach when you consider it was almost midnight in a lonely country lane – and for all he knew, I could have been a nutter with a gun. I was so shocked he was talking to me that I hesitated for a moment, then told him who I was. He seemed relieved and I grabbed at that opportunity.

'I can see from both of you that these marriage rift stories aren't true.'

'Yep. Load of nonsense,' came the reply from my genial Liverpudlian host.

'I suppose you wish these gossips would stop,' I carried on.

'Yep. Sure do,' came the next reply.

'Would you call them muckspreaders?' I added.

'Yep.'

'These rumours first surfaced a year ago. They're obviously no more truthful now than then.' I was pushing my luck at this stage.

'Yep. Now why don't you go off home?'

It was my turn to say 'Yep' because that signalled the end of the interview.

Two days later, readers of the *Sunday Mirror* were treated to a marvellous page-three 'Exclusive' headlined 'PAUL'S FURY AT LOVE RIFT LIES'. The opening paragraphs read:

Superstar Paul McCartney has hit back at the rumours that his marriage is on the rocks. 'I want the world to know that Linda and I are as happy as ever,' he insisted. 'I just wish these gossips would go away and stop talking rubbish.'

Paul, 40, was speaking on the eve of a West German court case in which a 20-year-old girl, who says she is his illegitimate daughter, is claiming millions of pounds' maintenance from him. He was tight-lipped about the court case – but with Linda by his side he angrily denied show business rumours of a rift in their fourteen-year marriage.

'We're targets once again for these malicious muckspreaders,' he said.

'Last time these rumours started was about a year ago and they are no more truthful now than they were then.'

Paul spoke exclusively to the *Sunday Mirror* at his cottage in the East Sussex countryside, near Rye.

LANGUAGE STUDY

Reporting verbs

1 *'I want the world to know that Linda and I are as happy as ever,'* he **insisted**.

The following example shows how the reporting verb **insist** can be used to put the sentence into reported speech.

Paul **insisted (that)** he and Linda were as happy as ever.

2 Reporting verbs use these following patterns.

1 *He* **insisted (that) they were** happy.
   VERB 1 + that + someone + VERB 2

2 *She* **persuaded him to tell** the truth.
   VERB 1 + someone + INFINITIVE (with to)

Other verbs: **advise, ask, encourage, persuade, remind, tell, warn**

3 *He* **denied** stealing the handbag.
   VERB 1 + VERB 2 + ing + (something)

Other verbs: **admit, suggest**

4 *His teacher* **suggested (that) he should become** a journalist.
   suggest (that) + someone + should + INFINITIVE (without to) + something

3 Put these sentences into reported speech using the reporting verb at the beginning of the second sentence.

1 'If I were you I wouldn't print that story,' he said. TO
   He advised me *NOT TO PRINT* story.

2 'I didn't take those photographs!' she said. TAKEN
   She denied *taking* photographs.

3 'Please don't print my name,' she said. TO
   She asked me *NOT TO PRINT HER* name.

4 'Don't give him an interview!' he warned me. TO
   He warned me *NOT TO GIVE HIM* an interview.

5 'I invented the story,' Julian said. HAD
   Julian admitted *HAVING* invented the story.

6 'Why don't you phone the editor?' he said. SHOULD
   He suggested *THAT I should phone* the editor.

7 'Get a photograph of the accident,' she said to her secretary. TO
   The editor told *her to get a photograph of* the accident.

8 'Tell me what happened,' he said. I did. TELL
   He persuaded *me to tell him what* happened.

THE IMPERIAL WEIGHTS/DISTANCES

Handwritten notes (top):
1 YARD = 0'93 METRES.
1 YARD 3 INCHES = 1 M.
1 YARD = 36 INCHES = 3 FEET
1 FOOT = 12 INCHES
1 INCH = 2'56 CM.
1 pound = 456 grams.
¼ pound = 4 ounces = 113 grams.
1 HUNDREDWEIGHT = 8 STONE.
1 stone = 14 pounds = Approx 6 kg.
12 ounces = 3/4 de litre (pound)
1 pound = 16 ounces.
1 MILE = 1754 YARDS = 1608 M.

Tricked! → Engañado

You are going to read two newspaper articles about two English girls who were arrested for smuggling rare birds' eggs. → Traficar (contrabando)

1 Work in pairs. One of you reads article **A** while the other reads article **B** on the opposite page.

Answer as many questions as you can, then exchange information with your partner. (*Don't worry if you can't understand all the vocabulary.*) defraudada

The species in dying out →

1 Where is Kathy from? From Oxford
2 What is special about the eggs?
3 How much did they weigh? 12 ounces
4 How does Kathy feel now? She feels that
5 Where were the eggs hidden?
6 What was the girls' destination?
7 Who else was involved?
8 What penalties does each girl face? Kathy probably to become extinct.

defraudada.

INOCENTE o INGENUA.   carcel/cell

From a POPULAR PAPER →

A

Too naive for this world?

sollozar

Hot tears ran down the cheeks of Oxford girl KATHY GRAHAM as she tried to reach out to touch me through the bars of her cell. 'Why was I such a fool?' she cried, her whole body shaken by **heartrending sobs**. 'I'll go crazy if I have to stay in this place,' she screamed. What started out as a luxury holiday for Kathy (18) and a friend has turned into a nightmare! Kathy is told she faces a long prison sentence if she is found guilty of trying to smuggle six priceless parrot eggs out of a small Caribbean state whose government is determined to prevent the bird from dying out. (Only 50 female birds are known to exist.) A top professor has been arrested in connection with the eggs' disappearance. Kathy's friend, Jennifer, who isn't yet 18, will probably escape with deportation. 'I know people won't believe us, but we were taken in, tricked, by people we thought were our friends. We didn't have a clue what we were carrying,' said Kathy, one minute laughing hysterically, the next in **floods of tears**. → inundación de lágrimas. Perhaps next month's **trial** will help us to get to the bottom of this story.

unable in a hostage way

enorar

juicio/proceso.

B

Two women arrested for smuggling 'chocolates'

Trafican →

TWO YOUNG WOMEN are awaiting trial in the Caribbean after being arrested for trying to smuggle out the rare eggs of a near-extinct parrot. One of the women, 18-year-old Kathy Graham, spoke from the cell where she is being held in custody, saying that she saw herself not as a criminal but as a victim. She had been tricked, she said, by 'professional' smugglers.

Kathy and a friend, Jennifer Roberts, were about to fly to London when they were stopped by suspicious customs officers who discovered six eggs weighing just 12 ounces hidden in a box of luxury chocolates. The eggs could be worth a considerable amount of money to dishonest dealers who would sell them to collectors.

'We had no idea what we were carrying. Someone asked us to deliver the box to a relative,' Kathy claimed.

The strange tale began in Oxford where Kathy and Jennifer met a group of wealthy young students at a party. 'This guy called Norman invited us on a luxury holiday on his father's yacht in the Caribbean. Norman fixed us up with visas and tickets but at the last moment said he wouldn't be able to join us until a few days later. It all seemed too good to be true... and it was.'

2 Quickly read the article you have not yet looked at.

Which one do you think comes from a 'popular paper' and which one comes from a 'quality paper'?
Which one:

• carries more information? *Article B.*
• has more human interest? *Article A.*
• is more 'emotional'? *Article A.*
• do you find more difficult? *Article A → less information to understand the truth story.*

SPEAKING

What kind of person do you think Kathy is? *She is a Naïve girl because she's tricked.*
Do you believe her story? *Yes I can believe*
What effect do you think the stories had on the girls' families? *to advice their girls about bad effect. the fact.*

WRITING

I thought you should know...

Write a letter to two friends who are travelling around the world. Tell them all about Kathy and Jennifer.
Remember to say if you believe their story and what *you* think should happen to them.
Give your friends some advice about accepting gifts from strangers.
Begin the letter like this:

Dear Megan and Janet,
I hope you get this letter before you leave Australia. I thought you should know about the two girls who've been arrested for smuggling.

LISTENING

The news

1 Listen and write down the three news headlines. What will they be about?

2 Now listen to the whole of the news. Were your predictions correct?

3 Listen again to the first news item about changes in the traffic regulations.

When do the new regulations come into force? Which vehicles will they apply to? What arrangements are being made to make the changeover easier?

4 Listen again to the news item about the fire and fill in the gaps.

A (1) ...Blaze... at the Local Examinations Board (2) ...has destroyed... a wing of the building. The (3) ...Mystery... fire (4) ...broke out... at around 3 o'clock this morning and it took until 9.00 for firemen to bring it (5) ...under... control. Fortunately, damage (6) ...appears to be... limited to the Science examinations section. A (7) ...spokesperson... has said that a (8) ...thousand..., I'm sorry I'll read that again, a hundred (9) ...thousand... who took the November (10) ...examination... will have to re-sit. A group of students is (11) ...helping... police with their (12) ...enquiries... .

5 Which tenses are used in the first two news items? Can you explain why?

WRITING

Newspaper articles

1 Expand these notes to complete a 'nonsense' news item.

1 Bad weather–cause–destruction–this year's spaghetti crop–Northern Italy.
2 crop–destroy–exceptionally cold weather–this time of year.
3 Farmers–wake up–this morning–find–spaghetti–freeze–branches–their trees.
4 This mean–ruin–thousands–Italian farmers–who–depend–this year's harvest.
5 This be–third year–spaghetti harvest–be disaster.
6 Farmers–must–wonder–if–they–be–rescue–European Community again.

2 Here is another 'nonsense' article to expand.

1 Finally–World Animal Fund–announce–plans–save–penguins–extinction.
2 want–build–electric fence–penguin breeding grounds–Antarctic.
3 believe–only way–prevent–hungry polar bears–eat–all the penguins.
4 polar bears–eat–bananas instead.
5 Next Monday–group–pop stars–make a record–raise money–the project.

Were the words you used 'information words' or 'grammar words'?

3 In pairs, or small groups, think of a 'nonsense' news item. Write it down and then choose one person from each group to read it to the rest of the class.

WRITING
PREPARATION

Composition writing

1 Read the composition and look at its relationship with the plan on the right.

Every day popular papers print stories about the private lives of public people. Journalists believe they have the right to invade their privacy; their victims disagree.

After all, isn't what the famous do behind closed doors their own business? A politician's unhappy marriage is unimportant. What matters is how well he does his job.

There again, how he acts in private may show us his true nature. Public figures must also realize that the loss of privacy is the price of fame.

There is no clear answer. Let's hope the journalists and their subjects (behave) in an honest and decent way.

↳ comportarse.

Popular newspapers - stories, private lives of public people.
Journalists/photographers think OK - victims disagree

Private life = own business
Good at job = important, not marriage

Private life reflects true nature
Fame = loss of privacy
↳ means.

No right answer

2 Now make a plan for this composition.

Television is one of this century's most important inventions. However, are we its master or its slave? Some say that it has killed the art of conversation.

In other words, people no longer know how to (amuse) themselves because they are so used to the instant entertainment it provides.

There again, it has brought many benefits. The news keeps us informed of world events, it can educate us and we can even watch a live football match on the other side of the world.

To sum up, it has changed our lives, but it is up to us whether we let it enrich or dominate them.

entretenerse

Television is the most important invention in the communications world.
Some people think OK - other people says It's a problem for communication.
T.V. shouldn't be the only way of entertainment. Can be an education.
People should do other things = read, play sports etc.
T.V. programs can give us benefits
— with educational programs
— Giving us information about the world news
— Giving entertainment watching a football match

Decide for yourself.
enrich or dominate?

3 Make a plan for this composition: *Newspapers should be politically independent.*

13 Evolution

Look at the cartoons and the captions. Imagine you wanted to explain the jokes to someone who hadn't seen them. What would you say?

THE FAR SIDE By GARY LARSON

The real reason dinosaurs became extinct

Suddenly, Bobby felt very alone in the world.

pie de página = The caption

Disaster befalls Professor Schnabel's cleaning lady when she mistakes his time machine for a new dryer.

[handwritten: unicada. TO DWELL = Habitar]

VOCABULARY

1 Dictionary definitions

This key vocabulary will help you with the listening and reading in this Unit.
Use the words in the box to complete the dictionary definitions. Note the context and forms in which any of these words appear in this Unit.

meteor   mammal   dwell   drought   genetics   fossil   reptile   ancestor

1 ...REPTILE.... /'reptaɪl/ a rough-skinned creature whose blood changes temperature according to the temperature around it.
2 ...DWELL.... /dwel/ formal; to live in a place.
3 ...METEOR.... /'miːtjə^r/ a small piece of matter floating in space that forms a line of light if it falls into the earth's air.
4 ...FOSSIL.... /'fɒsəl/ a hardened part or print of an animal or plant of long ago, that has been preserved in rock or ice.
5 ...DROUGHT.... /draʊt/ a long period of dry weather when there is not enough water. *[handwritten: celula]*
6 ...GENETICS.... /dʒənetiks/ a study of how living things develop according to the effects of those substances passed on in the cell from the parents.
7 ...MAMMAL.... /'mæməl/ an animal of the type which is fed, when young, on its mother's milk.
8 ...ANCESTOR.... /'ænsestə^r/ a person, esp. one living a long time ago, from whom another is descended.   *[handwritten: especially]*

2 Science and scientists

See if you can complete the names of the sciences and their scientists.

[handwritten: between (+ de 2)]   *[handwritten: to gaze = looking very much]*

1 (Amongst) other things, Galileo was an ast**RONOMER**.... Gazing at the stars is called ast**RONOMY**....
2 Some anth**ROPOLOGIST**... went into the jungle to study the life of an Indian tribe. They were never seen again. The science of anth**ROPOLOGY**.... will miss them!
3 Geo**logy**.......... is a very important science when people are searching for oil. Geo**logist**.......... take rock samples and analyze them.
4 Arch**AEOLOGY**... is the study of the remains of ancient times. Indiana Jones is a famous arch**AEOLOGIST**.... from the cinema!

• Which one of these sciences is the most/the least interesting? Which one do you think is the most useful?

SPEAKING

Time travellers

A new time machine means that expeditions can be made to: the Age of the Dinosaurs; the Ice Age; the Age of Columbus; the year 3000.

1 Discuss which three people you would choose for each expedition: astronomer, geologist, painter, poet, anthropologist, soldier, nurse, botanist, priest/nun, astrologer, archaeologist, linguist, explorer.

[handwritten: Botánico.] *[handwritten: Astrólogo.]*

2 Which expedition would you like to go on? Choose one of the roles. Discuss what you might find and what the Earth will be like.

A little chap/fellow = A little child = Bloke = guy.

Tail = coba.

LISTENING

Living dinosaurs

hija

Patricia Osborne has just been to the 'Living dinosaurs' exhibition with her daughter, Katie. They have just got home to their flat where Pop Osborne is doing some housework.
a man

This listening is in two parts.

1 Part A

Patricia is talking to Pop Osborne.
Listen to their conversation and find out:
- what is special about the exhibition.
- how suitable it is for children.

POP OSBORNE:	Hello Pat. What have you been (1) ...up two...?
PATRICIA:	I've just taken Katie to an exhibition.
POP OSBORNE:	(2) ...Poor you..., you (3) ...must be tired...
PATRICIA:	Tired! (4) ...I am... exhausted.
POP OSBORNE:	(5) ...Never mind... I'll make a nice cup of tea. So, what did you see?
PATRICIA:	Well, it was called 'Living Dinosaurs'.
POP OSBORNE:	'Living Dinosaurs'! You (6) ...can't be serious...!
PATRICIA:	Of course they were models which look like dinosaurs. They're operated (7) ...by computer... They do all the right things. Move and (8) ...breathe... and make horrible (9) ...noises...
POP OSBORNE:	Katie (10) ...must have been scared...
PATRICIA:	Actually she (11) ...loved... it. One little chap was (12) ...terrified... He (13) ...can't have been... more than four.
POP OSBORNE:	Oh (14) ...dear... , (15) ...what a shame...! He'll probably have (16) ...nightmares...

2 ▭ Sincerely sympathetic!
showing compassion

1 Pop Osborne uses the following expressions to show sympathy. *to compassion.*
Listen to the recording and practise saying them aloud, copying Pop Osborne's intonation as closely as you can. In the first one, a line shows what happens to his voice. Do the same for the other examples.

a Poor you!   c Oh dear!
b Never mind!   d What a shame!

2 How could you reply to the following statements? Sometimes more than one answer is possible!

a 'I've got an awful headache!' *oh dear! / Never mind!* ! I'll get you some aspirin.
b 'I'm sorry, I can't find that book you lent me.' *Never mind!* ! It's not important.
c 'My dog has been run over by a bus!' *What a shame!* ! He was such a nice dog.
d 'I can't do this exercise!' *oh dear! / Never mind!* ! I'll explain it to you.
e 'The last bus left ten minutes ago.' *oh dear! / What a shame!* ! That means we'll have to walk!

3 Part B

Katie is telling Pop what happened to the dinosaurs. Listen to their conversation and find answers to these questions.

1 When did the dinosaurs die out? *60.000.000 years ago*
2 Why did they disappear? What did people use to think? *change in the weather*
3 What do scientists believe these days?
4 What made them change their minds? *It's too much to believe*
5 Why didn't all the other animals die as well? *to be warm blooded*
6 How long did dinosaurs live on the Earth? *116.000.000 years*

LANGUAGE STUDY

Making intelligent guesses DEDUCTIONS.

1 Look at these sentences from the recording.

1 You **must be** tired. → POSITIVE (PRESENT) (SURE)
2 It **might have been** a change in the weather. → POSSIBILITY (POSITIVE)
3 Katie **must have been** scared. → POSITIVE (PAST)
4 He **can't have been** more than four. → NEGATIVE (PAST)
5 It **could have been** a meteor. → NEGATIVE (PROBABLY)
6 You **can't be** serious. → NEGATIVE (PRESENT)

Which sentences are:
• certain, in a positive sense?
• certain, in a negative sense? *Can't have died.*
• uncertain? *Must have gone +*
• talking about now/talking about the past? *Must have been / ought*

What happens to their structure when they go from the present to the past?

2 🔲 **Stress patterns**

Listen to sentences **1** and **2** again. Notice where the **stress** lies and how the unstressed words are pronounced (e.g. 'be' in sentence **1**).

1 *You **must** be **tired**.*
2 *It **might** have been a **change** in the weather.* *couldn't have survived*

Try to copy their pronunciation as closely as you can.

How do you think the other sentences will be pronounced? *Must have → told.*

3 Complete the text using one of these forms.

For *definitely*, a form based on **must**.
For *definitely not*, a form based on **can't**.
For *possibly*, a form based on **might** or **could**.
Be careful! Some of the sentences use the passive.

There are many strange cases of 'living fossils'. These are creatures which come to life after millions of years when they are freed from inside rocks. The most extraordinary event was in 1856 in northern France, where engineers were making a railway tunnel. They broke open a rock and a big ugly bird, with two legs and a beak full of sharp teeth, flew out. It flapped its wings a few times but then died. *Must have been · Must have been trap.*

They took its body to a museum where an expert said that the bird (1) *definitely be* a pterodactyl. Its form could be seen in the rock where it (2) *definitely trap*. Scientists *might have fallen* believed it (3) *possible fall* into a swamp (an area of soft, wet land). The bird (4) *definitely not die*; instead, it (5) *definitely go* into a kind of coma, like a deep sleep. It (6) *definitely catch* in the swamp at least a hundred and fifty million years ago, before the swamp turned to rock. Some of these prehistoric birds (7) *definitely* → *Must have been* be much bigger; some (8) *possible have* *might have had* wings which were fifteen metres across. Some people did not believe the engineers' story; they said the creature (9) *definitely not* survive all that time, but I feel they (10) *definitely tell* the truth.

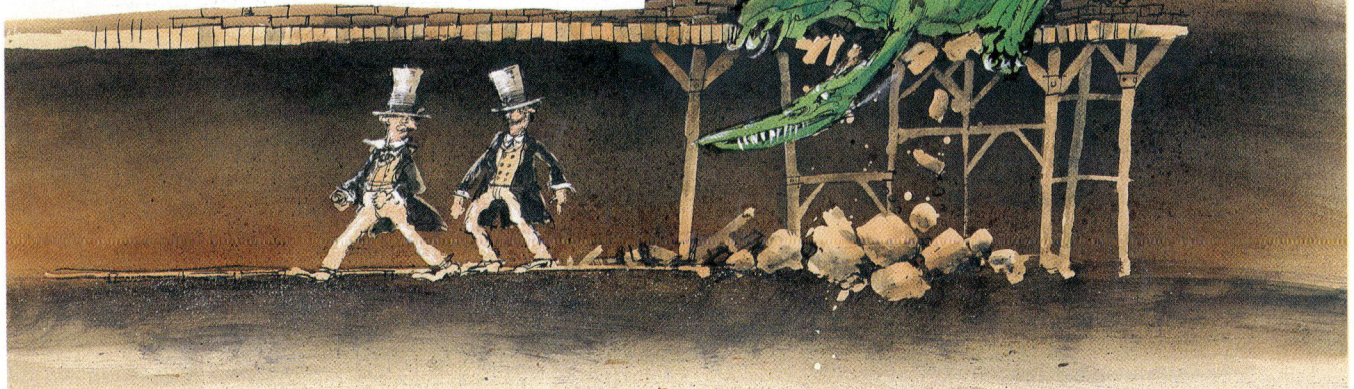

α SPEAKING

Mystery cultures

Work in pairs. Each of you is an archaeologist with a different interest.

STUDENT A look at page 141.
STUDENT B look at page 145.

STUDENT A look at page 141.
STUDENT B look at page 145.

READING

'Man After Man'

1 Before you read, think about these questions:

• How much longer will man survive?
• What do you understand by 'genetic engineering'?

2 Match the headings **A–E** to the paragraphs (1–4). There is one letter you do not need to use.

A Homecoming. (return) 4
B Catastrophe. 1
C A Brighter Future.
D Evolution in the laboratory. 2
E Dependence. 3

3 Read the text carefully and answer questions 1–6 by choosing the answer (**A**, **B** or **C**) which fits best.

1 What destroys man as we know him?
A War.
B Famine.
C Disease.

2 Which is the most successful in the *long* term?
A Technically adapted humans.
B Farmers and fishermen.
C The humans who leave in their space ships.

3 Which species is *not* developed?
A One which can live in the sea.
B One which can fly.
C One which can live in rainforests.

4 What happens to the Earth's climate?
A It becomes hotter.
B It becomes colder.
C It becomes wetter.

5 Which of the new species goes through the greatest changes?
A The Tundra dweller.
B The Woodland dweller.
C Piscanthropus profundus.

6 Which of the species survives the 'newcomers'?
A Piscanthropus profundus.
B The food creature.
C The Woodland dweller.

4 Word search

Search the text and find the different ways which are used to express the idea of something dying or ending.

We know how mankind has evolved till now, but what is his future? In his fascinating anthropology of the future, Man After Man, Dougal Dixon makes some suggestions.

1 ▪ B   He predicts that, within 200 years, man will have reached crisis point. Overpopulation and industrial pollution will have made life impossible for most of us. Civilization will have broken down and billions of people will starve and die. A few specially chosen human beings will leave Earth on giant spaceships in search of new planets. On Earth, scientists will try two ways of adjusting man to the changing environment. In a first attempt, a tiny number of adapted humans will live on, helped by high technology. But they will become extinct in a thousand years along with the last remaining farmers and fishermen. Man as we would recognize him will no longer exist.

2 ▪ D   The scientists' second attempt to preserve mankind is more successful: they genetically engineer five new species based around humans. What would normally take three and a half million years, only takes thirty years. One of the new species lives in tropical forest, another can survive in the desert. A third (Piscanthropus profundus) can live and breathe deep in the oceans. The two remaining species are particularly interesting. They are the Tundra Dweller, who inhabits the land of the melting ice caps, and the Woodland Dweller.

3 ▪ E   These two eventually depend on each other because the Tundra Dweller migrates to the woods in winter. At first they are enemies but eventually they rely on one another – the Tundra Dweller carries the Woodland Dweller and provides it with warmth. In return, it depends on the intelligence of its passenger. They start to die out but, as the Earth becomes hotter, the Tundra Dweller adapts by losing its hair and growing fat. Instead of warmth, its body provides food for the transformed Woodland Dweller.

SPEAKING

- How likely do you think Dixon's predictions are?
- Make your own prediction of how Man will look in five million years!

Will he still be around? How many eyes, legs, arms will he have? How will he communicate/travel/reproduce etc?

4 But nothing lasts for ever. After five million years, descendants of the men who left Earth return in giant spacecraft. They too have evolved and come back to exploit the Earth's resources. All the land creatures suddenly die out except for genetically engineered workers and an ugly food creature: the final form of the Tundra Dweller. Their work complete, the 'newcomers' leave and everything dies. Yet deep in the oceans there is 'Piscanthropus profundus', which has managed to escape all of these changes. Perhaps this last descendant of man will eventually come out of the sea to evolve into other creatures who will inhabit the land.

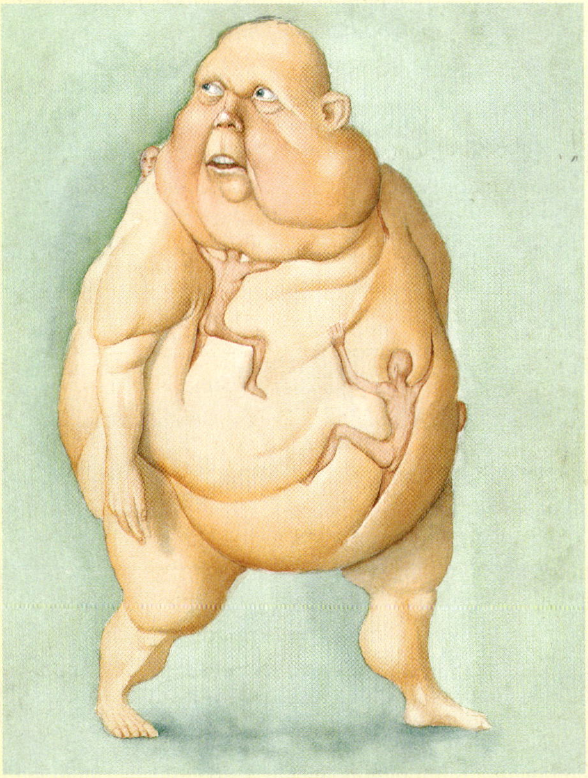

LANGUAGE STUDY

Future predictions

A few specially chosen human beings **will leave** Earth on giant spaceships in search of new planets.
Civilization **will have broken down**.

- We often use the simple future (**will**) for predictions.
- The 'future perfect' (**will have done**) is used when we predict that, by a point in the future, something has already happened.

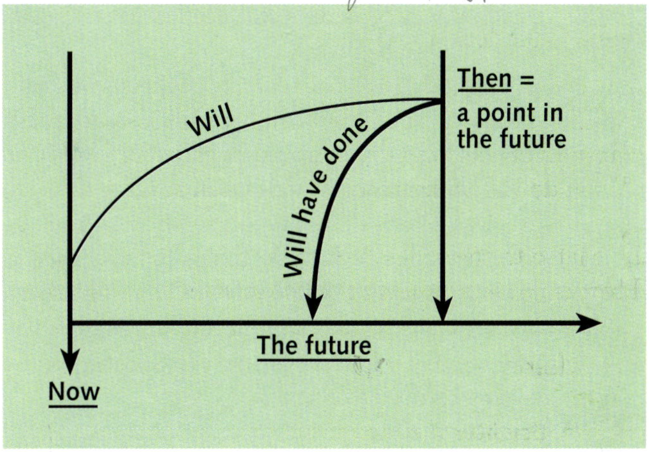

1 *Imagine ...*

The year is 2200. Yonotot Nartrog has just taken off in one of the spacecraft. She has extremely regular habits. She plans to take a food pill three times a day, write a page in her diary once a day, play chess once a week, watch a video every month and drink a bottle of Happy Juice on her birthday! Calculate what she will have done by the year 2250. Fortunately a new 'Space Year' is 500 days (not 365) and has 50 ten-day weeks! Each space month is five weeks.

2 Make some predictions about your own life.

Example: *By the time I'm 30 I'll have ...*

TO BARTER = *system del Trueque cambiarios.*

por el contrario = instead

Linking, explaining and contrasting

In earlier units we looked at some of the ways we can join phrases and short sentences to make longer sentences, talk about 'cause and effect', give explanations and make contrasts. Choose the words and expressions which can be used to complete the text about the evolution of money. Sometimes, more than one possibility is correct.

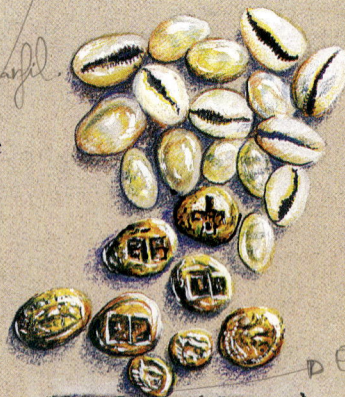

It is difficult to imagine a world without money, though of course, it hasn't always been around.

1 **A** *First of all,* **B** *Once upon a time,* **C** *Firstly,* **D** *In the beginning,* people would exchange sheep for ivory, or goats for weapons.

2 **A** *Sincerely,* **B** *Of course,* **C** *Naturally,* this could be inconvenient.

3 An easier way of trading was needed, **A** *so that* **B** *because* **C** *that's why* money had to be invented.

4 **A** *Lately,* **B** *Once,* **C** *Eventually,* four-and-a-half thousand years ago in Mesopotamia (now southern Iraq) someone had a brilliant idea.

5 They realized that it would be easier **A** *for* **B** *in order to* **C** *to* buy and sell by using standard weights of silver.

6 This was a marvellous invention because **A** *unless* **B** *otherwise* **C** *instead* we might still be swapping things for sheep and goats!

7 However, it wasn't **A** *before* **B** *by* **C** *until* the seventh century BC that the first coins appeared in the ancient kingdom of Lydia (now Turkey).

8 **A** *During* **B** *By* **C** *Over* the next few centuries, the use of coins spread to other civilized countries.

9 Rulers wanted to control the issue of coins, **A** *because* **B** *so* **C** *so that* **D** *that's why* they were stamped with the head of the ruler and their value.

10 **A** *As* **B** *While* **C** *Because* precious metals like silver and gold were used, they were actually worth the weight of the metal.

11 Chinese copper coins were **A** *so* **B** *too* **C** *very* **D** *really* heavy to carry that people kept them with merchants

12 **A** *which* **B** *whom* **C** *that* **D** *who* gave their customers receipts written on pieces of paper.

13 **A** *After* **B** *Afterwards* **C** *–* they would use them

14 **A** *like* **B** *as* **C** *for* **D** *instead* money.

15 **A** *Eventually,* **B** *Lastly,* in the fourteenth century, the Chinese government introduced the first paper money.

16 **A** *Because* **B** *Although* **C** *Despite* people were suspicious at first, they accepted it.

17 Nowadays, nobody thinks twice about using paper money, **A** *despite* **B** *although* **C** *while* it only has symbolic rather than intrinsic value. (This is true of coins, too).

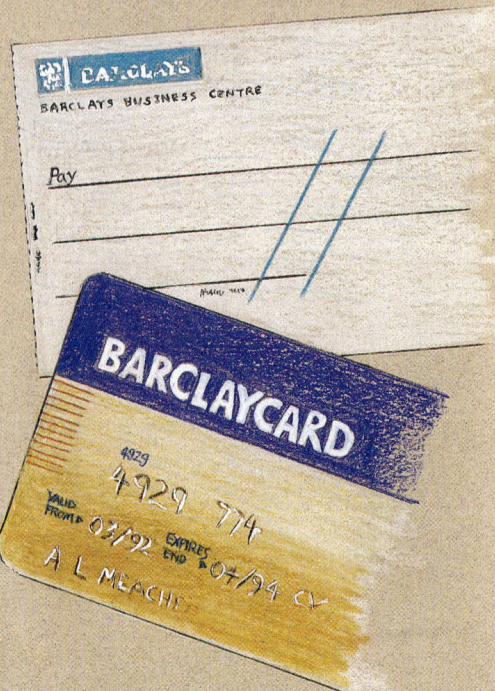

18 There is nothing new in this **A** *so* **B** *because* **C** *that's why* **D** *as* tribes have traded for centuries using shells and even feathers as currency.

19 **A** *Nowadays,* **B** *These days,* **C** *Actually,* less and less cash is used and we pay for expensive items like CD players and cars by cheque and credit card.

20 **A** *In fact,* **B** *Really,* **C** *Nevertheless,* people predict that, by the end of the century, coins and paper money will have been completely replaced by plastic money.

LISTENING

→ diapositiva.

→ armadura

1 You are going to hear a short talk about the evolution of armour. Before you listen, look at the pictures and see how many of these items you can find.

→ muralla.

| helmet | breast plate | sword | chain mail | spear | shield | = *escudo.* |

→ HELMET.

→ BREAST PLATE.

→ Lanza.

2 While you listen, complete the notes for each picture as the lecturer discusses it. Then compare your notes with a partner and listen to the passage again.

Slide one:
In classical times soldiers used to fight (1) .... ~~H.......~~ *ON FOOT* using (2) .... *SPIERS and SWORDS.* The armour was (3) .... ~~.......~~ so that soldiers could move. It only protected the (4) ...*HEAD AND UPPER*... body. *→ FAIRLY LIGHT*

Slide two:
The helmet from (5) ....*Greece*... *even do it* covers the face but leaves enough room for the soldier to (6) .....*see through*... .

Slide three:
Roman soldiers wore armour made of strips because it was (7) .....*more*..... *→ long pieces for ~~......~~ flexible* than armour made from one/a single piece.

Slide four:
In the Middle Ages a lot of the fighting was done on (8) .....*horse back*.....*→ HEVIER* *A SUIT OF ~~CHAIN~~ OVER HOLE BODY.* This allowed soldiers to wear (9) .... armour which gave more protection. Knights wore (10) .... of chain mail which was popular until about 1300. However, there was a return to plate armour because (11) .... became powerful enough to penetrate the chain mail. *→ BOWS*

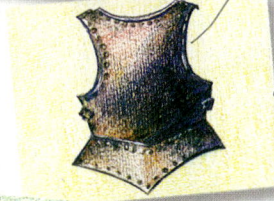

Slide five:
The best plate armour came from (12) .....*Italy and Germany*.....

Slide six:
When gunpowder and guns were invented armour became (13) .....*less and less effective*..... for a while.

Slide seven:
People realised the best protection against bullets was to be a (14) .....*difficult target*..... . For the next few centuries soldiers had (15) .....*very little protection*..... *returned to foot and lightly on soldiers with bales.*

Slide eight:
In the last (16) ......*fifteen*...... years new materials offer protection against bullets and (17) .....*flying metals*..... .

WRITING

From your notes write a composition on the evolution of armour. Use the exercise about the story of money as a guide.

Talking about family relationships

Queen Victoria's descendants have married into most of the royal families of Europe. Study the family tree of the House of Windsor.

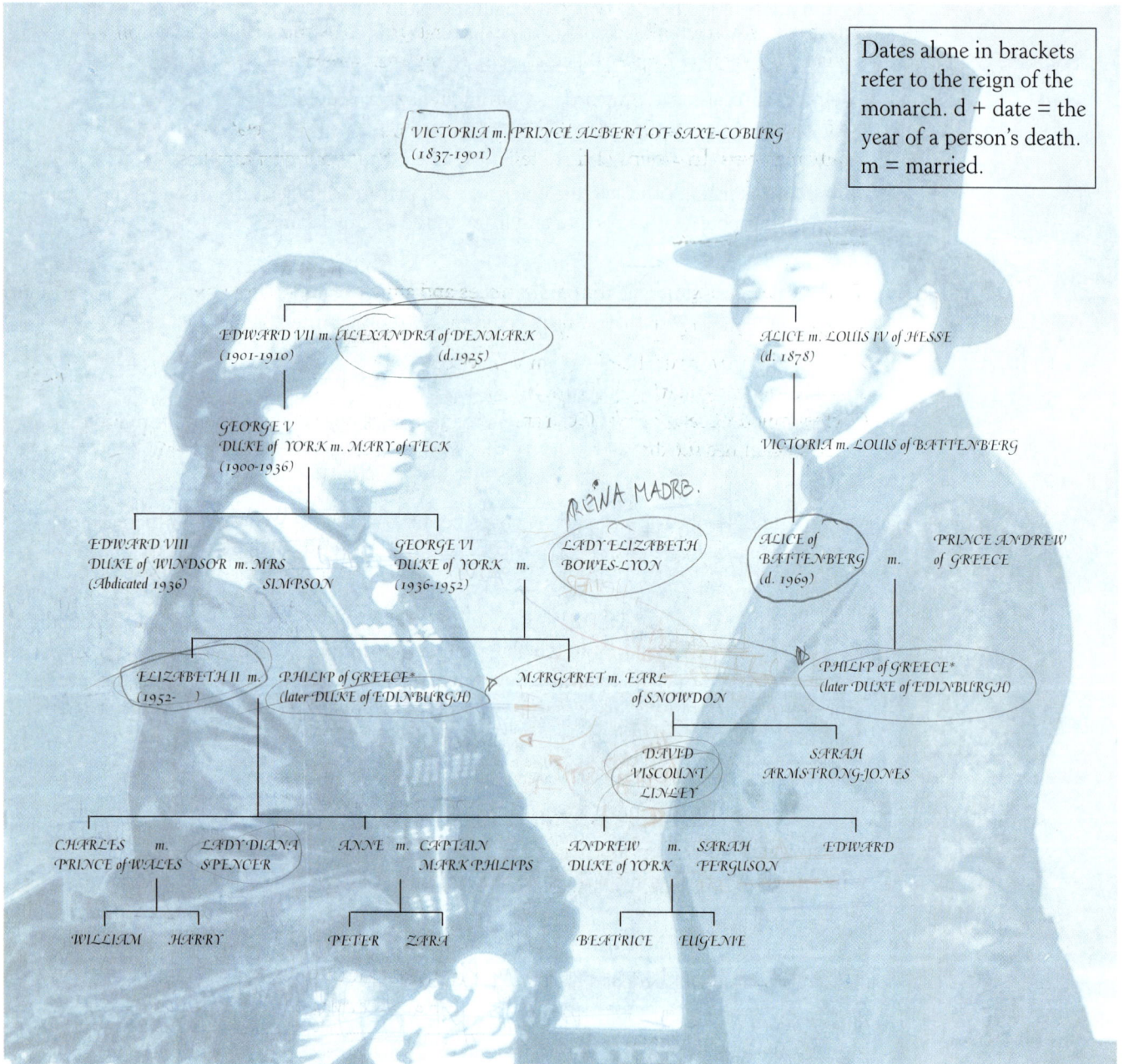

> Dates alone in brackets refer to the reign of the monarch. d + date = the year of a person's death. m = married.

VICTORIA m. PRINCE ALBERT OF SAXE-COBURG
(1837-1901)

EDWARD VII m. ALEXANDRA of DENMARK
(1901-1910)   (d.1925)

ALICE m. LOUIS IV of HESSE
(d. 1878)

GEORGE V
DUKE of YORK m. MARY of TECK
(1900-1936)

VICTORIA m. LOUIS of BATTENBERG

REINA MADRE.

EDWARD VIII
DUKE of WINDSOR m. MRS
(Abdicated 1936)   SIMPSON

GEORGE VI
DUKE of YORK   m.
(1936-1952)

LADY ELIZABETH
BOWES-LYON

ALICE of
BATTENBERG   m.
(d. 1969)

PRINCE ANDREW
of GREECE

ELIZABETH II m.
(1952-   )

PHILIP of GREECE*
(later DUKE of EDINBURGH)

MARGARET m. EARL
of SNOWDON

PHILIP of GREECE*
(later DUKE of EDINBURGH)

DAVID
VISCOUNT
LINLEY

SARAH
ARMSTRONG-JONES

CHARLES   m.   LADY DIANA
PRINCE of WALES   SPENCER

ANNE m. CAPTAIN
MARK PHILIPS

ANDREW   m.   SARAH
DUKE of YORK   FERGUSON

EDWARD

WILLIAM   HARRY   PETER   ZARA   BEATRICE   EUGENIE

1 Using the family tree, answer these questions.

1 Who was Queen Elizabeth's mother-in-law? ALICE OF BATTENBERG.
2 What is the relationship between Queen Elizabeth and:
  • David Viscount Linley? • King Edward VIII of England? NEPHEW; UNCLE
3 Who is Queen Victoria's eldest great-great-great-great-grandson? PETER. GREAT GREAT
4 What is the relationship between Queen Victoria and the Duke of Edinburgh?
5 What is the relationship between Prince Andrew of Greece and Louis of Battenberg?
6 Who are Prince William and Prince Harry's cousins? PETER, ZARA, BEATRICE AND EUGENIE.

2 Vocabulary

Make a list of words to describe family relationships, e.g. *mother, cousin, uncle*.

3

Do you still have a royal family in your country? If so, is there any connection with the British royal family? Could you extend the family tree shown here?

4

Draw your own family tree. Write sentences to describe your relationship with other family members. In groups of three tell each other about your own families.

READING

Heirs to the throne

1 Read the passage about the royal princes and answer the following questions.

1 Who are second and third in line to the British throne? *PRINCE WILLIAM and HARRY.*
2 When is it predicted that William will succeed? *2030*
3 What will be special about him? *MOST ENGLISH MONARCH FOR ABOUT FOUR HUNDRED YEARS.*
4 How much Greek, Polish, German, Russian and Danish blood do the princes have? *all together 32'5 (6'5%)*
5 How often has the throne gone to the second child in the House of Windsor? *OFTEN GONE.*

Prince William, born on 21st June 1982, is second in line to the throne, (1) .... his father, Prince Charles. This means that in the normal course of events, he should succeed (2) .... the throne in around 2030. He is likely to be (3) .... most English monarch (4) .... about four hundred years!

He is 39% English, 16% Scottish with 6.25% each (5) .... Irish and American. The rest is an interesting mixture of Greek, Danish, German, Russian and Polish. He gets most of (6) .... through his grandfather, Prince Philip, (7) .... is able to trace his family through (8) .... every royal house of Europe.

His younger brother Harry, who was born (9) .... September 1984, is third in line. It is worth remembering (10) .... , in the House (11) .... Windsor, the throne (12) .... often gone to the second child. Edward VII was Queen Victoria's second child (13) .... he succeeded to the throne because the eldest child was a girl. George V became King (14) .... his elder brother died young, and George VI came to (15) .... throne because his brother (16) .... to abdicate so that he (17) .... marry Mrs Simpson. Because of past history, and in case (18) .... accidents, Harry will never be (19) .... to fly in the (20) .... plane as his brother, William.

2 Now fill each of the blanks with one word only.

Handwritten notes (top margin):
A WILL (TO INHERIT) = TESTAMENTO ; " HEREDAR ; INHERITANCE = HERENCIA.
TO TAKE AFTER = TO RESEMBLE SOMEBODY IN YOUR WAYS. = Parecerse en la conducta/gestos.

READING

Forbidden love

1 Read the text and make a list of the important dates and events.

2 Match sentences **A–E** with the gaps in the text (**1–5**).

(3) **A** Edward had long had a poor relationship with his parents who considered him to be immature and easily bored.

(4) **B** For eight years she had been bedridden and cared for day and night by a team of nurses.

(5) **C** This caused great bitterness.

(4) **D** Public opinion would not let a twice-divorced American woman become Queen.

(2) **E** She spent the next couple of years hopping from city to city and spent some happy months in Peking.

In 1986 the Duchess of Windsor died in Paris, a lonely old woman. **1** B Yet fifty years earlier, as Mrs Wallis Simpson, she had been at the centre of the abdication of Edward VIII. Her father had been a wealthy American businessman but his sudden death meant she was **brought up** in relatively poor circumstances. Her mother remained socially ambitious and Wallis took after her. In 1916 she married for the first time, her husband was the dashing airman, Winfield Spencer. Sadly, he **turned out** to be a drunkard and Wallis left him. **2** E She returned to New York where she met Ernest Simpson, an Anglo-American who had come into a family fortune. They married in London in 1929 and Wallis soon established herself as a successful high-society hostess. She first met the Prince of Wales on 10th July 1931 and they soon received an invitation to be his guests. She soon became bored with Ernest, and a firm friendship developed between her and Edward, the heir to the throne. They went on a skiing holiday to Austria which was extended to include visits to Budapest and Vienna. This meant **calling off** several official engagements which made King George V absolutely furious. **3** A Out of loyalty to the Royal Family, the British press kept the story of the relationship a secret and any foreign papers which reported it were kept out of Britain. On January 20th 1936 King George died and from that moment Edward became king and the final crisis was near. Edward's mother, Queen Mary, **looked down on** Wallis and was completely against any idea of marriage. She and the Prime Minister tried to make Edward end the relationship. For his part Edward neglected his duties.

The story finally became public when the Bishop of Bradford publicly denounced the affair. Wallis ran away to France. **4** D The King would have to choose between Wallis and the throne. On 11th December 1936, he abdicated, and left England for a life of exile with the woman he loved.

With the new title of the Duke of Windsor he eventually married Wallis in France. No members of his family were present. As the ultimate insult, Edward received a message from his brother saying although Wallis could call herself the Duchess of Windsor the title of 'Your Royal Highness' would be denied to her. **5** C In the period before the Second World War the Duke damaged his reputation by flirting with fascism and meeting Adolf Hitler in Germany. When war broke out he became governor of Bermuda but was viewed with suspicion by those who believed he would be prepared to re-occupy the throne if Germany was victorious. The years which followed the war were empty ones and the Duke was consistently denied a role by his family. In 1953, shortly before the coronation of the Duke's niece, Queen Elizabeth II, the couple moved to a magnificent chateau in the Bois de Boulogne in Paris. His health rapidly declined as he entered his seventies and in 1972 he died. His body was buried in St George's Chapel, Windsor.

Handwritten margin notes: Edwar; Kept = Mantener; Good looking = handsome; bad reputation = borracho; "braguetazo" = ambitious; Herederos; Cancel; provocarse; MIRAR POR ENCIMA DEL HOMBRO = DESPRECIAR; bedridden = postrada; Dando saltos; Abandonar = dejar al lado.

3 Answer the following questions about the text.

1 What do you imagine Wallis's childhood was like? *IN RELATIVELY POOR CIRCUMSTANCES*
2 When she went to London, how did Wallis become popular so quickly?
3 Why did so few people know about the relationship between Wallis and Edward?
4 What happened after Edward's abdication?

VOCABULARY

Phrasal verbs in context

1 Six phrasal verbs are highlighted in the text in **bold type**. In the infinitive decide which ones mean:

1 to inherit a characteristic or physical feature from a parent. ⇨ TO TAKE AFTER.
2 to inherit money or property. ⇨ TO COME INTO
3 to consider someone else as inferior to oneself. ⇨ To Look Down ON.
4 to raise/to educate. ⇨ TO BRING UP.
5 to cancel ⇨ TO CALL OFF
6 to become apparent. ⇨ TO TURN OUT.

2 Write a sentence of your own for each of the phrasal verbs.

3 Word search

Go through the text and make a list of any words to do with royalty.

SPEAKING

Evaluating the text

1 What would you have done in Edward's place?
2 Do you feel sorry for anyone in the story?
3 Who do you feel was responsible for his abdication? Put these people in order of their 'guilt': the Bishop, Wallis, the press, Queen Mary, Edward, Wallis's mother, the Prime Minister.

WRITING

Imagine you are one of the principal characters and write a 100-word paragraph giving your point of view about what happened.

LANGUAGE STUDY

Make and let

1 Study these two sentences which show how **make** and **let** are used.

1 *She and the Prime Minister tried to **make** Edward end the relationship.*
   Here **make** means oblige or **force**.
2 *Public opinion would not **let** a twice-divorced American woman become Queen.*
   Here **let** means **allow**. → permit

2 Using the word in **bold type**, continue the second sentences so that they have the same sense as the ones above.

1 Brothers and sisters in ancient Egyptian and Inca royal families could marry each other. **allow**
   Brothers and sisters in ancient Egyptian and Inca royal families WERE ALLOWED TO MARRY WITH other.
2 In some societies men can have more than one wife. **let**
   Some societies... LET MEN HAVE MORE THAN one wife.
3 She had to marry him even though she didn't love him. **made**
   Her parents... MADE HER MARRY HIM even though she didn't love him.
4 Child marriages are allowed in gypsy communities. **let**
   Gypsy communities ... LET THEIR CHILDREN GET married.
5 In the Tallensi culture of Ghana, young men are obliged to look for wives outside their tribe. **make**
   Tallensi tribes ... MAKE THE YOUNG MEN LOOK FOR WIVES outside their tribes.
6 The prince's parents wouldn't let him marry the actress. **allowed**
   The prince ... WASN'T ALLOWED TO MARRY the actress.

SPEAKING

Marriage customs → barra de pan.

In some parts of Southern Germany, the bride receives a loaf of bread and the bridegroom a glass of beer. Then, together, they saw a log in half. What do you think this custom means? La sierran un tronco por la mitad.
Work in groups. Write your answers on separate pieces of paper and then compare them. Did any two in the group have the same answer?

(handwritten notes at top: MEANWHILE .909 AFTER. ACTUALLY = REALLY   DURING = NAMED PERIOD NOT A NUMBER FOR A SPECIFIC PERIOD OR A NAMED PERIOD. CURRENTLY = Actualmente   EVENTUALLY = FINALLY.)

LANGUAGE STUDY — Time expressions

Decide which of the two words in brackets best completes the following sentences.

1 Queen Victoria reigned (for/during) 64 years.
2 The Prime Minister changed 27 times (for/during) Victoria's reign.
3 (While/Meanwhile) she ruled her empire, her heir, Edward, was preparing to become King.
4 (While/Meanwhile) he gained a reputation as a playboy. *(handwritten: RECENTLY)*
5 Edward VII (lately/eventually) became King on her death in 1901.
6 Film of his coronation has (lately/eventually) been discovered in an attic.
7 He died in 1910 (after/afterwards) a short but popular reign.
8 (After/Afterwards) his son became George V.
9 Wallis had already been married (before/previously) she met the heir to the throne.
10 She had (before/previously) been married to a pilot.

(handwritten: D + TO + GERUND (FOR GENERAL CASE).)

WRITING — Writing a story from notes

Study these notes and then write the story of Juan Carlos and Sofia's royal romance. Decide which information you will/won't include. Try to use some of the time expressions from the previous exercise.

(handwritten notes in left margin: HOMELAND = TIERRA. TO ENCOUNTER = REENCONTRARSE o ENCONTRARSE. TO BE SWORN IN = TO GIVE AN OATH = PRESTAR JURAMENTO.)

1931	Alfonso XIII leaves Spain for exile in France.
1938	Juan Carlos, his grandson, is born in Rome. Princess Sofia is born in Athens.
1941 –46	Juan Carlos's family takes refuge in Switzerland. Princess Sofia goes into exile. *(handwritten: TO SOUTH AFRICA)*
1946	Sofia returns to Greece.
1948	Juan Carlos goes to Spain to continue his education.
1954	Sofia's mother, Queen Federika, arranges a cruise on her yacht for the young royals of Europe. Sofia and Juan Carlos meet for the first time.
1958	Juan Carlos and Sofia meet again at a wedding in Stuttgart.
1960	They meet at the Sailing Olympics in Naples.
1961	They sit together at a wedding reception in England. They start to go out with each other. In September, they announce their engagement. *(handwritten: COMPROMISO.)*
1962	They get married on May 14th.
1963	Their first child, Elena, is born.
1965	A second daughter, Cristina, is born.
1968	A son, Felipe, is born.
1969	General Franco announces that Juan Carlos will succeed him as head of state.
1975	Franco dies. Juan Carlos becomes King of Spain.

[handwritten top margin: JESTER = BUFÓN / POR CASUALIDAD / WHAT DID YOU HAPPEN TO SEE? = / = QUE VISTE POR CASUALIDAD.]

LANGUAGE STUDY

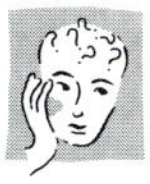

Subject–object questions

Not all love stories end happily. Look at this summary from a programme of the play *Romeo and Juliet* by William Shakespeare.

1 Read it through quickly and find out how many characters are mentioned and how many deaths are involved.

[handwritten: forbidde to entrance = kind of exit.]

[handwritten: THERE ARE NINE CHARACTERS AND FIVE DEATHS.]

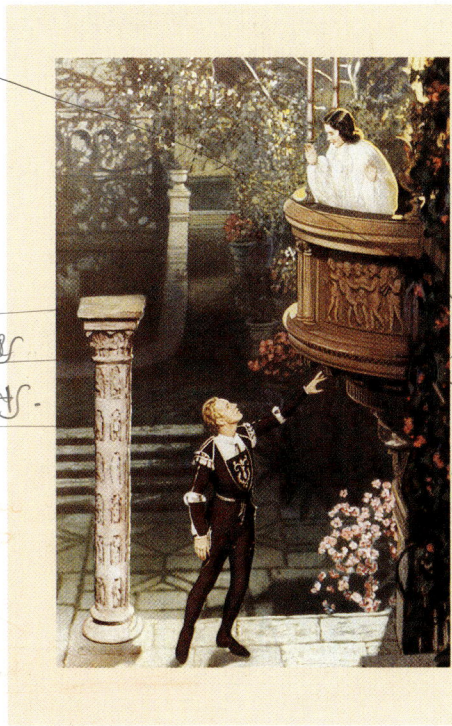

[handwritten: banquete/festejo]

The Montagues and Capulets are the two most important families in Verona but hate each other. Romeo, Lord Montague's son, and Juliet, Capulet's daughter, meet by chance at a feast and fall in love. The next day Friar Laurence marries them in secret. Following an argument about Romeo's presence at the feast, Tybalt, a member of the Capulet family, murders Romeo's friend, Mercutio. Romeo takes his revenge and kills Tybalt. Prince Escalus banishes Romeo from Verona. Capulet, who knows nothing of the secret marriage, tries to make Juliet marry Prince Paris. Juliet wants to escape this marriage. Friar Laurence gives her a drug to make her appear dead but Romeo does not hear about the trick. He returns to Verona and kills Prince Paris, whom he blames for Juliet's death. He drinks some poison by Juliet's side and dies. When she awakes, she realizes what has happened and kills herself with a dagger.

[handwritten: CULPAR A ALGUIEN]

2 Look at these questions and answers.

Who loves Romeo? ⟶ Juliet. Juliet does. *[handwritten: Juliet loves Romeo.]*
SUBJECT   OBJECT
Who does Romeo love? ⟶ Juliet. He loves Juliet.
OBJECT   SUBJECT

So, when **who** or **what** is the SUBJECT of a question, we don't use the auxiliary **do/did**.

3 Using the prompts on the left, make questions for the answers on the right.

1   Where/the lovers/meet?   → At a feast. *[handwritten: WHERE DID THE LOVERS MEET?]*
2   Who/marry them?   → Friar Laurence. *[handwritten: WHO MARRIED THEM?]*
3   Who/kill/Mercutio?   → Tybalt. *[handwritten: WHO KILLED HIM?]*
4   What/Romeo/do?   → He kills Tybalt to avenge Mercutio. *[handwritten: WHAT DID ROMEO DO?]*
5   What/happen/Romeo?   → He is banished from Verona. *[handwritten: WHAT HAPPENED TO ROMEO?]*
6   What/make/Juliet/appear dead? → A drug Friar Laurence gives her. *[handwritten: WHAT MADE JULIET APPEAR D...]*
7   Who/Romeo/kill?   → Prince Paris. *[handwritten: WHO KILLED ROMEO? OR WHO DID ROMEO KILL?]*
8   Why/Romeo/kill/him?   → Because he blames him for Juliet's death. *[handwritten: WHY DID ROMEO KILL HIM?]*
9   What/kill/Romeo?   → The poison he drinks. *[handwritten: WHAT KILLED ROMEO?]*
10   What/happen/Juliet/wake up? → She sees Romeo's body and kills herself. *[handwritten: WHAT HAPPENS TO JULIET WHEN SHE WAKES UP?]*

READING

The best job in the world?

Imagine that you are the Editor of a magazine for young people. One of your journalists has given you this article to be included in the next edition.

1 Match the opening sentences **A–G** with each of the paragraphs (**1–7**).

What does each of the opening sentences do?

> **A** Possibly the worst thing is the lack of privacy. (6)
> **B** Then, of course, there's the power and the foreign travel. (3)
> **C** Have you ever daydreamed and wondered what it would be like to be the Queen? (1)
> **D** While I wouldn't mind the money, it must be a minor consideration for such a rich woman. (7)
> **E** To begin with, the money's not bad. (2)
> **F** It is the perfect job if you like going abroad. (4)
> **G** Now let's look at the minuses. (5)

2 Read the text again and see if there is anything in it that you find surprising or amusing. What is the balance between the light and humorous, and the more serious elements?

3 Make a list of all the points the writer makes and decide if they are important (**I**), of secondary importance (**SI**), or light and humorous (**LH**).

Example: advantages: £4 million a year (**I**), no stamps (**SI**), black blotting paper (**LH**)

4 **Understanding the organization of the text**

Search the text for ways that the writer: orders points, gives opinions, balances arguments and draws conclusions.

5 **Writing**

Your magazine has just been given a big advertisement. In order to make room for it, you have to cut the article about the Queen by 50%. How will you do it? Look at your list of points and decide which points you will cut. Show your teacher your list of points and then write the shorter version.

1 **C** Just for fun, let's treat it like any ordinary job and weigh up its good and bad points.

2 **E** She gets a 'salary' of four million pounds a year from the British government. There is no tax on any of her income* and, when she dies, her heirs won't have to pay a penny. What's more, she doesn't have to put stamps on letters: the royal seal is enough. She also uses special black blotting paper to dry the ink on letters. (It has to be black so nobody can read any state secrets from it!)

3 **B** She can declare war, dismiss the government and pardon everybody in prison!

4 **F** The Queen travels all round the world in style, visiting fascinating places. There are some great presents as well: on two of her trips she was given a crocodile and two hippos.

5 **G** There are lots of boring, formal dinners to attend (bad news if you've got a weight problem) and speeches to give. She always has to be diplomatic and isn't allowed to speak her mind. It must also be hard knowing who your real friends are and who are just 'yes men'.

6 **A** True, on the one hand she has lots of homes where she can hide away, but on the other hand, there are always photographers trying to take pictures of her whatever she is doing. It must be very difficult trying to keep a balance between public life and a private family life.

7 **D** I'm sure there is part of her which would rather live in peace and quiet, enjoying her wealth. Fortunately for the British people, the Royal Family's tradition of service means we have a monarch prepared to bear the heavy responsibility of the Crown. I wouldn't want the job.

*Since April 1993, the Queen has been paying tax on her private income.

SPEAKING

Spitting images?

Here are two pictures of the Royal Family. One is a real photograph; the other is a photograph of puppets which are used in a satirical TV comedy programme. Match each person in the satirical photograph with one in the real photograph. What do you think of this photograph? Is it funny/fair/cruel?

LISTENING

The British Royal Family

You are going to hear four passers-by giving their points of view about the Royal Family.

1 Listen once and look at the photographs. Decide who said what. Then listen a second time and make a list of the points made by the people being interviewed. Decide whether they are positive, negative or neutral.

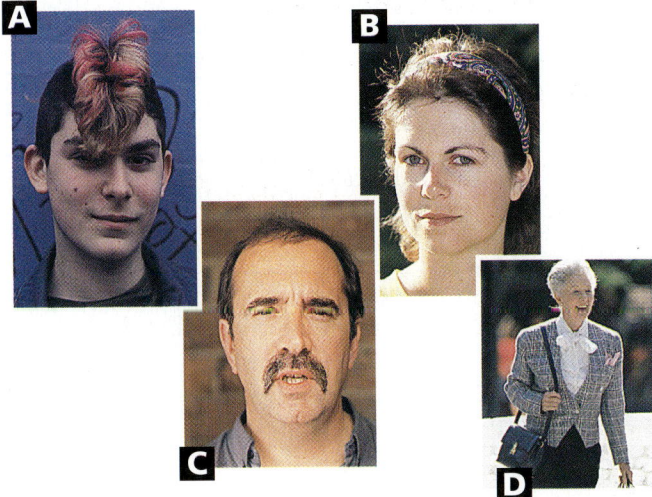

A

B

C

D

2 ▭ Leading questions

Listen to these ways of asking someone's opinion and try to mark their stress and intonation.
Example: **What** do you think of the Royal Family?
1 **Could you tell me what you think** of the Royal Family?
2 **Do you think** the Royal Family does a good job?
3 **Would you mind telling me** what you think of the Royal Family?

3 Using the types of question used by the interviewer, find out the opinions of some of your classmates.

4 ▭ Linking words in connected speech

Listen, and then read this extract from the tapescript. Notice where the **stress** lies and how words link up (⌢) in connected speech.
It's **not** like⌢in the⌢**old**⌢days when the **King led** his⌢**armies**⌢into **battle**.

Now listen to this extract and mark the stress and links in the same way.
Me, I'm unemployed and I have to live off £50 a week but they've got millions.

WRITING

Balancing arguments

You are going to write a follow-up magazine article called: 'What ordinary people think about royalty'.

- In pairs or groups, compare the lists of points you made in the listening exercise. Decide on four positive and four negative points you are going to use in your articles.
- Now describe your own opinions and what your conclusion will be. Make notes, and plan your article. When your plan is ready, show it to your teacher.
- Now write the article. This introductory paragraph will help you to get started.

What do ordinary people think about royalty? Does it still have a role in this day and age or should it be abolished? We decided to go out on the streets and find out from ordinary men and women what they thought of royalty and its future.

LISTENING

Henry VIII and his six wives

1 Henry VIII (reign 1509 – 1547) had six wives. Listen to the interview and complete the table.

Wife's name	What happened to her
Catherine of Aragon	....
Anne Boleyn	....
.....JANE.... Seymour	....
.... of Cleves	divorced
....	executed
Catherine Parr	....

2 Listen again and choose the best answer (**A, B** or **C**) to the questions.

1 According to the interviewer, how is Henry VIII best remembered?
A As the king who married six times.
B As the founder of the navy.
C As a religious reformer.

2 What does the interviewer say about Henry's behaviour?
A He was a man of his times.
B He was capable of great kindness.
C He was worse than many other monarchs.

3 Why did Henry want a divorce from his first wife, Catherine?
A He needed an excuse to break with the Pope.
B He wanted a male heir.
C He no longer loved her.

4 Why was Henry grateful to Thomas Cromwell?
A He found him a new wife.
B He made Henry extremely rich.
C He got on well with the great Lords.

5 Why did Henry search abroad for his fourth wife?
A He was suspicious of English women.
B There was a lack of suitable English candidates.
C He wanted a wife who was Catholic.

6 How did Henry feel when he saw Anne of Cleves' picture?
A He was furious with Cromwell.
B He immediately wanted to marry her.
C He was ready to accept Cromwell's advice.

3 Look at the tapescript on page 166.

a Which ways are used to express obligation?
b Which phrasal verbs mean:
  (i) to continue?   (ii) to hate/consider someone as inferior?
  (ii) to attack?   (iv) to maintain?

4 Tell each other about a 'larger than life' figure from your country's history.

READING

1 Read the short biographies about some of the most important kings and queens from English history. Answer the questions which follow by writing **B** (for Boudicca), **A** (for Alfred), **W** (for William I), **E** (for Elizabeth), **C** (for Charles I) and **V** (for Victoria) in the boxes after each question.

1 Which monarchs had literary giants in their reign? ☐☐
2 Which two monarchs had particularly unpleasant deaths? ☐☐
3 Who caused a civil war? ☐
4 Who is the subject of an amusing legend? ☐
5 Who successfully invaded England? ☐
6 Who fought against invaders? ☐, ☐ and ☐
7 Who had the least personal but the most symbolic power? ☐

BOUDICCA (DIED AD 60)

Queen of the Iceni – a tribe of ancient Britons – she led a revolt against Rome which had colonised England. It is said that 60,000 Romans and their supporters were killed. Her followers must have been a terrifying sight as they covered themselves with a blue dye. Legend says she drove a chariot with sharp knives attached to its wheels into battle. When she was finally defeated she took poison to avoid capture.

VERDICT: Noble and savage, she dared to challenge the might of the Roman Empire. She led her people to disaster.

ALFRED 849-99 (KING OF WESSEX 871-99)

As King of Wessex in the South West of England, Alfred fought many battles to save England from conquest by the Danes. A funny story tells of how he took shelter in a peasant woman's hut one day. Deep in thought about the future of England, he let the cakes in her hearth burn. The woman returned and told Alfred off, not realising he was the King of the English. Alfred also revived learning and actually translated works of Latin into old English, a language unrecognisable today.

VERDICT: A brave soldier and leader. A scholar and virtuous man. Deserves his title The Great. A poor cook!

WILLIAM I (THE CONQUEROR) 1027-1087 (KING OF ENGLAND 1066-87)

William, as the Duke of Normandy, invaded England and defeated the English under their king, Harold, at the battle of Hastings. 1066, the year in which this happened, is the best known date in English history. He swept away the Anglo-Saxon monarchy and established his rule systematically and mercilessly. Norman feudalism was introduced i.e. a system in which land was given to William's followers in return for their loyalty. The Normans and their descendants continued to speak French. Words of Norman French origin eventually found their way into the English language e.g. beauty, pork, veal. The Domesday book, a survey of England, was completed in his reign.

VERDICT: A brave but ruthless soldier, honest and religious. A capable king.

QUEEN ELIZABETH I 1533-1605 (REIGNED 1558-1603)

Daughter of King Henry VIII and the executed Anne Boleyn, she survived imprisonment and intrigue. She was a skilful politician and one of England's greatest monarchs. She established much needed religious and political stability. During her reign England started to become an important overseas power. Plots to establish Mary Queen of Scots on the throne ended in Mary's death. Elizabeth's navy defeated an invasion attempt by the Spanish Armada in 1588. Her reign saw a great flowering of artistic talent, notably that of William Shakespeare (1564 - 1616). Elizabeth never married.

VERDICT: A skilful politician and a great monarch. Manipulative and vain, she loved to be flattered.

CHARLES I 1600-1649 (REIGNED 1625-1649)

Charles believed in the absolute power of the crown and ruled England for long periods without Parliament. Eventually he had to call one to raise taxes. When he tried to arrest five members of Parliament who were particularly critical of him, this signalled the start of a long and bitter civil war. The two sides were the Roundheads and the Cavaliers. Charles was eventually defeated and was executed for treason (crimes against the state).

VERDICT: Great personal courage and a good family man. A stubborn man who did not keep his word.

VICTORIA 1819-1901 (REIGNED 1837-1901)

During her reign Britain became the dominant political and industrial power of the world. Was queen through nineteen governments. She married Prince Albert of Saxe-Coburg and they had nine children. After Albert's death in 1861, she virtually retired from public life. An almost perfect example of the constitutional monarch, she symbolised Britain's greatness but had little real political power. Charles Dickens, Britain's greatest novelist, wrote many stories exposing the hardship and poverty of the lives of ordinary English people.

VERDICT: Made monarchy respectable at the height of Britain's power. A devoted wife and mother. Dull with little sense of humour.

2 Which of the monarchs you have just read about strikes you as the most interesting?

3 Which people would you select as being representative of important periods in the history of your country?

READING

1 Read the text.

What is the connection between the ghostly piper and the castle in the picture below?

There is a terrible tale associated with this Scottish castle. In the seventeenth century it belonged to **1 A** *one* **B** – **0** *the* Campbell family, **2 A** *their* **B** *whose* **C** *which* deadliest enemy was 'Left-Handed Coll Macdonnel'. Macdonnel wanted to find a way of killing his enemies, **3 A** *whom* **B** *they* **C** *who* were safely behind the castle's walls, **4 A** *as* **B** *because* **C** *so* he sent his piper to spy on it.

The piper disguised himself and **5 A** *being* **B** *had been* **C** *was* welcomed by the Campbells, **6 A** *what* **B** *whom* **C** *which* he entertained. Unfortunately for him, the Campbells became suspicious and locked him in a tower. The piper had to warn his friends **7 A** *outside* **B** *underneath* **C** *away* that the Campbells were prepared for an attack so he played a famous tune now known **8 A** *about* **B** *of* **C** *as* 'The Piper's warning to his Master'. Macdonnel understood **9 A** *that* **B** *what* **C** *which* had happened and turned **10 A** *out* **B** *off* **C** *back*.

The Campbells were so furious **11 A** *so* **B** *because* **C** *that* they cut off the piper's hands and the brave man died. **12 A** *When* **B** *While* **C** *After* the castle's present owners **13 A** *have* **B** *have had* **C** *had* it restored, workmen discovered a handless skeleton under the cellar floor. His spirit **14 A** *yet* **B** *still* **C** *always* lives on in the castle, **15 A** *when* **B** *where* **C** *which* even today you can sometimes hear him playing.

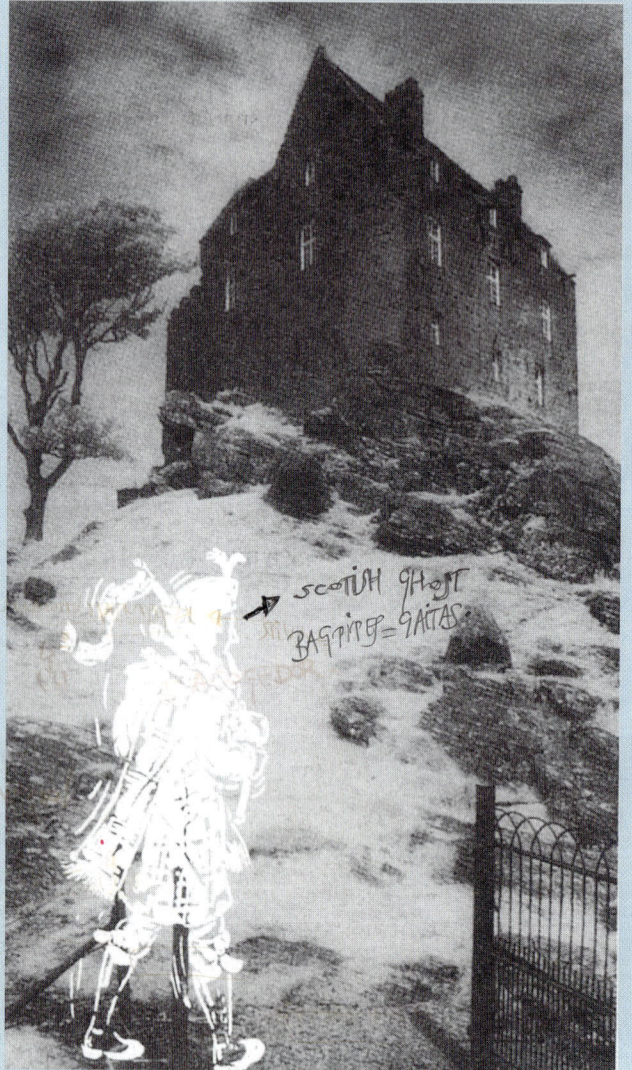

2 Read the text again and, for each number, decide which of the three choices (**A**, **B** or **C**) is correct.

3 Discussion

- What do you think of the story?
- Was the piper brave?
- Do you think he really does haunt the castle?

Do you know a place with a history like this? Tell your classmates the story.

[handwritten: To CHIME = RUIDO DEL RELOJ. (TIC-TIC, TAN, TAN)]

[handwritten: FOOTSTEPS.]

VOCABULARY

🔲 Common sounds

These words all describe common sounds. Study the definitions of the sounds and write down the order in which the sounds appear on the recording.

[handwritten: 2] a **bark** /bɑːk/ the sound that dogs make.
[handwritten: 1-4] b **slam** /slæm/ to shut loudly, with force.
[handwritten: 7] c **gasp** /gɑːsp/ to catch one's breath suddenly because of a shock. *[handwritten: (metal with metal)]*
[handwritten: 9] d **rattle** /ˈrætl/ to make a lot of quick metallic noises.
[handwritten: 8] e **scream** /skriːm/ to cry out loudly on a high note.
[handwritten: 5] f **snore** /snɔː/ to breathe noisily through the nose and mouth while asleep. *[handwritten: (RONCAR)]*
[handwritten: 3] g **squeak** /skwiːk/ a very high but not loud sound. *[handwritten: (RUIDO FUERTE – CHIRRIDO AL ROMPERSE ALGO)]*
[handwritten: 7] h **tap** /tæp/ to strike lightly against something. *[handwritten: (GOLPEAR CONTRA ALGO CON LA MANO)]*
[handwritten: 1] i **yawn** /jɔːn/ to open the mouth wide and breathe in and out, as when tired. *[handwritten: (BOSTEZAR)]*

WRITING

A night to remember

1 You are going to hear a story made up of different sounds and then write it. Before you listen to the sounds, look at the picture and answer the questions. This will help you develop the background.

- When and where was the house built? What kind of history do you think it has?
- Who are the people? How do they feel?
- How would you describe the figure in the doorway? Use your imagination!

[handwritten margin notes: BARREN = DESOLATE = = desolado. / IN THE WILDERNESS = = En la soledad del lugar.]

[handwritten: BROKEN DOWN (THE CAR) = = AVERIADO.]

[handwritten: SKINNY = THICK.]

[handwritten: NOISES]
[handwritten list: – GASP. – SQUEAK. – BARK. – SLAM. – RATTLE (CLICK). – YAWN. – TAP – GASP. – SCREAM.]

2 Listen to the sounds, make notes and plan your story. Then write the story in the PAST. If you need to remind yourselves about narrative tenses, look at pages 34–35.

TO BE DRINKABLE = POTABLE.
STILL MINERAL WATER = WITH GHOST.
After Dark = AGUAL MINERAL WITH GHOST.
[= A RESERVOIR = PRESA
– A DROUGHT = SEQUIA.
– TO DRILL = EXCAVAR.]

fin gap
STILL SPRING WATER = PLAYABLE = FACTIBLE.

READING

= AGUA de ORIGEN (RÍO)

Haunted houses

1 Here are two different stories about houses with mysterious problems. The paragraphs are mixed up and in the wrong order. Read the paragraphs and reconstruct the two stories. Paragraph A is the beginning of one of the stories. Which story does the picture illustrate?

A Most doctors and scientists refuse to believe in ghosts and psychic happenings. Yet in the 1950's in Yorkshire, in the north of England, two doctors almost changed their minds. A house which they used as their surgery started to make strange noises. *→ CONSULTA*

B Almost immediately, the husband changed from a hard-working, stable individual to lazy and bad-tempered. Kathleen felt that she was being controlled by something outside her power.

C As the foundations of the house settled, the rest of the house moved too. As final proof, the bangs and noises were at their worst at high tide. *→ altamares (nivel)*

D On a November morning in 1974, one of the sons of the De Feo family took a rifle and murdered the other six members of his family. For the next thirteen months the house in Amityville in the USA stood empty. *→ TO BE EMPTY* *→ not in life*

E In the garden they discovered an old disused sewer which was connected with a nearby river. It turned out that, at high tide, river water forced its way up the sewer and was making the earth under the house wet and unstable.

F The 'ghostbusters' noticed that the walls of the surgery were cracked and that the roof needed repairing where it dipped in the middle. This suggested that the house had problems with its foundations, so the team decided to investigate. *→ cimiento.*

G None of the local people wished to buy it and the newspapers were full of stories of demonic possession. Eventually, a young couple called George and Kathleen Lutz, believing they had found a bargain because of some ridiculous stories, moved in. *→ mudanza* *George*

H Things got worse. Their children started to get hurt around the house, and Kathleen Lutz had terrible nightmares about the De Feo family. The couple had the horrible feeling that history was about to repeat itself. Just after the Christmas period, unable to stand it any longer, they fled. *→ TO FLEE – FLED – FLED = TO ESCAPE = TO LEAVE.*

I These included loud explosions and the sound of banging, which even made the walls shake. The doctors called in a plumber, who looked over the water pipes, and they had the gas and electrical systems examined. Nobody was able to find out the cause of the noises. By now, the doctors were seriously wondering whether their surgery was haunted and they called in some psychic researchers to investigate.

J Over the next few weeks, thousands of flies appeared in the bedrooms; windows and doors opened and closed for no reason; the toilet bowls turned black and a statue moved around their home on its own. The house was either boiling hot or freezing cold, and they could do nothing to change the temperature. *Alcantarilla.*

PICTURE IS ABOUT FIRST STORY

2 Can you think of a logical explanation?

3 Answer the questions about the texts by choosing the best answer (**A**, **B** or **C**).

1 What effect did the events have on the doctors?
A They felt foolish and embarrassed.
B They became more open to supernatural explanations.
C Their belief in a rational explanation was confirmed.

2 How did the doctors feel after the first investigations?
A Disappointed.
B That there might be a supernatural explanation.
C They had no idea what to do next.

[handwritten top margin: SURGEON = CIRUJANO. · CIRUGIA · OPERATING THEATRE = QUIROFANO. · CONSULTA]

3 What was the fundamental cause of the noises?
A Poor foundations.
B An old sewer.
C Rising water.

4 Why did the Lutz family buy the house?
A Nobody else wanted it.
B They had been put off by the stories.
C They thought it was good value for money.

5 What happened shortly after the Lutz family moved into their new home?
A The wife had a religious experience.
B They started to repair the house.
C Things they couldn't explain.

6 Why did the Lutz family finally leave?
A The parents believed something terrible was going to happen.
B They went away for Christmas.
C The children had bad dreams.

LANGUAGE STUDY

Have something done and need

1 Look at these two sentences

a *They had the gas and electrical systems examined.*
b *They examined the gas and electrical systems.*
Which sentence means:
• someone did it for them? *a*
• they did it themselves? *b*
The first sentence uses the construction 'have something done'.
*She **had** her picture **taken** (by a professional photographer).*
Have + something + PAST PARTICIPLE

2 In the text it says: *[handwritten: ANY TENSE]*

The roof needed repairing.
Something + need + VERB + -ing
We can rephrase this without changing its meaning by saying:
The roof needed to be repaired.
Something + need to be + PAST PARTICIPLE

[handwritten: I have my car fixed by professional]

3 Imagine that the surgery has been repaired by workmen. The doctors are now showing a friend around the house and garden. Rephrase these sentences using one of the forms we have just looked at.

1 Some workmen repaired the roof.
We *HAVE HAD THE ROOF REPAIRED BY THE WORKMEN*

2 The wall still needs fixing.
The wall needs to *BE FIXED*

3 We had the hall redecorated.
A painter *REDECORATED THE HALL FOR US*

4 A plumber fixed the pipes and the central heating.
We *HAVE HAD THE PIPES AND THE CENTRAL HEATING FIXED*

5 A builder filled in the old sewer.
We *HAD THE OLD SEWER FILLED IN.*

6 We are going to have the garden dug.
The garden needs *DIGGING / TO BE DUG*

4 What would you need to have done to make the Lutz's house in Amityville habitable?

[handwritten: Haber hecho algo]

[handwritten: — A CATCH INSTALLED ON THEM = UN CERROJO INSTALADO EN ELLAS (WINDOWS AND DOOR)]

[handwritten bottom: — They Local streets need to be clean up. — " " " streets needs cleaning up.]

WARDROBE = CLOTHES.
CUPBOARD = THINGS.

VOCABULARY

All around the house

Martina is a university student studying away from home.
Look at the picture of her room and label it with the words in the box.

ALFOMBRA

cooker fireplace wallpaper desk bookcase sofa
basin bed rug radiator wardrobe chest of drawers

FIREPLACE *COOKER* *COJÍN* *A CUSHION*

WRITING

A room of my own

1 Read Martina's letter and compare it with the picture. What has she forgotten to mention?
What changes would you make to it?

A BUILT-IN WARDROBE = = ARMARIO EMPOTRADO

FITINGS = INSTALACIONES

AL ALCANCE.

ACOGEDOR.

Dear Mum and Dad,

I thought I'd write and tell you about where I'm living. I've got an attic room in a large old house which has been turned into flats. The landlord lives on the ground floor, he seems o.k.

The room is a bit small but it's cosy. There's a nice big sofa by the radiator and a lovely old fireplace with a mirror above it. My desk is right next to a big bookcase where I've got all my books – so they're all within easy reach when I'm working!

There's a little basin where I can have a wash and a tiny cooker for simple meals and making tea. The bathroom and toilet are just down the corridor. The wallpaper is horrid but I've put some posters up.

Anyway, I must go – I've got a lecture in half an hour.

    Love,
    Martina

VERY LITTLE

HORRIBLE.

– wallpaper!

CONFERENCE AT UNIVERSITY.

AN EXPRESSION

2 Using her letter as a guide, write to a friend describing your favourite room.

WRITING

The story of Princess Elizabeth Bathory

→ IN PAST (NARRATIVE)

Elizabeth Bathory was one of history's most beautiful and terrible people. She was born in 1560 in Hungary and was related to the King of Poland and the Dracula family.
Finish the story. Expand the notes and put the verbs into their correct forms.

1 When–she be fifteen–she marry–famous count–who be–Hungary's greatest general–who be often away.
2 At–age–twenty-five–her beauty start–disappear. *started to disappear*
3 She believe–she can stay beautiful–have baths–blood–young girls! *she could*
4 She send servants–find young women–who be promised–good jobs.
5 Once they reach–castle–they–be thrown–deep dungeons.
6 The girls' blood–be drained–for–countess' bath. *WAS (UNCOUNTABLE)*
7 After five hundred girls disappear,–the King–hear–rumours.
8 When he–have–castle–search–many terrible things–be found. *WERE FOUND.*
9 Because–her noble position–she not be executed–but she be–sealed–small room–until she die. *SEALED (ALUACÓ).*
10 Nowadays,–dark nights,–you can hear–screams–countess and her victims–near ruins–castle!

LISTENING

What a bargain!

Miranda Short is visiting a house with Liz Balfour, an estate agent.

1 Listen and make notes on the good things and bad things about the house.

• What are Miranda and Liz like?
• Would you live in this house?

2 Checking and confirming

Study these two sentences from the tape and listen to how they are said.

a It's really big, isn't it?
b They only stayed six weeks, didn't they?

Which one is a real question?
Which one is just checking?
How do you know?

3 Listen to these sentences from the recording and decide which ones are real questions and which ones are just checking.

1 It's been empty for quite a while, hasn't it?
2 You don't believe that, do you?
3 But there had been a murder, hadn't there?

Listen again and practise saying the sentences.

4 Turn to the tapescript on page 167 and read the dialogue in pairs.

Estate Agent
E. Balfour

READING

The late arrival

Read the text and answer these questions.

1 Who was 'the late arrival'?
2 What happened to the storyteller?
3 Which of the three pictures below fits the description of 'the late arrival'?

We decided to hold a 'horror' fancy-dress party before we had our flat decorated. There were mummies, monsters and people dressed up as Frankenstein. Everyone was making lots of noise and having fun. I had a headache, so I went to my room …

While I was sleeping, I heard a sound at the window so I got up. When I pulled back the curtains, I almost fainted. Outside, there was a woman dressed all in black. I was so surprised, I cried out. I'll never know how she got there because we live on the top floor. Then, somehow, she managed to come through the window which had been stuck for years. If it hadn't been a fancy dress party, I would have been terrified. As it was, I was scared.

She lifted her hood … she was bald and her skin was smooth and as white as paper. Then she looked at me. She had the strangest eyes I'd ever seen. They were bright green with red pupils! Although I was shocked, I felt attracted by her.

'Where did you get those contact lenses?' I asked.

'That's my little secret,' she whispered, 'but unless you come closer, you won't see my teeth.'

I can't remember what happened next. Since that night, I've felt awful. And these marks on my neck, they won't go away. What on earth's wrong with me, do you think?

LANGUAGE STUDY

Revision of key language

1 Complete the second sentence in each case using the word in **bold type** so that it means the same as the one above.

1 I went to my room because I had a headache.   **so**
I had .... my room.

2 When I heard a sound, I was sleeping.   **was**
While .... sound.

3 It was such a surprise, that I cried out.   **so**
I .... out.

4 She succeeded in coming through the window.   **to**
She managed .... window.

5 It was a fancy-dress party. I wasn't terrified.   **would**
If .... terrified.

6 I'd never seen such strange eyes.   **had**
She had the .... seen.

7 Despite being shocked, I was attracted to her.   **felt**
Although .... by her.

8 Come closer, otherwise you won't see my teeth.   **come**
Unless .... teeth.

9 I've forgotten what happened next.   **remember**
I can't .... next.

2 Now check your answers by looking through the text about 'the late arrival'.

LISTENING

Vampire rumours

You are going to listen to an interview in which a boy and a vampire are discussing some of the myths and rumours concerning the powers of vampires and the dangers they face.

Decide whether each rumour is **true** or **false**.

RUMOURS	TRUE	FALSE
1 Vampires can fly.		✗
2 Vampires are scared of crosses.	✗	✗
3 Sunlight hurts vampires.	✗	
4 The only way to kill a vampire is with a stake through the heart.	✗	
5 Garlic will protect you against this vampire.		✗
6 He has a lonely existence.		✗

Pairwork

Unit 1 SET A PAGE 8

VOCABULARY

Clothes and fashion

Using the words in the exercise, label dummy 2's clothes. Tell Student B what it is wearing and he/she draws the clothes on his/her dummy 2. Then 'dress' your dummy 1 following Student B's instructions.

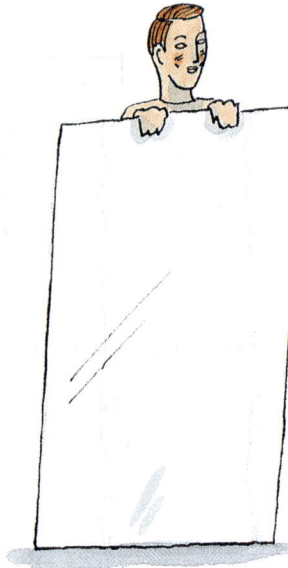

Unit 2 SET B PAGE 21

SPEAKING

An interview with Chris Caine

You are Chris Caine. You are going to be interviewed for *Mondo Movie* magazine. Here are some personal details.

You are fifty-five years old (you say you're forty!). You were born in a poor part of London. Life was hard and you had a poor but happy childhood.

You started your show business career as a singer in a London club. You went to drama school and acted in many plays. You were always so nervous that you were sick before going on stage. This is a long time in the past now!

In 1963, you went to Hollywood and had very small parts in films. Life was hard at first and you slept in your car in car parks. In the first two years you had six accidents because in England everybody drives on the left. You were very homesick and missed your family. Your big opportunity came in 1965 when you played an eccentric English teacher in *Here Comes Lulu*. Since then, you have made thirty films and millions of dollars.

You are now happy in the US and have changed your nationality. You still hate hamburgers though! You have been married three times. (Invent your story!) Now you live alone with six dogs.

Unit 3 SET D PAGE 33

SPEAKING

Booking a hotel

You are the receptionist at the Avonbury Hotel. It is a two-star hotel five minutes' walk from the station. It is a ten-minute bus ride to the centre of town where the Festival is being held. You are busy next week because of the music festival and only have a few rooms left. Here are details of the rooms that are still free.

Room		Mon	Tues	Wed	Thurs	Fri
322	Single room with bath	X	....	X	X	....
441	Single room with shower	X	....	X	....	....
201	Double room with shower	X	X	....	....	X
303	Double room with bath	X	....	....	....	X

Double rooms are £50 per night; single rooms are £30. All prices include breakfast.

Unit 5 SET B PAGE 48

SPEAKING

Giving advice

You don't have regular meals, you love chocolate and sweets, never take any exercise and only sleep four hours a night.

You feel unhappy and want to ask your friend, (Student B), for advice.

Unit 6   SET B   PAGE 57

SPEAKING

Describing a painting

Describe your painting to Student B, who should try to draw it.

Unit 11   SET A   PAGE 97

SPEAKING

The newest continent

You are going to complete a map of the main sights of Australia. The underlined information is the same on your map and Student B's map, but the other information is different. Complete your map by exchanging information with Student B. Do NOT show your map to him/her.

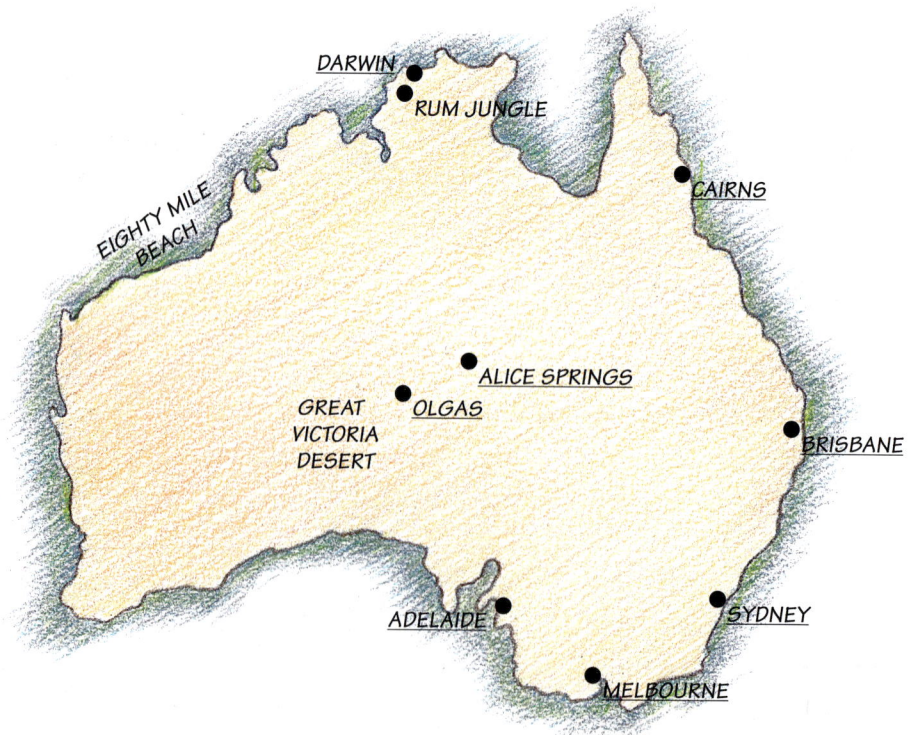

Unit 12   SET A   PAGE 105

SPEAKING

Getting the facts straight

You are Kit Lucas, an international reporter with the *Daily Planet*. You are in Zblinkski, the capital of Moronia. You are calling your editor in London with a big story. You spoke to him/her yesterday but the line was bad and the situation has changed. Your editor will tell you the details he/she has. Correct him/her where necessary.

> YESTERDAY MORNING AT 6 P.M., THE PRESIDENT OF MORONIA WAS ASSASSINATED BY A BOMB IN A BOX OF CHOCOLATES. A REVOLUTION HAS BEGUN, LED BY THE GREEN SHIRTS. THEY HAVE CAPTURED THE POST OFFICE, THE BRITISH EMBASSY AND THE AIRPORT. 50 PEOPLE HAVE BEEN KILLED AND THIRTEEN MINISTERS HAVE BEEN ARRESTED. THE ARCHBISHOP OF ZBLINSKI SUPPORTS THE GREEN SHIRTS. IN GROZNY, SOUTH OF ZBLINSKY, THE ARMY IS SUPPORTING THE REVOLUTION. YOU ARE GOING THERE BY PLANE TOMORROW MORNING. YOU CAN'T SEND MANY PHOTOGRAPHS BECAUSE THE POLICE HAVE ARRESTED YOUR PHOTOGRAPHER.

Unit 13   SET C   PAGE 116

SPEAKING

Mystery cultures

You have found these objects. What culture do you think they belong to? Show the pictures to Student B and tell him/her what you think.

Pairwork

Unit 1 SET A PAGE 8

VOCABULARY

Clothes and fashion

Using the words in the exercise, label dummy 1's clothes. Then listen to Student A's instructions and draw the clothes on your dummy 2. Finally, describe your dummy 1 to Student A and let him/her 'dress' his/her dummy 1.

Unit 2 SET B PAGE 21

SPEAKING

An interview with Chris Caine

You are a journalist from *Mondo Movie* magazine. You want to find out as much as you can about Chris Caine so you can write an article for your readers.

Find out about:

- background
- early career
- number of films made
- first big opportunity
- unhappy marriages
- reputation as a bad driver
- reputation for being nervous before acting

Unit 3 SET D PAGE 33

SPEAKING

Booking a hotel

You and a friend want to spend three days next week at the Avonbury music festival. A friend has given you the number of the Avonbury Hotel. You want to find out where it is and how far it is from the festival. You would rather have single rooms but don't mind sharing if necessary.

Unit 5 SET B PAGE 48

SPEAKING

Giving advice

You are Student A's friend and are worried about his/her lifestyle.

Find out how she/he is and what problems she/he has. Talk about his/her habits and lifestyle and give advice. Think of these topics: eating habits, exercise, sleep, luxuries and spending.

Unit 6 SET B PAGE 57

SPEAKING

Describing a painting

Describe your painting to Student A, who should try to draw it.

Unit 11 SET A PAGE 97

SPEAKING

The newest continent

You are going to complete a map of the main sights of Australia. The underlined information is the same on your map and Student A's map, but the other information is different. Complete your map by exchanging information with Student A. Do NOT show your map to him/her.

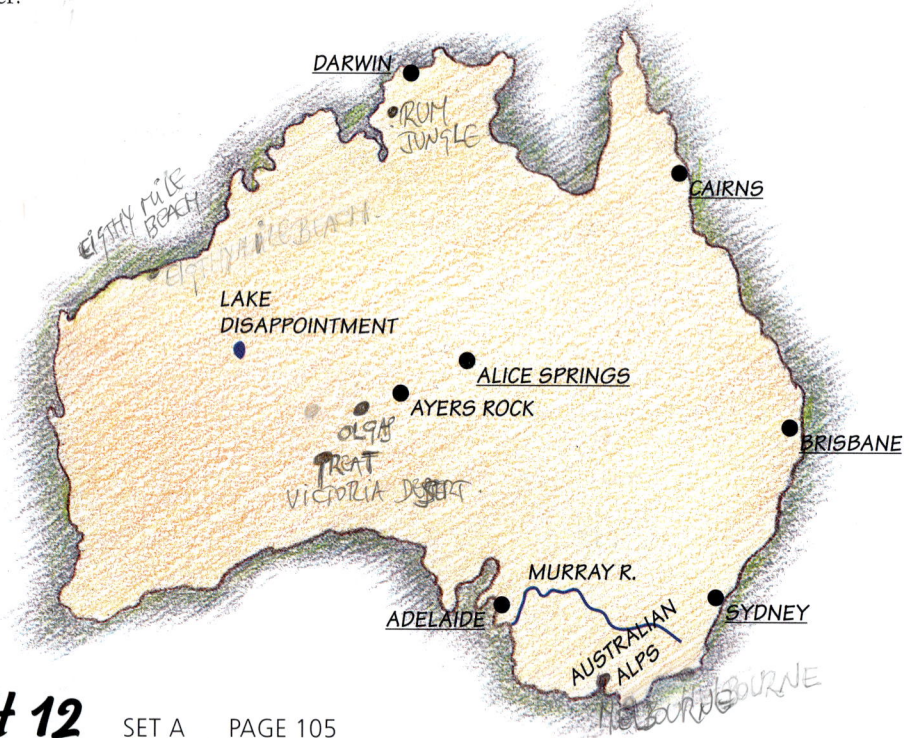

Unit 12 SET A PAGE 105

SPEAKING

Getting the facts straight

You are the Editor of the *Daily Planet*. You are phoning your correspondent, Kit Lucas, who is covering the events in Moronia. You want to check the story you received yesterday. Tell Kit what you know and he/she will correct you or add extra information where necessary.

THE PRESIDENT'S WIFE HAS BEEN KILLED. ATE A POISONED CHOCOLATE. A REVOLUTION HAS BEGUN. ORGANIZED BY THE GREEN SKIRTS. THEY HAVE CAPTURED THE POST OFFICE AND THE BRITISH SCHOOL. 15 PEOPLE HAVE BEEN KILLED AND 30 MINISTERS HAVE BEEN SHOT. THE BISHOP OF ZBLINSKI SUPPORTS THE GOVERNMENT. IN GROZNY, NORTH OF ZBLINSKY, THE ARMY IS SUPPORTING THE REVOLUTION. KIT IS GOING THERE BY TRAIN TOMORROW MORNING BUT CAN'T SEND ANY PHOTOGRAPHS BECAUSE THE ARMY HAS ARRESTED THE PHOTOGRAPHER.

Unit 13   SET C   PAGE 116

SPEAKING

Mystery cultures

You have found these objects. What culture do you think they belong to? Show the pictures to Student A and tell him/her what you think.

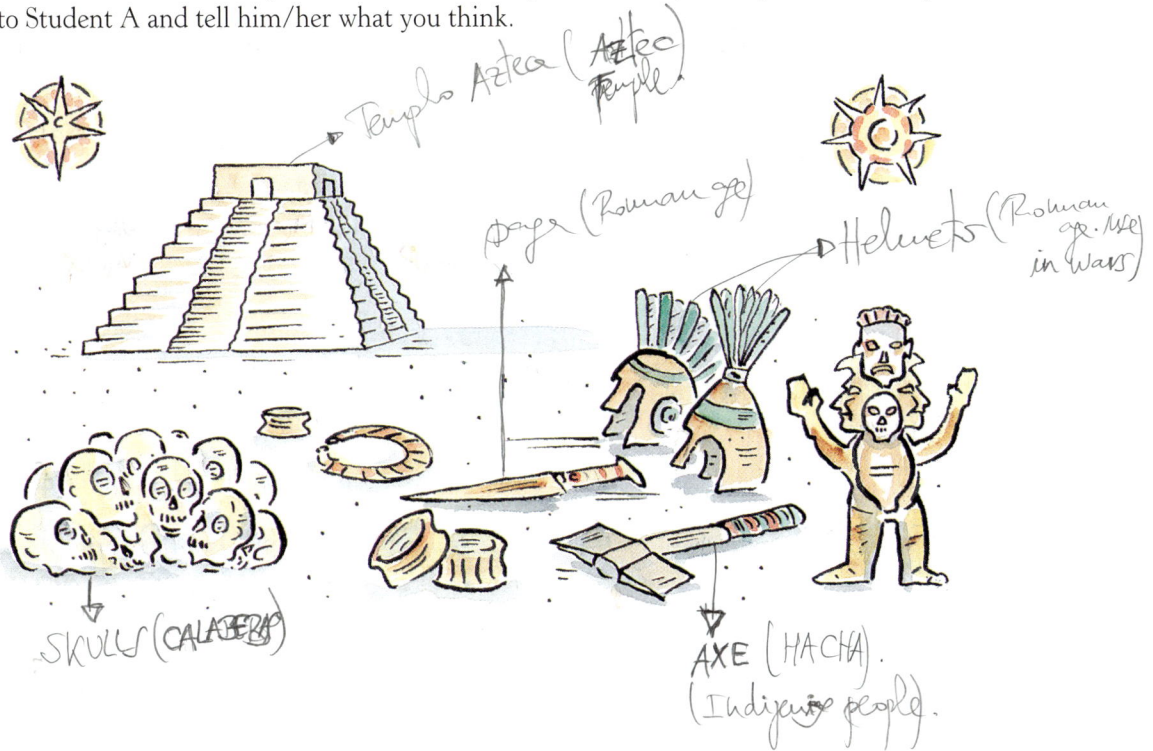

Handwritten annotations on the illustration:

Templo Azteca (Aztec Temple)

Daga (Roman age)

Helmets (Roman age. Used in wars)

SKULLS (CALAVERAS)

AXE (HACHA). (Indigenous people).

Irregular Verbs

Here are some of the most common irregular verbs in English.
Add the missing form to complete each 'set'. The first 'set' has been done for you.

INFINITIVE	PAST SIMPLE	PAST PARTICIPLE
be	was/were	**been**
become	BECAME	become
begin	began	BEGUN
BREAK	broke	broken
bring	BROUGHT	brought
build	built	BUILT
buy	BOUGHT	bought
CATCH	caught	caught
choose	chose	CHOSEN
come	came	COME
cost	COST	cost
do	DID	done
drink	drank	DRUNK
drive	DROVE	driven
EAT	ate	eaten
fall	FELL	fallen
feel	FELT	felt
fight	fought	FOUGHT
find	FOUND	found
fly	flew	FLOWN
forget	forgot	FORGOTTEN
get	got	GOT
give	GAVE	given
go	went	GONE
HAVE	had	had
hear	HEARD	heard
hide	hid	HIDDEN?
hold	HELD?	held
HURT	hurt	hurt
keep	KEPT	kept
know	knew	KNOWN

INFINITIVE	PAST SIMPLE	PAST PARTICIPLE
lead	LED	led
leave	LEFT	left
let	let	LET
lose	LOST	lost
make	made	MADE
MEET	met	met
pay	PAID	paid
put	put	PUT
read	READ	read
RING	rang	rung
run	RAN	run
say	SAID	said
see	saw	SEEN
sell	sold	SOLD
sing	SANG	sung
sit	sat	SAT
sleep	SLEPT	slept
speak	spoke	SPOKEN
spend	SPENT	spent
stand	stood	STOOD
steal	stole	STOLEN
swim	SWAM	swum
take	took	TAKEN
teach	TAUGHT	taught
THINK	thought	thought
wear	WORE	worn
WIN	won	won
write	wrote	WRITTEN

Prepositions

Revise the prepositions you know by completing the text. Study the pictures and select one of the prepositions from the box.

Before he became a film star. Sid the snake worked in the circus with Fred the snake charmer.

Most of the time he lived 1 ....IN............ a basket which was 2 ...UNDERNEATH.... Fred's bed.

In the evenings, Fred took Sid 3 ...IN TO *movement*...... the ring and their act began.

Fred started to play his flute and Sid would rise 4 .....OUT OF.... the basket and dance around for a bit.

Then he climbed 5 ....OVER.. the edge and down 6 ...ON TO.... the floor.

When Fred clapped his hands Sid jumped 7 ...THROUGH... a burning hoop.

After that he wriggled 8 ....ACROSS....... some burning coals and 9 ....BETWEEN.... a pair of extremely sharp knives!

The last part of the act was when Sid pretended to escape! He went slowly 10 ....TOWARDS........ the audience and everybody started to scream.

They screamed even louder when he went 11 ...AMONG.... them.

The last thing Sid did was to curl 12 .....AROUND... the neck of the most beautiful girl.

She always screamed the loudest and fell 13 .....ON TO.... the floor.

Life was quite dangerous for Sid, but as we can see it was lots of fun too!

Narrative tenses

Change the verbs in brackets into appropriate narrative tense.

Last month I (1) ..HAD.. (have) the strangest experience of my life. I (2) HAD STUDIED (study) hard for my exams so I (3) ..WAS.. (be) pleased to stop for dinner. Afterwards, while I (4) WAS WATCHING (watch) a programme about astronomy, I suddenly (5) ..FELT.. (feel) tired. I (6) ..WENT.. (go) upstairs and (7) ..FELL.. (fall) into a deep sleep. A few hours later I (8) BECAME (become) aware of a strange smell and (9) WOKE UP (wake) up. At first this (10) ..MADE.. (make) me angry as I (11) WAS HAVING (have) a wonderful dream about my favourite film star. Then I (12) ..SAW.. (see) two tall grey creatures at the end of my bed. They (13) LOOKED/WERE LOOKING (look) at me with golden insect-like eyes. I (14) HAD TRIED (try) to scream but I (15) ..COULDN'T.. (cannot). When they (16) ..TOOK..

(take) my arms I (17) ..FELT.. (feel) completely powerless and I (18) REALISED (realise) I (19) WAS BEING KIDNAPPED (be kidnapped). We (20) WERE TRAVELLING (travel) up a beam of light to their spaceship and I (21) WAS WONDERING (wonder) if I (22) WAS WONDERING (will ever) see my family again. One of the aliens (23) WAS HOLDING (hold) me in a chair while another (24) WAS EXPLAINING (explain) they (25) ..WERE.. (be) the only survivors of a planet that (26) HAD EXPLODED (explode) many years earlier. They (27) HAD TRAVELLED (travel) thousands of light years in search of somewhere else to live. One (28) ..CAME.. (come) towards me with a kind of saw when the spacecraft (29) ..STARTED.. (start) to rock violently. The next thing I (30) ..KNEW.. (know) I (31) ..WAS.. (be) back in my room. My mother (32) WAS SHAKING (shake) me, trying to wake me up.

Handwritten annotations in margins:
CONSCIOUS OF
SERRUCHO/SIERRA
A BIGAP
A RAY OF LIGTH

Phrasal Verbs

Here are the twenty-five most important phrasal verbs which appear in *Think Ahead to First Certificate*.

1 Match the phrasal verbs on the left with their equivalent on the right. The unit in which they appear is given (e.g. U1).

1 find out U1 *e*	a	care for
2 get on with U1 *m*	b	criticize
3 take on U1 *q*	c	find by chance
4 look for U1 *t*	d	despise
5 give away U1 *i*	e	discover information
6 turn up U3 *g*	f	reduce
7 set off U3 *r*	g	arrive
8 run out U3 *o, f*	h	invent
9 hold on U3 *l*	i	tell a secret
10 put through U3 *p*	j	inherit – money/property
11 come across U4 *c*	k	begin something new
12 make out U4 *y*	l	wait – on the telephone
13 look after U5 *a*	m	have a (good) relationship
14 give up U5 *v*	n	do something – usually wrong
15 cut down on U5 *f*	o	finish/consume
16 take up U5 *k*	p	connect – on the telephone
17 make up U6 *h*	q	employ
18 get over U5 *w*	r	leave on a journey
19 come up with U6 *x*	s	raise/educate
20 tell off U7 *b*	t	search
21 be up to U7 *n*	u	inherit – characteristic
22 look down on U14 *d*	v	stop
23 bring up U14 *s*	w	recover
24 take after U14 *u*	x	think of a solution *or an idea*
25 come into U14 *j*	y	see with difficulty

BRAIN WAVE = UNA INSPIRACIÓN.

2 There are four types of phrasal verb.

Type 1: intransitive e.g. *come to* (recover consciousness) These don't take an object.

Type 2: transitive inseparable e.g. *look into* (investigate) These must take an object which always comes after the verb.

Type 3: transitive separable e.g. *put off* (postpone) The object can either come between the verb and the particle or after the verb. If we use a pronoun then it must go between.

Type 4: three-part e.g. *put up with* (endure) *TO BEAR = TO SUPPORT = AGUANTAR.* These are always transitive inseparable.

Using the unit references and your dictionaries find out which of the categories the phrasal verbs above fall into. Write the type after each of the phrasal verbs in the list.

HE PUT ME OFF : ME desconcentro.

3 Use each of the phrasal verbs once only to complete the following sentences which provide a context.

1 She **made up** such an incredible story nobody would believe her.
2 They **came across** some valuable paintings in their grandmother's attic.
3 He **came into** a fortune on his father's death.
4 Have you seen my glasses? I've **looked for** them everywhere but I still can't find them.
5 When we **found out** the terrible news it really ruined our holiday.
6 Even though I've completely **given up** chocolate, potatoes and beer I still can't lose weight.
7 She loves cooking. She **takes after** her mother who is an excellent cook.
8 I had to **tell off** your son again for being naughty in class.
9 Oh no! What was he **up to** this time?
10 When we **set off** it was so early there were hardly any other cars on the road.
11 On the death of his parents in a plane crash, he was **brought up** by his grandmother.
12 I had to leave my old job because I just couldn't **get on with** my boss.
13 Could you **look after** my suitcase for five minutes while I make a phone call?
14 I can't **make out** what this says, it's so old the writing has almost disappeared.
15 You want to speak to Maria? **Hold on** I'll check if she's here.
16 After his heart attack he **took up** yoga to help him relax.
17 There is just too much work; we need to **take on** an extra person.
18 By the time they **turn up** all the tickets had been sold.
19 It isn't fair to **look down on** the unemployed.
20 He doesn't work in this office; I'll **put you through** to his extension.
21 He just can't seem to **get over** his wife's death, the poor man.
22 So you don't like my idea! Can you **come up with** something better?
23 We **ran out** of petrol and had to walk five miles to the nearest garage.
24 I'm not telling you to stop smoking entirely; I just think you should **cut down on**.
25 He was shot for **giving away** his country's military secrets.

Functions

Often it is useful to look at language in terms of what we do with it, i.e.: its 'function', as well as its structure. Here is a list of key functional areas which are dealt with in *Think Ahead to First Certificate*. Turn to the references and write down some examples. The references direct you to the pages where they are dealt with in the most depth, although there are many examples of the different functions throughout the course.

Agreeing and disagreeing UNIT 9, SET D

....

Asking indirect questions UNIT 4, SET D

....

Comparing and contrasting UNIT 7, SET C

....

Describing ability UNIT 6, SET D

....

Describing dress UNIT 1, SET A

....

Describing geographical features/a country
UNIT 11, SET A

....

Describing objects UNIT 4, SET D; UNIT 4, SET E

....

Describing past and present habits
UNIT 2, SET B (*used to do/ing*)

....

Describing people: faces UNIT 7, SET A

....

Describing a process UNIT 11, SET D

....

Describing a room UNIT 15, SET C

....

Describing a painting UNIT 6, SET B

....

Expressing number and quantity UNIT 4, SET A

....

Expressing obligation UNIT 14, SET B

....

Expressing plans and intentions UNIT 10, SET A

....

Expressing opinions UNIT 6, SET B

....

Expressing reason and purpose
UNIT 2, SET B (*so/because*)

....

Expressing sympathy UNIT 13, SET B

....

Giving instructions UNIT 1, SET E

....

Giving and requesting advice UNIT 5, SET B; UNIT 10, SET D

....

Giving street directions UNIT 8, SET D

....

Making complaints UNIT 1, SET C

....

Making decisions UNIT 10, SET A

....

Making polite requests UNIT 8, SET D

....

Making questions UNIT 2, SET C; UNIT 8, SET A

....

Making suggestions/agreeing and disagreeing with suggestions UNIT 2, SET A

....

Narrating UNIT 3, SET E

....

Ordering actions
UNIT 1, SET E (*after/afterwards/after that*)

....

Ordering actions
UNIT 2, SET B (*then, finally, first of all*)

....

Telephoning UNIT 3, SET D

....

'Language Study' Index

DO YOU REALIZE = TE DÁP CUENTA

Turn to the references given and complete the examples to make your own 'Language Study' Index.

Adjective + preposition: UNIT 7, SET C.
Ratan Patel is ..*GOOD AT*.... languages.

After and *afterwards:* UNIT 1, SET E.
I put the blindfold on her. ..*AFTERWARDS*. I went into the audience.
...*AFTER*.... I had put the blindfold on her, I went into the audience.

Comparatives and superlatives: UNIT 7 SET C.

Countable and uncountable: UNIT 4, SET A.
I'm looking for ...*SOME*.... treasure.
HOW MUCH. luck have you had so far?
Well ..*SOME*./*NONE*.

Describing physical appearance: UNIT 7, SET A.
Angela ....*HAS*...... beautiful blue eyes, long red hair, pale skin and freckles.
Mr Gilbert, a big man ...*WITH*...... a bald head and glasses.

Despite and *although*: UNIT 4, SET C.
DESPITE....... the poor man's warning, Shovell kept on his course.
ALTHOUGH. he escaped drowning, he was murdered.

Different types of description: UNIT 9, SET B.
What's she like? *Physical/personal description*
How is she? *She is better/she lós flere.*
What does she look like?
What does she like?

Expressing ability: UNIT 6, SET D.
She ..*is able*.... to hum the melody.

First and second conditional: UNIT 8, SET C.
......*IF*....... you move to Rome, ..*you'll become*...a Roman too.
......*IF*......... you moved to Rome, *you would become* a Roman too.

Future predictions: UNIT 13, SET C.
A few specially chosen human beings ..*will inhabit the* Earth.
Civilization ..*will*...*disappear*...

Going to or *will?*: UNIT 10, SET A.
I'm going to a policeman when I grow up.

Have something done and **need:** UNIT 15, SET B.
She ....*HAD*......... her picture *DONE/TAKEN*... by a professional photographer.
The roof ....*NEEDS*..... repairing.

If, unless and *otherwise*: UNIT 5, SET A.
........*IF*......... you don't eat more fruit, your teeth will fall out!
..*UNLESS*....... you eat more fruit, your teeth will fall out!
You ...*MUST/NEED TO*.. eat more fruit ..*OTHERWISE*.. your teeth will fall out!

In case: UNIT 10, SET D.
I'll take a map ...*IN CASE*... I get lost.

Indefinite pronouns: UNIT 7, SET B.
Say you're sorry when you hurt...*SOMEBODY/SOMEONE*.
Share ...*WITH*...*SOMEBODY/EVERYTHING*

Indirect questions: UNIT 4, SET D.
Could you tell me where he was from?
Do you know what it's worth?

The infinitive and the gerund: UNIT 3, SET B.
Casanova ....*KEEP*....... him quiet.
They ..*MANAGED TO*.... one of the roof-tiles.
SUCCEEDED IN REMOVING *REMOVE*

Linking, explaining and contrasting: UNIT 13, SET D.

Make and *let*: UNIT 14, SET B.
She and the Prime Minister tried to ......*MAKE*.... Edward end the relationship.
Public opinion would not ....*LET*...... a twice-divorced American woman become Queen. *=ALLOW = PERMITIR*

Making intelligent guesses: UNIT 13, SET B.
You *LOOK/SEEM* tired. /*APPEAR TO BE*
It *LOOKS AS IF* a change in the weather.
THERE IS / THERE IS GOING TO BE.

Narrative tenses: UNIT 3, SET E.
Paul *WAS HAVING*.. drinks at the bar, when disaster struck. *SPREAD (extend down)*.
Within seconds, a fire *BROKE OUT*. and ...... to lots of gas-filled balloons, which ...*BEGAN*.... to explode.
Paul .....*RUN/CAME* to me at midnight.

Passive: UNIT 11, SET C.
They *ARE REPORTED* the hostile tribes of the Lower Xingu.

Prepositions of position and direction: UNIT 3, SET A.
Then he climbed ......*OVER*..... the edge and ...*DOWN*...... onto the floor.

'Language Study' Index

Present perfect and past simple: UNIT 5, SET C.
I ......WAS...... a pharmacist.
I ...WORKED... as one and I'VE BEEN WORKING .... for a few years.
TRAINED/GRADUATED

Reflexive verbs: UNIT 5, SET A.

Remember, forget and remind: UNIT 10, SET C.
I ...REMEMBER/forgot... going to India.
Don't ......FORGET !... to keep your hands in your pockets.
Can you ...REMIND...... me to post this letter.

Reported speech: UNIT 6, SET B.
Jane said (that) it was awful and (that) she didn't like it at all.

Reporting verbs: UNIT 12, SET B.
He ...insisted...... on paying the bill.
She ...told......... him to tell the truth.
He Accused me of stealing the handbag.
His teacher Advised him (that) he should become a journalist. suggested

Revision of adverbs: UNIT 7, SET D.
He plays ..WELL/PERFECTLY/wonderfully
She writes ...LOVELY / BEAUTIFULLY.

Revision of key language: UNIT 15, SET D.

Revision of past forms: UNIT 2, SET B.

Separable phrasal verbs: UNIT 6, SET D.
Ellen Boudreaux knows when to ....TURN........ the radio
........UP OR DOWN

Sequencing/Reason and purpose: UNIT 2, SET C.
→ BECAUSE
Wanda was always sick ...... she was so nervous.
She slept in car parks ...... save money.
→ IN ORDER TO.

Past simple passive: UNIT 6, SET A.
Hamlet WAS WRITTEN BY Shakespeare.

So and such: UNIT 2, SET C.
It was ......SUCH..... a challenge that it took four months to film.
It was ....SO....... challenging that it took four months to film.

Subject object questions: UNIT 14, SET C.
Who loves Romeo?
Who does Romeo love?

Subjects, verbs and objects: UNIT 3, SET C.
We drove the car.
Night had fallen.

Tense review: UNIT 1, SET D.

Third conditional and wish: UNIT 9, SET E.
If he HAD HAD..... an EC passport, probably nothing WOULD HAVE..... happened.
He ...WISHED..... he HAD KNOWN about these regulations.

Time expressions: UNIT 6, SET C AND UNIT 14, SET C.
We always eat ....AT......... 7 o'clock.
I'll wait ..UNTIL........ 7 o'clock.
Queen Victoria reigned ......FOR...... 64 years.
The Prime Minister changed twenty-seven times ...DURING.... her reign.

Uses of a/an, the and some: UNIT 11, SET B.
She's ....A......... travel agent.
........THE..... kangaroo was running fast.
There's ......SOME.... water in this bottle.

Uses of used to: UNIT 2, SET B.
I ....USED TO... watch The Flintstones when I was a kid.

Tapescripts

■ SET A   ■ PAGE 9

Women's fashions since the 1950s

1 In this photograph she's wearing a pinkish patterned shirt and trousers. They're quite short and stop above her ankle. She's also wearing a pair of sandals. Her hair is up and she seems to be wearing a lot of make-up and, um, false eyelashes. Looks quite nice, I suppose.

2 Um, I think this is really fashionable. Really simple but very smart and practical too. She has just got on a black one piece suit and a pair of white trainers. She has got long straight hair and is wearing some bright red lipstick. Apart from that no other make-up.

3 She looks really weird in this one. I mean, lots of black lipstick and her hair is in a mess. She is wearing trousers and a loose yellow top with a scarf tied around her waist. She looks a bit like a pirate. Awful.

4 Wow! This one is really too much. She is wearing a really short skirt and high heeled shoes. She has also got on a leopard skin top. Hope it wasn't from a real leopard. You could have worn this to a party but not for anything else surely.

5 This must be the oldest one. She is formally dressed and looks terribly old-fashioned. She is wearing a matching skirt and jacket with high-heeled shoes and she is carrying a tiny bag and has got a funny little hat on her head. Her clothes look really tight and uncomfortable.

■ SET C   ■ PAGE 12

Making complaints

Assistant: Can I help you?
Colin: Yes, it's about this this sports shirt. I washed it the other day. The colour ran and it shrank.
Assistant: Oh dear, I see. Do you have the receipt?
Colin: I'm afraid not, but it was in one of your bags.
Assistant: I'm sorry, but I'm not allowed to change anything without a receipt.
Colin: Do you think I could speak to the Manageress.
Assistant: Yes, of course. I'll fetch her for you.

Manageress: Are you the gentleman who brought this shirt in?
Colin: Yes, could you change it? It's a well-known brand.
Manageress: Where did you get it? Did you buy it here?
Colin: Actually it was a present from my girlfriend. Is something the matter?
Manageress: I'm afraid there is. You see, it's an imitation.
Colin: An imitation? Are you sure?
Manageress: I'm absolutely positive. The crocodile is even the wrong way round.
Colin: I don't know what to say.
Manageress: Forget it. But if I were you, I'd have a word with my girlfriend!

Intonation in questions

Where did you get it?
Did you buy it here?

■ SET E   ■ PAGE 16

A 'Mentalist Act'

Interviewer: How did you start in show business, Arthur?
AC: As a magician's assistant for 'The Great Marvella'. I helped out mostly with the mentalist act.
Interviewer: What was that?
AC: Oh, a kind of telepathic act where she guessed the names of objects while wearing a blindfold. Um … I put the blindfold on her. Afterwards I went into the audience. People handed me objects like watches or rings and things and then 'The Great Marvella' guessed what they were.
Interviewer: And how did this trick work then? She didn't have any special powers, did she?
AC: No, not at all. Actually she could see through the cloth.
Interviewer: So it was as simple as that!
AC: Not really. After I had blindfolded her she couldn't actually see the objects. They were too small, and don't forget the theatres were dark.
Interviewer: So how was it done?
AC: I spelled out the name of the object by the way that I was standing. For example, if I had my head on the left, that told her that it began with 'r': or if both of my arms were bent that there was an 'ing' sound in the word …
Interviewer: So she could guess that you'd been given a ring. And did anybody ever realize what you were doing?
AC: No. Never. I also misled the audience. I said things in a funny way – you know – changed my intonation so that people would think I was signalling with my voice.
Interviewer: Clever. And did it work? I mean did the boss always manage to guess the objects which were handed to you?
AC: Oh yes. Ninety-five per-cent of the time.
Interviewer: And for the other five?
AC: She just said that the vibrations weren't right. The audience loved it.

■ SET A   ■ PAGE 18

Film fantasy

Main stress in words

A Western
A Thriller
A Cartoon
A Comedy
A Musical
An Adventure
A Documentary
A Horror Film
A Love Story
A Science Fiction Film

■ SET A ■ PAGE 19

Organising an evening out.

Annabel: What shall we do this evening? Have you got any ideas, Martin?

Martin: Why don't we go out for a meal? Or maybe we could go and see a film. What about you, Rick?

Rick: I think I'd rather go to the cinema.

Annabel: So would I.

Martin: OK. That's fine by me. What's on?

Annabel: Well, there's *Robot Cop*. It's a kind of science fiction thriller.

Rick: Mm, I know. It's great but I've already seen it.

Martin: Well, let's go and see *Back to the Future III* then.

Annabel: That sounds like a good idea. I haven't seen it yet.

Rick: Neither have I. I really enjoyed the first two.

Annabel: Look. It's 6 o'clock now and the film doesn't start until 8.30. I'm going home to change.

Martin: ... and I'd like to get something to eat!

Rick: Me, too. Why don't you come back to my place for a snack?

Martin: Thanks, that would be really nice.

Rick: What about you, Annabel?

Annabel: Thanks for the offer, but I want to go home and change first. But I can pick you up at Rick's place in my parents' car, if I can borrow it. Would 7.45 be OK?

Rick: Great. We'll see you then. Could you give us a ring if there's a problem?

Annabel: I promise. See you later then. 'Bye.

■ SET A ■ PAGE 19

Pronunciation

Why don't you come back to my place?
Could you give us a ring if there's a problem?

■ SET B ■ PAGE 20

The changing Mickey Mouse

Rachel: Oh great. *The Flintstones* are on telly. I used to watch *The Flintstones* when I was a kid. What about you, Barry?

Barry: Me too. My favourite's Tom and Jerry though.

Rachel: That's because of all the violence!

Barry: Don't be silly … It's just a cartoon!

John: But they are really cruel. I agree with Rachel.

Barry: It's just harmless fun!

Rachel: But kids still copy them. I mean, these things have more of an effect than we like to think. Tom and Jerry seems to get more and more violent too.

Barry: Oh come off it! They're exactly the same …

John: That's not true, you know, Barry. Characters do change. Take Mickey Mouse.

Barry: Mickey Mouse?

Rachel: Yeah. I read an article. It – the article – said in the old days, in the early cartoons, he was really horrible. You know, he was always doing cruel things.

Barry: Cruel things?

Rachel: Yeah. Like, in one cartoon he makes the animals play a tune by pinching and squeezing them, to erm make them squeal.

John: That's right. We're not used to seeing that kind of Mickey these days. He's too busy being nice to everybody.

Barry: Goody goody.

John: That's right, Barry. He never does anything naughty.

Barry: Even so. This article, did it say anything else?

Rachel: I'm trying to think. Oh yeah – it said that his face gets rounder and softer as time goes on … How can I explain? Have you seen any of the early cartoons?

John and Barry: Yes.

Rachel: Well, in the early ones he looks quite rat-like, doesn't he? He has got this long pointed nose and little eyes.

Barry: And?

Rachel: Well later on his face changes. His head gets as big as his body. Or almost. His eyes get bigger, too.

Barry: Strange, isn't it?

Rachel: Yeah, he grows backwards! He gets younger instead of older. I wonder if they did it on purpose?

John: Mm, it makes him much cuter I suppose.

Barry: An acceptable symbol for the US of A.

Pronunciation of *used to*

I used to watch *The Flintstones* when I was a kid.
We're not used to seeing that kind of Mickey these days.

■ SET D ■ PAGE 25

People in films

1 Cut, cut. We're going to have to do it again. That was just fine Angela, but you need to concentrate on the feelings. Now remember, this is the man who you think murdered your brother, but you've got to try to hide your suspicions because you're afraid something might happen to you. OK, let's have another go, shall we? When you're ready … action.

2 Yeah, it was a really difficult shot. It was continuous, from the moment Angela leaves the place where she has hidden the money to when she gets to work, about four minutes in all. We did it all with one camera as a single take. It took two days to get it right.

3 One of the erm biggest problems we had was how to explain the motivation of the main character, Angela. In the original book, the writer describes her inner emotions, so it is quite clear why she does such crazy things later on. After all, on the surface she is a really ordinary housewife, the kind of person who you meet every day. But ordinary housewives don't steal drug money from the Mafia. So for the film we had to create an extra character, someone she worked with who was involved, so that Angela had someone to talk to.

4 I've got to say Angela was one of the most difficult roles I've ever had. One thing which made it really tough was the leading man. He had such an ego, you know, such a high opinion of himself. Although, to be fair, I found the part challenging too. I'd always been in comedies before and found changing to drama very hard.

5 Of course these days there's a lot that you can do with video and with er, computers – lots of the special effects are generated by computer. Having said that I think that there will always be a need for people like me who can jump out of high windows and fast cars because somehow it makes the film look much more realistic. It was me, by the way, in the helicopter scene in *Angela*. It can be dangerous but it is a calculated risk.

6 There's a lot of waiting around but it's fun … It means that I can make a few dollars to help get me through college. You also see some of the stars close up … Anyway, it's a beginning and who knows, some day, a director may notice me in the crowd and give me a bigger part. You know, one day you're a face in the crowd and then you might get a small part with a couple of lines and then who knows..? Lots of the big names in Hollywood started out just the same way so why not me?

7 Well, I suppose I'm the guy everybody loves to hate. The one with the big cigar except that I don't smoke any more. Once we decide to make the film, I have to get the money together to do it, which means convincing a lot of people who are going to expect a good profit too. Then I have to sort out the contracts and locations and make sure that we can get the support of the theatres. Film making is an art, it is creative but it's big business too and you need someone like me who really knows what they're doing …

UNIT 3

■ SET A   ■ PAGE 27

She's leaving home

Wednesday morning at 5 o'clock as the day begins.
Silently closing the bedroom door,
Leaving the note that she hoped would say more,
She goes downstairs to the kitchen clutching her handkerchief.
Quietly turning the back door key,
Stepping outside, she is free.

She is leaving home
We gave her most of our lives.
Sacrificed most of our lives.
We gave her everything money could buy.
She's leaving home after living alone for so many years.

Father snores as his wife gets into her dressing gown.
Picks up the letter that's lying there.
Standing alone at the top of the stairs,
She breaks down and cries to her husband
'Daddy, our baby's gone,
Why would she treat us so thoughtlessly?
How could she do this to me?

She is leaving home.
We never thought of ourselves.
Never a thought for ourselves.
We struggled hard all our lives to get by.
She's leaving home after living alone for so many years.

Friday morning at 9 o'clock she is far away,
Waiting to keep the appointment she made,
Meeting a man from the motor trade.

She is leaving home.
What did we do that was wrong?
We didn't know it was wrong.
Love is the one thing that money can't buy.
Something inside that always denied for so many years.
She's leaving home.

Bye, bye.
She's leaving home.
Bye, bye.
She's leaving home.
Bye, bye.

■ SET C   ■ PAGE 31

A narrow escape

Janice: Goodness! That was lucky … It reminds me of one I had years ago. I was studying Italian in Rome.

Carole: Huh, huh.

Janice: One erm night I went to a to a pop concert in an indoor stadium. We all set off in a party mood; we'd been looking forward to it for ages. Anyway, around this time people used to invade cinemas and theatres without paying because they said prices were just too high.

Carole: Sounds like a good idea.

Janice: Not if you'd paid. Well that evening, about two hundred of them got in. Every seat was taken. It was packed.

Carole: Go on.

Janice: So then the riot police turned up and told everybody to leave. Then the troublemakers started throwing things at the police. They'd come prepared for a fight, they had sticks and helmets. Fighting broke out around the stadium.

Carole: Wow!

Janice: Then the police started hitting their sticks against their shields. It was a really terrifying noise. Anyway, the troublemakers kept throwing things at them and several got hurt by flying chairs and things. Eventually they just ran out of patience and started firing tear gas and hitting people.

Carole: What just the troublemakers?

Janice: No anybody. Discipline just broke down.

Carole: … and did you get hurt?

Janice: Almost. A policeman told me to move but I answered back in English. Roberto did though. He got hit on the head so I stayed by him until he came round. Finally we got away, they hadn't blocked off one of the exits. Of course we were coughing and blind from the tear gas but it was great to get outside.

■ SET D   ■ PAGE 33

Booking by telephone

Part A

Telephonist: Breakaway Travel.

Mrs Roberts: Good morning. I'm phoning about your weekend escapes to Berlin.

Telephonist: I'll put you through to someone who can help you. Hold the line please madam. I'm afraid all lines are busy. If you'd like to leave me your name and number I'll get someone to return your call as soon as possible.

Mrs Roberts: The name is Mrs Roberts and my number is 675982.

Telephonist: Right Mrs Roberts. I'll pass the message on.

Part B

Mrs Roberts: Hello. 675982.

Sharon Grey: Hello. This is Sharon from Breakaway Travel …

Mrs Roberts: Oh hello, thanks for ringing back. I'd like to know about your weekend escapes to Berlin for the last weekend of next month.

Sharon Grey: Let me see. Yes, madam, three nights departing the 27th is available. That's £320 per person for scheduled flights, and a double room in a three star hotel with continental breakfast is also included.

Mrs Roberts: That sounds fine. I'll come in to book this afternoon.

Sharon Grey: I look forward to seeing you then, Mrs Roberts.

Mrs Roberts: Goodbye.

UNIT 4

■ SET C   ■ PAGE 41

Sunken treasure

PJ: So Frances, is there very much pirate treasure left?

FG: I'm not sure. You see they mostly spent what they stole or else it was taken back. Kidd's famous treasure might not even exist. But there are lots of sunken wrecks out there.

PJ: Sunken treasure. That's really romantic. What advice would you give listeners who want to get rich quick?

FG: Basically I'd tell them not to bother. The ships carrying it often sank in bad weather. Then over the next few hundred years they move and get covered in sand.

PJ: All the same, it's just lying out there waiting for someone to pick it up!

FG: Well, treasure hunting's a bit more complicated than that. For one thing it's an incredibly expensive activity. It nearly always ends in disappointment too.

PJ: I see, but there are success stories, aren't there? I seem to remember one where lots of porcelain was found.

FG: Mm, that was the Dutch ship, the 'Geldermalsen'.

PJ: The thing that amazed me was that it was in such fantastic condition.

FG: Yes, it looks new, doesn't it? That's because it had been packed in tea which was the rest of the cargo.

PJ: Oh, right. Have there been any other big finds?

FG: Quite a few. Mostly because of improvements in technology. One of the biggest was in 1985 off the coast of Florida. Someone called Mel Fisher found the wreck of a galleon called 'La Nuestra Señora de Atocha'.

PJ: Did he find it while he was fishing or something?

FG: Not quite. Actually he had been looking for it for fifteen years! It has been worth it because so far they have recovered over four hundred and fifty million dollars worth of silver.

PJ: But it's not the biggest?

FG: Actually no. That's the Russian treasure ship, the 'Admiral Nakhimov'. It was sunk during the Russian–Japanese war at the beginning of the century. Its cargo was two billion dollars worth of gold and platinum.

PJ: Wow!

■ SET D   ■ PAGE 42

Treasure in our attic

1

George Brown: Well, hello young man, and what's your name?

Robin: Robin.

George Brown: And how old are you then?

Robin's mother: He was seven last week.

George Brown: Seven eh! What have you brought to show us? It's a lovely old teddy bear. It's golden brown but the poor chap's fur's rather worn now and one of his eyes is loose. Where did you get it from Robin?

Robin: My grandfather gave it to me. It was his when he was little.

George Brown: Could you tell me where he was from?

Robin's mother: Actually, he was German.

George Brown: Just as I thought. And if we look at the bear's ear we should find a little button with the manufacturer's name. Yes here we are. Do you know what you have here?

Robin's mother: Grandad Martin's teddy, I suppose.

George Brown: But it's very special. You see this is a very early teddy made by Margaret Steiff in Germany. She is the lady who invented the teddy bear. Now what do you think it's worth?

Robin's mother: A few pounds? I've no idea really.

George Brown: Well, let me tell you something. Young Robin is a lucky young man. These bears are quite valuable. This one is worth about a thousand pounds.

Robin's mother: Do you know if someone would like to buy it?

Robin: Come on mummy, give me back my teddy bear. He's mine …

2

Rupert Andrews: Yes, sir. What is it we have here? Let's have a look. Um. I have just been handed an old golf ball. It's not often you see one of these. Can I ask where you got it?

Mr Crown: I actually came across it in the attic along with some old clubs and other things, but I just thought I'd bring this in to show you.

Rupert Andrews: Well, I'm extremely glad that you did. If I can just describe it to the listeners at home. It's not perfectly smooth like one of the plastic coated golf balls we have these days. In fact it's made of pieces of leather which have been stitched together. This is a real collector's item. A year or two ago a ball similar to this was sold for four thousand pounds! This one is rather cracked I'm afraid but is still valuable. It just goes to show that you should never throw anything away; most people would take one look at this and think it was worthless. Personally, I find an antiques handbook an invaluable source of useful information.

3

George Brown: Now what do we have here? It is a figure of Charlie Chaplin … um … It looks like one which was made in England in around 1918. Oh dear. Unfortunately it isn't genuine. I'm afraid that it is an imitation. A real one would be worth around two thousand pounds now. Never mind. This doesn't make this entirely worthless. I would say you could probably get around fifty pounds for it. Would you mind telling me how much you paid for it?

Man: Not really, I suppose, it cost me ninety pounds.

George: Pity.

4

Rupert Andrews: A young lady has just brought me something which a lot of people will be interested in. It's an early Beatles record which was issued in the mid-sixties. Where did you get this, young lady?

Girl: It belongs to my dad.

Rupert Andrews: Well. What makes this interesting is that it has all of the Beatles' signatures on it and is signed 'All the Best George Harrison'. Are they genuine?

Girl: Yeah. My dad got it from George Harrison. He was working as a waiter in a hotel and he asked them if they'd sign it for him.

Rupert Andrews: Do you know what it's worth?

Girl: Well, as far as my dad's concerned it's priceless, he'd never part with it.

Rupert Andrews: Well he might if you tell him it could be worth around a thousand pounds at auction.

Girl: A thousand pounds. Wow!

Language Study

Intonation in questions

a What have you brought to show us?
b Could you tell me where he was from?
c Do you know what it's worth?

UNIT 5

■ **SET A**   ■ **PAGE 47**

A monster or a saint?

Robert: So, what did you think about that article, Jasmine?

Jasmine: The one about the doctor.

Robert: Yeah …

Jasmine: I thought it was awful. I mean the job of a doctor is to save patients' lives not to end them, I mean, it goes against the erm ethics, you know principles of their profession.

Thomas: I don't agree. I think he did the right thing for his patient. She was in terrible pain and there was no chance of recovery. Anyway, he didn't actually kill her, she did it herself, he only helped her.

Robert: Mm. It amounts to the same thing, though, doesn't it? Without the doctor she wouldn't have been able to do anything.

Thomas: So are you saying he shouldn't have helped her, Robert?

Robert: Not really. I think he probably did the right thing. After all, we should think about the quality of life someone has. Nowadays, it is possible to keep someone alive even though their lives are hell. Doctors don't let them pass away naturally. It's just not fair.

Thomas: I quite agree. I mean we ourselves wouldn't want a pet to suffer, would we? I don't really understand you, Jasmine. People should be allowed to die with dignity.

Jasmine: I see your point, but we're not animals are we? We're human beings.

Robert: So we should be allowed to decide for ourselves.

Jasmine: But very often when people are ill they aren't able to think straight or make good decisions.

Thomas: That's a good point. I suppose one thing that worries me about, erm people being able to decide for themselves, is what the next step might be. We could end up with doctors making these decisions themselves on behalf of patients.

Robert: I'm quite sure that happens anyway, Thomas ….. It could be easily abused. I don't think it was in this case …

Jasmine: Maybe not, but I don't think the doctor should be allowed to get away with it.

Thomas: But he's not, is he, according to the article the police looked into the case which is why he is on trial. And unless they lock him up he'll do it again.

■ **SET B**   ■ **PAGE 48**

Discussing a problem

Frank: I'm so overweight. It's making me depressed.

Angie: So that's it. I thought you looked a bit fed up.

Frank: And the more I worry about it the more I seem to eat.

Angie: Frank, just between you and me, what have you had to eat today?

Frank: Well I didn't have breakfast so I ate a bar of chocolate on the way to school. Then I had a packet of crisps at breaktime.

Angie: And what about at lunch?

Frank: Um … a hamburger and a cola.

Angie: It's no surprise you're getting fat. What you need is a balanced diet.

Frank: What are you getting at?

Angie: Obviously, you're taking in too many calories. You should give up chocolate completely for a time and cut down on all the snacks you eat. Also, have you tried one of those slimming clubs? You get advice on nutrition and they weigh you each week. It really works.

Frank: How come you know so much about it?

■ **SET C**   ■ **PAGE 50**

An interview with an iridologist

Annie: So how long have you been an iridologist?

Paola: Oh, I've been practising for about seven years now.

Annie: And do you have an ordinary medical background too?

Paola: Actually yes. I have been a pharmacist. I trained as one and practised for a few years.

Annie: Really? Why did you give up?

Paola: I decided to stop when I noticed how many people are made sick by the medicines they are prescribed.

Annie: What, from the side effects?

Paola: Not just that. Fortunately, I have never taken sleeping pills in my life but lots of people get addicted to them.

Annie: How come this happens?

Paola: Quite simply the doctor often makes the wrong diagnosis. The wrong medicine is prescribed to people who are already ill and weak.

Annie: So that explains why you're fed up with conventional medicine; but why iridology?

Paola: Because it gives an accurate diagnosis and cares about prevention as much as cure. Conventional medicine is only interested in you once you get sick.

Annie: Mm, I'm not sure that's always true. But anyway, how can you tell someone's health by looking at their eyes.

Paola: We start with the colour which tells us about your basic constitution. Erm … people with blue eyes tend to have allergies and rheumatism, things like that. Those with brown eyes have problems with circulation and their digestion.

Annie: Huh, huh. And what about hazel eyes like yours?

Paola: Well, hazel and green eyes are actually false colours. Hazel is a mixture of brown on blue. Green eyes are also basically blue but liver problems gives them a yellow overlay.

Annie: And what can you tell from my eyes?

Paola: OK then … Mm … Now, eyes wide open, look straight in front. Good. Well, you've got a good constitution. There's something wrong with your left knee though. I can see that you have hurt it at some time.

Annie: Goodness! That's right. I had quite a bad skiing accident two years ago. I had an operation but it has bothered me ever since. How on earth did you see that?

Paola: Well there's a mark on the iris here at about six o'clock … let me show you on the chart.

Annie: Well that's quite incredible. I'll have to come to you for a consultation. And can you see …

■ SET D   ■ PAGE 52
Medical treatment

1   Well, it was terrible. My sister, she's seventy seven, she fell down the stairs at home and we had to wait two hours for the ambulance. And when we got to the hospital this young doctor examined her. She was really inexperienced, she can't have been more than twenty three? We were really dissatisfied … after all, we both worked for almost fifty years and paid a lot in taxes. It is a scandal, really it is. I think it is so unfair, I mean people with money they don't have to queue, do they? They can just go to an expensive clinic straightaway.

2   When I asked if my daughter could see a specialist that week they told me it was impossible. You see there is a waiting list which means we'll have to wait at least four months for a minor operation. The doctor was sorry but said the delay was unavoidable. I just don't know what she is going to do at school, if she can't hear properly she won't be able to follow the lessons. She might never catch up again.

3   I think it is unforgiveable … she'd been waiting six months for the operation but it was cancelled at the last minute. Poor mum, she's been in terrible pain with her hip but they said there was an emergency and they needed to operate on someone immediately. This is the second time it's happened. There should be more surgeons and facilities so people don't have to wait. She was so looking forward to walking properly again.

4   I think it's a scandal that we misspend so much money on weapons and bombs but that there's never enough for things like hospitals and education. It's completely immoral. The government has got completely the wrong priorities. It should be illegal to cancel operations and send people away.

5   As your local Member of Parliament I am fully aware of the problems affecting the City hospital and can fully sympathise with your dissatisfaction at the ineffecient running of the hospital. However, I would like to remind your readers that this unsatisfactory state of affairs is largely the result of the irresponsible behaviour of members of Trade Unions. The last strike was totally unnecessary and could have been avoided but they didn't want to talk.

UNIT 6

■ SET A   ■ PAGE 54

Lookalikes

Corinne James: Now it's quite remarkable how closely you resemble John Major, the British Prime Minister. When were you first aware of it?

Douglas Royale: About four years ago. It happened by accident really … We were watching TV when my wife said ' You look exactly like John Major.' I was a bit upset at first, he's not the most attractive man in the world. Anyway it started from there.

Corinne James: Ha ha … I suppose not. And erm why did you start impersonating him?

Douglas Royale: Well, we wanted someone to present the prizes at our local tennis club and we thought it would be fun for me to pretend to be Mr Major.

Corinne James: Do you have to dress up?

Douglas James: Not at all. I just wear one of the suits I have for work … The only thing I have to do is put on a pair of glasses with a black frame, because I wear contact lenses normally.

Corinne James: Right. And has it led to other things?

Douglas Royale: Well, I've opened a couple of supermarkets and been on a TV show …

Corinne James: And is there any money in it?

Douglas Royale: A little bit. I charge £50 for an appearance which I donate to charity.

Corinne James: So what do you actually do for a living?

Douglas Royale: I'm an accountant.

Corinne James: Ever thought of being a full-time John Major?

Douglas Royale: Not really. I think he'll be out of work very soon!

Corinne James: So Janet, or should I call you Marilyn?

Janet Klein: Janet will do..

Corinne James: How did you become Marilyn?

Janet Klein: Well, I knew I looked a bit like her but then, when I was 19, some of the girls at work sent my photo off to an agency. They called me in and that was that. I became a full time Marilyn.

Corinne James: And what about your old job?

Janet Klein: Well, I was training to be a hairdresser but I'd always wanted to be an actress.

Corinne James: And does it take you a long time to turn into Marilyn?

Janet Klein: Oh yes … It takes about three hours to dress up and put on my make-up. I also have to dye my roots because I'm not naturally blonde.

Corinne James: I see. And do you make a living at it?

Janet Klein: Oh yes, quite a good one too. I charge five hundred pounds to do something like open a supermarket or car showroom. The most I've ever made was six thousand pounds for a TV advert.

Corinne James: Wow! What just for being there and looking like Marilyn?

Janet Klein: There's bit more to it. I've managed to copy her walk too, and her look and her smile, of course. That was really difficult … I sing a couple of her songs too, you know 'I want to be loved by you.'

Corinne James: Ha ha … And are there many of you around? Marilyns, I mean.

Janet Klein: Oh yeah, but me and another girl are the best so we get all the big jobs.

Corinne James: Now, Marilyn died about 35 years ago, why is she still so popular?

Janet Klein: She was just so beautiful and everything, she'll never go out of fashion.

Corinne James: Now Elvis. Can I call you that?

Elvis O'Neill: You can, 'cos it's my real name.

Corinne James: You're kidding.

Elvis O'Neill: No, my mum and dad have always been Elvis fans so they named me after their favourite musician.

Corinne James: I see … and when did you start to impersonate him?

Elvis O'Neill: Oh when I was a kid … There are pictures of me dressed up like Elvis when I was five. It was expected of me …

Corinne James: Really? And er, do you take off Elvis full time?

Elvis O'Neill: No I wish I could … but even though I look like him my voice isn't that good …

Corinne James: So what do you do?

Elvis O'Neill: I'm an electrician and plumber.

Corinne James: Right … And do you get fed up with people saying you look like the king of rock and roll?

Elvis O'Neill: Yeah. I only grease back my hair and wear the erm clothes at the weekends.

Corinne James: And does it take a long time to get ready?

Elvis O'Neill: It depends what I'm wearing. A tee shirt and jeans takes about ten minutes but if I want to put my full Elvis costume on it takes a lot longer, maybe an hour. I've got hundreds of pounds worth of costumes.

Corinne James: Wow … And have you made any money at it?

Elvis O'Neill: Not a penny.

Corinne James: So Juliet, you erm, you impersonate Queen Elizabeth the first. Is that right?

Juliet Ashe: Yes, that's right.

Corinne James: Forgive me for saying this, but you don't actually look much like her.

Juliet Ashe: This is true, but it is a case of putting on loads of make-up and then the costume and I think you'd be quite surprised at the transformation.

Corinne James: It must take ages.

Juliet Ashe: Only about half an hour. It's basically lots of white make-up and a wig.

Corinne James: And er, why do you do it?

Juliet Ashe: Well, it's great to be queen for a day or just for the evening. You get to order everyone around..

Corinne James: I see. And what do you do normally, then?

Juliet Ashe: I'm a history teacher.

Corinne James: Really! And is this why you chose Elizabeth?

Juliet Ashe: Yes. I've always been fascinated by her … She's always been a heroine of mine.

Corinne James: And what does your family think about this?

Juliet Ashe: Well, they think it's great. My husband, who's a doctor, looks a bit like Shakespeare so we make a wonderful couple. It's marvellous for going to fancy dress parties.

Corinne James: And would you ever do it professionally?

Juliet Ashe: Well, we've gone along to historical evenings for tourists. They love us! We get a meal and about twenty pounds and that's fine. We want to keep it as a hobby, that way it stays fun.

■ SET B   ■ PAGE 56

In an art gallery

Phil: What do you think of this, Jane?

Jane: Ugh! I think it's awful. I don't like it at all.

Phil: Why on earth not? I think it's fascinating.

Jane: It's just a lot of funny black lines. It does nothing for me. Ah, but look! What a marvellous picture! All those gorgeous colours.

Phil: Do you really think so? You have never seen grass that colour. It's terrible.

Jane: But it's not supposed to be realistic. Anyway, let's not argue. Do you like this one over here?

Phil: Oh yes, fantastic. That's what I call a painting.

Stress for emphasis

I think it's fascinating.
All those gorgeous colours.

■ SET C   ■ PAGE 57

Vincent

Starry starry night
Paint your palette blue and grey
Look out on a summer's day
With eyes that know the darkness in my soul.
Shadows on the hills
Sketch the trees and the daffodils
Catch the breeze and the winter chills
In colours on the snowy linen land.

Now I understand
What you tried to say to me
And how you suffered for your sanity.
And how you tried to set them free
They would not listen, they did not know how
Perhaps they'll listen now.

Starry starry night
Flaming flowers that brightly blaze.
Swirling clouds in violet haze
Reflect in Vincent's eyes of china blue
Colours changing hue.
Morning fields of amber grain
Weathered faces lined in pain
Are soothed beneath the artist's loving hand

For they could not love you
But still your love was true
And when no hope was left in sight
On that starry starry night
You took your life as lovers often do.
But I could have told you Vincent
This world was never meant for one as beautiful as you.

■ SET D   ■ PAGE 60

The sad geniuses

Unfortunately some children will never be able to lead ordinary lives because they have serious mental and physical disabilities. However, a tiny few are able to do things that ordinary people would find quite impossible. Take the case of Ellen Boudreaux. When she was four months old doctors realized she was completely blind. Yet two months later her parents noticed something extraordinary. Above her bed she had one of those musical toys which plays a tune. Ellen could copy it exactly by humming the tune. Other incredible things followed. Little Ellen couldn't walk until she was four. However, when she finally started she managed to get around without knocking into anything even though she was blind. Even outside in woods and forests she just knows where all the trees are and can avoid them. When she walks about she makes a little noise. Some doctors believe it is her own personal kind of radar. But let's go back to her remarkable musical ability. Ellen learned how to play the piano and the guitar like an expert. But what is amazing is her musical memory. She only has to hear a piece of music once and she can reproduce it exactly. What's more, she never forgets anything and can play and sing all the songs she has ever heard. These abilities are extraordinary particularly if we remember that she can't hold a simple conversation, she can only echo and repeat questions. All doctors also agree that she has a very low intelligence. Yet she has one more miraculous gift I would like to tell you about. Ellen has an incredible 'internal clock' inside her brain which tells her to the second what the time is. This means she knows exactly when to turn the radio on for one of her favourite programmes.

Language Study

Separable phrasal verbs

1 Turn it off.
2 Why don't you try them on?
3 I can't make it out.
4 Shall we take him in?
5 Could you turn it down?
6 If I were you, I'd give it away.
7 He made the story up.
8 When can you pay me back?
9 The operator cut us off.
10 The bad weather held us up.

UNIT 7

■ SET A   ■ PAGE 63

Crime and punishment in the classroom

I don't think I'll ever forget what happened that day in 1975. I was just seven years old and had fallen deeply in love for the first time. Angela had beautiful blue eyes, long red hair, pale skin and freckles. While the teacher's back was turned, I passed her a note which said 'Angela, I love you – Tim.' She looked at it and at once put up her hand. 'Mr Gilbert,' she shouted, 'Tim has been naughty, he wrote this.' Mr Gilbert, a big man with a bald head and glasses took the note and looked at it. He smiled and I thought he was going to let the incident pass. Instead, he called me to the front of the class and told me to read the note aloud. As I said the words I felt so ashamed that my face turned a deep shade of red. All the other children laughed and I returned to my desk. However, this was not the end of it, each time he turned away from the class to write something on the board Angela turned towards me and stuck out her tongue. After the seventh or eighth time I stood up, picked up a heavy dictionary and did something which would have the most terrible consequences …

■ SET D   ■ PAGE 68

A miraculous way to learn?

Part A

Kay Able: What is this fast method for learning languages, doctor?

Dr Green: Basically it gets us to use all our brain. The brain is divided into two halves. Each half has different jobs. The left half is the logical side. This is where language is stored. The right side deals with space, artistic ability and music.

Part B

Kay Able: So artists and musicians use the powers in the right half.

Dr Green: … that's correct. Now, most teaching methods depend on studying grammar and doing exercises. There is also a lot of repetition. This is all logical left brain activity.

Kay Able: But what's wrong with that?

Dr Green: Well, what happens is that students work hard but often don't learn a lot. By the next lesson they can hardly remember anything. It's slow. What they need to do is use all of their brain.

Kay Able: How exactly can you do this?

Dr Green: Well, you know how we can remember rhymes and songs from childhood …

Kay Able: Mm yes. The other day I sang a song to a child which I last heard, it must have been twenty years ago. I was surprised I could still remember it.

Dr Green: Well, it doesn't surprise me. The two halves of your brain were working together. The words were kept in the left part but you were able to remember them because the music from the right side helped to fix them there.

Part C

Kay Able: So we should learn languages through singing?

Dr Green: Not exactly, but let me quickly say something about the method which was invented by a Bulgarian professor called Lozanov. His method has lately been developed in the United States. The teacher speaks to the students using a special rhythm and intonation which helps us to remember the language longer. The lesson is also accompanied by slow music. All these things make the brain work more efficiently and the language learning process faster, easier and much less stressful.

Kay Able: So the two halves work together. It sounds fantastic. I think I'll take up German again.

Dr Green: It's never too late to learn, Kay.

UNIT 8

■ SET A   ■ PAGE 70

City thoughts

1 Oh no! This looks like trouble … He's coming towards us. What's that in his hand … we should have taken a cab.

2 Either you don't exist or they treat you like an animal in a zoo. Tourists! What do you expect – a big smile? You've got your photo – now how about some change?

3 What a jam! I'll never get my flight. The only thing that's moving is the meter in this funny old taxi.

4 Whee, this is great. What a neat birthday gift!

5 Drivers. Think they own the road; and all the pollution. I'm glad I've got this mask … The lights are going to change! Just watch me beat this guy! *↳ bloke/chap (Tho).*

■ SET B ■ PAGE 73

Two cities

Part A

Poppy: This is a lovely house, Mrs Hallam. Is it very old?

Mrs Hallam: Quite old. It's Victorian, you know. It was built about a hundred years ago. There are thousands like it. You see, in the last century London grew enormously.

Poppy: But how did people get to work?

Mrs Hallam: By train. People have moved further and further out. Loads of people commute. The quality of life is often much better. They can live in the countryside and maybe have a bigger house. You escape all of the social problems we have here.

Poppy: Social problems. What do you mean?

Mrs Hallam: Well, during my childhood it was lovely round here. Nowadays there's quite a bit of crime.

Poppy: Crime! Goodness! What kind of thing?

Mrs Hallam: Burglaries and muggings too. You see, you've got people like me who are reasonably well-off, then unemployed and homeless people. You have to be careful at night.

Poppy: Oh dear. And what else?

Mrs Hallam: There's all the litter and the dirty streets.

Poppy: You make it sound terrible! Why on earth do you stay?

Mrs Hallam: Because I love it really. You've got the theatre here, all of the cinemas and museums and things. It's interesting too just wandering around the streets. There are lots of lovely parks as well. We moved out into the country for a while but we were bored. It was green and beautiful and everything but it was just too quiet I suppose.

Part B

Mrs Hallam: Anyway, tell me about Athens. I went when I was a girl. I had a marvellous time sightseeing. It was marvellous – I'll always remember it.

Poppy: Well, I think it must have changed since you were there. We've got our problems too. Pollution mainly. There are too many cars. Sometimes Athens is just one big traffic jam. Sometimes we're covered by a yellow cloud we call the 'nefos'.

Mrs Hallam: … sounds like London in the fifties with our smog.

Poppy: It's terrible for the buildings like the Parthenon. The stone is just being eaten away.

Mrs Hallam: Oh dear. Can't the government do something?

Poppy: Well, it tried to cut down traffic in the centre. You can only go in every other day; according to whether your number plate is odd or even.

Mrs Hallam: Has it worked?

Poppy: It has helped a bit.

Mrs Hallam: What would you do if you were in charge?

Poppy: First of all, I'd try to improve public transport, then …

■ SET D ■ PAGE 77

Finding the way

Poppy: I wonder if you could help me, Mrs Hallam. I want to get to Covent Garden.

Mrs Hallam: Oh yes. That's easy. Let's look at the Underground map. Right, we're in West London, so you take the brown line – that's the Bakerloo line – to Piccadilly Circus. Then change to the Piccadilly line, and take the eastbound tube to Covent Garden.

Poppy: Thank you. How long do you think it will take?

Mrs Hallam: About half an hour.

Poppy: Excuse me. Could you tell me the way to Garrick Street ?

Passer-by 1: Sorry, I'm a stranger here myself.

Poppy: Oh dear. Excuse me. Can you tell me where Garrick Street is?

Passer-by 2: Yes, but you're walking the wrong way. Go back down this road, past the tube station, take the third or fourth turning on the left and cut through into Garrick Street. It's only a couple of minutes' walk.

Poppy: Thanks a lot. Do you happen to know the time, please?

Passer-by 2: Yes, it's 8.15.

UNIT 9

■ SET B ■ PAGE 81

Describing someone

Carmen: It's really kind of you to offer to meet my aunt.

....

Carmen: Well, she's quite short and plump. She's about fifty-five and has got curly grey hair. She wears glasses and loves bright clothes.

....

Carmen: Really nice. Very lively. I haven't seen her since my Uncle Pablo died.

....

Carmen: Oh yes. She was very sad at first but she's OK now.

....

Carmen: She doesn't speak a word. You'll be able to practise your Spanish.

....

Carmen: She adores shopping. The last time she came to England we went to Harrods. I'm sure she'd love to go again …

The whole conversation

Carmen: It's really kind of you to offer to meet my aunt.

↳ shame = not a good thing.

Roger: No problem. It's a (pity) you don't have a photo of her. What does she look like? *→ a little bit fat*

Carmen: Well, she's quite short and (plump.) She's about fifty-five and has got curly grey hair. She wears glasses and loves bright clothes.

Roger: I see. And what's she like? I mean, what kind of person is she?

Carmen: Really nice. Very lively. I haven't seen her since my Uncle Pablo died. *→ RECOVERING.*

Roger: Oh, right. How is she now? Has she (got over it?)

Carmen: Oh yes. She was very sad at first but she's OK now.

Roger: And what's her English like?

Carmen: She doesn't speak a word. You'll be able to practise your Spanish.

Roger: Great! And what does she like doing?

Carmen: She adores shopping. The last time she came to England we went to Harrods. I'm sure she'd love to go again.

Tapescripts

■ **SET D** ■ **PAGE 85**
Agreeing and disagreeing

Simon: Mm … he is just one kind of Englishman. Lots of black people are English too. Another thing, nobody dresses like him these days.

Shirley: That's just not true. What about on the tube every morning. All those businessmen and civil servants?

Simon: Alright … but the other day I went to the post office and there was this guy – you know behind the counter – a civil servant – and he had punkish hair and an earring.

Shirley: Did it bother you, the hair and that?

Simon: Not really. Surprised that's all …

Shirley: Mm. You might be right. Anyway, that bit about the typical English family, you know, dad at work, mum at home. I thought that was wrong.

Simon: Why's that?

Shirley: Well, a lot of kids are only brought up by one parent. Dad's living with someone else …

Simon: … he's not in the garden with his roses.

Shirley: Right, that bit about the daughter living with a punk was realistic … It always seems to happen with middle class families doesn't it?

Simon: Yeah, you're right. For me the best thing about the article was that it made me wonder what foreigners think of us. I'm sure if you spoke to them about the English gentleman they'd laugh.

Shirley: Absolutely, all those awful English holidaymakers. Mm, they probably think the typical Englishman is a drunk football fan …

Simon: That's right, wearing union jack swimming trunks and reading a copy of The *Sun*.

UNIT 10

■ **SET A** ■ **PAGE 88**

Toad-in-the-hole!

Moira: I wonder where Poppy is. I hope she hasn't got lost.

Martin: I'm sure she'll be here soon. Let's look at the menu.

Moira: I think I'll have the smoked salmon then the duck. What about you, darling?

Martin: I'll have the cheese and onion tart and the roast beef.

Poppy: Hello. Sorry I'm late. I got lost.

Martin: Never mind. Do sit down.

Moira: Well, Yorkshire pudding – it's a sort of cake made from eggs and flour and water. You cook it in the oven and eat it when it's crisp and brown …

Poppy: Oh, I think I see. And toad-in-the-hole? What a strange name!

Moira: Oh that's Yorkshire pudding with sausages cooked inside.

Poppy: I see. I really can't make up my mind.

Moira: Why don't you have the duck? That's what I am going to have.

Poppy: Alright then. And I'd like to start with the soup.

Waiter: Are you ready to order, sir?

Martin: Yes, I think so. Will you bring us a bottle of dry white wine with the first course and we're going to have …

Poppy: Thank you for a lovely meal. It was really delicious. I am afraid I am going to have to go.

Martin: What so soon?

Poppy: I am sorry to leave in such a hurry but I am worried about getting home.

Martin: Come on, stay for coffee. It's going to rain soon and you'll get soaked. We'll give you a lift.

■ **SET B** ■ **PAGE 90**

Five people talk about English food.

1 English food. Well it's difficult to say what it is really. There's no such thing really. It's a mixture of all kinds of cooking. At home I think you could say that it is erm European. If English people go out they hardly ever go to an English restaurant. It's usually something like an Italian, Chinese or Indian one. French for special occasions

2 Well, before I came to England I'd always thought that, you know, the saying that the English don't eat, they just take nourishment was true. But I must say I have changed my mind. The food here is not too bad at all.

3 Really, it's awful. It's a nightmare. The family where I am staying, well, really there is just one old lady … the food doesn't taste of anything. And the vegetables. All the time potatoes, potatoes, and other vegetables like carrots or cabbage … she cooks them for hours! All the stories people have about English food are true. I'm sorry but it's true. One evening she said she wanted to give me pasta and she gave me spaghetti but from a tin – it was horrible.

4 Mmm, at Easter we usually go to France for a week, we go to a cottage or something like that, but this year we decided to go to the countryside in England, on the east coast. Now it was a nice holiday in many ways and there were lots of interesting places to visit but the food. Finding somewhere to eat out was a problem and when we did, frankly the food was awful. All you could really get was fish and chips or steak and chips, stuff like that. A disappointing choice. Next year it's France again.

5 Definitely, it's things like roast beef and Yorkshire pudding on Sunday, or lamb with mint sauce. Then you've got delicious desserts like bread and butter pudding or apple pie or summer pudding, you know, made with all the soft summer fruits. It's nonsense to say there's no such thing, cooked well they can be as delicious as anything from anywhere in the world.

■ **SET B** ■ **PAGE 90**

How to make bread-and-butter pudding

Now today's quick recipe is for bread and butter pudding. It's a simple but delicious dessert. Now, you'll need the following ingredients: three quarters of a litre of milk, two hundred grams of butter, four large or six small eggs, two hundred and fifty grams of sugar, some dried sultanas, the big juicy ones, you'll need about one hundred and fifty grams – or if you can't get sultanas some little raisins. Oh, and I almost forgot you'll need about half a dozen slices of white bread, it's actually better if it's a day old!

So what you do is this, break the eggs into a bowl and mix in the sugar, then add the milk and beat the mixture well until it's nice and smooth. Now take the slices of bread and spread them generously with butter, cut off the crust and cut each slice into three or four strips. Take a medium sized shallow dish, something that can go in the oven, and butter it so that it doesn't stick. Then put the strips of buttered bread along the bottom of the dish to form a layer. Take about half the sultanas or raisins and sprinkle them on ... you can be quite generous. Then put down another layer of bread and butter strips and sprinkle on the rest of the sultanas. Now pour the egg and milk mixture over the bread and butter and sultanas and leave it for a couple of hours. Then, when the bread is nice and wet, put it in a medium hot oven, around two hundred degrees for about forty-five minutes or until it starts to rise and go nice and crisp. It's best not to eat it straight away. I think it tastes much better if it's warm rather than boiling hot.

■ SET C　　■ PAGE 92

Watch your body language

Carol Jones: When we're abroad, it's not just the spoken language that can cause problems. Most travellers can remember accidentally upsetting someone because a gesture which is harmless at home causes great offence abroad. On 'Travel Wise' today, we have Dr Ian Williams, an expert on international gestures.

Dr Williams: Good evening.

Carol Jones: Now, Ian, I believe that even experts like you are sometimes caught out.

Dr Williams: Oh indeed, Carol. Why, I remember being in India and misunderstanding a conversation. You see the person I was talking to kept shaking his head. I thought he was disagreeing with me. In fact it turned out to be the opposite.

Carol Jones: So his head shake meant yes?

Dr Williams: More than that, it meant 'carry on talking because I'm interested'.

Carol Jones: So we can't even take simple head movements for granted. What about closer to home?

Dr Williams: Well, in Europe some gestures are universal. Thumbing your nose means the same whether you are in Oslo or Madrid. But very often a gesture is either unknown or else means something entirely different. For example the thumbs up sign we use to mean OK is known throughout northern Europe. But if you go to Greece or Italy people won't understand what you're on about.

Carol Jones: Mm ... talking of Italy I'm reminded of that strange gesture, you know, the one where they hold the tips of their fingers together and move them up and down ...

Dr Williams: Oh yes, the 'hand purse'. Um, we never see it over here but it's used all around the Mediterranean. Unfortunately it's probably the most confusing gesture around.

Carol Jones: Why's that?

Dr Williams: Well in Italy you'll remember it means 'What are you getting at?' or 'I don't understand' ... Yet in France it can mean that you are afraid, and if you go to Greece it means that something is good, while in Spain it simply means 'a lot'.

Carol Jones: What a minefield! Sadly, the news is about to begin, so we don't have time to go into this any further. But Ian, what one piece of advice would you give to travellers going abroad?

Dr Williams: Never copy local gestures as it can seem strange and cause offence. Steer clear of local taboo gestures too.

Carol Jones: So probably the best thing on your next trip is to remember to keep your hands in your pockets. It's by far the safest way! Dr Ian Williams, thank you for coming in. And now ...

UNIT 11

■ SET B　　■ PAGE 99

The world's favourite Australians

When explorers came to Australia they couldn't believe their eyes. The continent was full of strange and wonderful creatures. There was the kangaroo which moved along in huge jumps, and all kinds of new snakes and insects. The strangest one of all was the duck-billed platypus, basically because nobody could work out what it was. Let me explain why.

It's a bit like a duck because it's got a bill and webbed feet and lays eggs. It spends most of its time in the water digging around in the mud with its bill but instead of feathers it's covered with fur so it can't be a bird. In the end scientists decided it was a mammal because it's warm-blooded and produces milk for its young.

Everybody's favourite, though, is the koala. Koalas are rather interesting. They are active at night and because of this, spend most of the daytime asleep in the fork of trees. They don't have tails which is strange for animals which live in trees but they have a hard pad of skin which lets them sit for hours. They have pouches for their young like kangaroos but theirs open downwards! Baby koalas spend about six months in the pouches before riding on their mothers' backs.

Over the past two hundred years they have had a varied history. In the old days dingoes ate them and they were hunted by the aborigines. When the Europeans colonized Australia they shot the dingoes and the aborigines started eating different food. This was great for the koalas and the population grew incredibly. Unfortunately they were hunted for their fur and in 1924 two million koala skins were exported. Nowadays, they are no longer hunted but there are other dangers. Koalas eat enormous amounts of leaves from gum trees but since many of the forests have been cut down food is getting scarce. Disease and cars are two other major threats. Luckily people are aware of the problems and are trying to protect them so their future doesn't look too bad.

Even though they look so cute and cuddly don't be taken in! One famous politician saw a koala and picked it up for a group of photographers. The koala wasn't interested and scratched him with its sharp claws. By the way, in case you were wondering, the name 'koala' comes from the aborigine language which means: 'I don't drink'. Even though they can drink water, they get most of the liquid they need from the leaves they eat.

■ SET D　　■ PAGE 102

Don't be so green!

Frank: Just look at these pictures! Why doesn't your government do something?

Maria: Are you accusing me of burning down the forest again?

Frank: It's somebody's fault. You can't blame us.

Maria: But I do. Indirectly you're responsible. Your banks lent us too much. And we can't pay it back ...

Frank: What are you getting at?

Maria: Well, interest rates are high and we're desperate for dollars. We have to clear the forest to provide land for cattle.

Frank: That's still no excuse. You shouldn't have borrowed so much. Anyway, what about coffee? Couldn't you export that?

Maria: We do. But there's more money in beef than coffee.

Frank: Come off it! I paid two pounds sixty p for this jar.

Maria: But we get hardly anything … about fifty p, I think.

Frank: How come?

Maria: It's the processing – the roasting and the grinding – which adds value. That's done over here.

Frank: So why not process it yourselves? Or put up the price?

Maria: Because importing countries are too powerful.

Frank: Even so … there must be another way.

Maria: Yes and no. You can't prevent people from clearing the forest if that's the only way they've got of making a living. We have to show there's an alternative by encouraging people to buy more products which grow in the forest; you know – like nuts and rubber.

Frank: No morality, just economics. You're a hard woman, Maria.

Maria: And you, Frank, darling … sometimes you're just a bit too green!

UNIT 12

■ SET A   ■ PAGE 104

BRITISH NEWSPAPERS

Hans: Can you tell me something about newspapers in Britain, Jackie?

Jackie: Right, well, there are two types of newspaper. There are the popular papers, you know the tabloids like the *Sun* and the *Daily Mirror* and the quality papers like the *Times*, *Guardian* and *Independent*. Oh, and of course the *Daily Telegraph*.

Hans: Are there big differences politically?

Jackie: Um, the *Mirror* and *Guardian* are the only two which are fairly left wing. All the rest are on the right, you know, the *Sun*, the *Times* are right wing in my opinion. So is the *Telegraph*. The *Independent*, a fairly recent paper, tries to be independent of all the major parties and is in the centre.

Hans: And who reads which papers?

Jackie: Well, I think this is largely to do with social class, education and, of course, which political party you tend to support. Tabloids are mostly read by ordinary working class people but there is a middle class tabloid called the *Daily Mail*. The tabloids are dreadful, they're full of pictures of pretty girls and competitions, stories about the private lives of famous people, TV stars and so on. They've got no real news in them.

Hans: And do political parties own newspapers?

Jackie: No, except for some papers with tiny circulations. Most papers are owned by rich businessmen. All the same, national papers support a party especially at general elections. In fact the *Sun* claims that it won a general election for the Conservative party.

Hans: Really! And do many people buy the *Sun*?

Jackie: Goodness, yes. It has a circulation of about 4 million; its left wing equivalent, the *Mirror*, sells about 3 million, I think. All the quality papers added up together don't equal the circulation of the *Sun*.

Hans: And do you have any kind of censorship?

Jackie: Not really. I suppose it's because we have a long tradition of freedom of the press. And in a way this can be a problem. Recently there was an awful photo on the front of several of the tabloids of a woman news presenter. She was sitting on a beach somewhere hot and sunny, looking very fat and unattractive, a million miles from her normal TV image. I think it's unfair to print pictures like that. After all, she was just a private person trying to relax on holiday. But in Britain we have far too much of this, there aren't really any privacy laws which can protect people from the Press. Telephoto lenses mean that nobody is safe.

■ SET A   ■ PAGE 105

How to get an interview

Julian: What's so funny?

Annabel: It's this book. It's about this journalist who would do anything for a story.

Julian: Who did he work for?

Annabel: The tabloids, the popular papers.

Julian: One of those …

Annabel: Anyway, he got up to some real tricks.

Julian: Like what?

Annabel: Well, you know Oliver Reed?

Julian: The film director?

Annabel: That's Oliver Stone. Oliver Reed, the actor.

Julian: Oh him? … a bit of a playboy wasn't he?

Annabel: Mm that's right. There was a lot of gossip a few years ago, he married a schoolgirl …

Julian: Who, this reporter?

Annabel: No, Oliver Reed.

Julian: What! He must have been twice her age.

Annabel: Three times, actually. Anyway, Wensley, you know, the journalist, he realized that this would be a great story so he followed them to the West Indies.

Julian: Oliver Reed can't have been happy.

Annabel: You're right! He refused to talk to anyone. Of course Wensley couldn't go back to England without a story – his editor would have killed him.

Julian: I can imagine …

Annabel: Anyway Wensley was desperate. What he did was invite Reed's minder, you know a kind of bodyguard, to his hotel.

Julian: Crafty.

Annabel: And guess what. His minder actually turned up with the girl and Wensley got them to tell him the whole story!

Julian: And where was Reed while this was going on?

Annabel: At home in bed with a cold. Anyway, the best bit is that Wensley told the other two …

Julian: The girl and the minder?

Annabel: Yeah … so he told them that he was going out to get some food because everyone was feeling hungry. Anyway, instead, he went off to find Reed. He just walked into the villa.

Julian: What a cheek!

Annabel: Reed was furious and chased him out of the house. All the while though, Wensley was asking him questions.

Julian: And did he get him?

Annabel: No, he got away, although Reed spent the next day checking every hotel on the island. It was worth it though, Wensley had his interview and his editor was happy. The story made the headlines.

■ SET D   ■ PAGE 110

The news

This is the eight o'clock news on Wednesday 1st April. First the main news headlines read by Arthur Robinson.

- New regulations for Britain's motorists are to come into force from midnight tonight.
- A blaze has destroyed examination buildings in Cambridge
- Bad weather has caused the destruction of Italy's spaghetti crop.

And now for the news in depth from your newscaster, Annie McCleod.

The Minister of Transport, Mr Alfred Murphy, has announced that as of midnight tonight new regulations for road users will come into force. From midnight cars and buses will have to drive on the right-hand side of the road. To avoid unnecessary confusion bicycles and lorries will not have to comply with the changeover until February 29th of next year. All traffic will be banned from roads between 11.30 this evening and midnight to ensure that the changeover goes smoothly.

A blaze at the Local Examinations Board has destroyed a wing of the building. The mystery fire broke out at around three o'clock this morning and it took until nine o'clock for firefighters to bring it under control. Fortunately damage appears to be limited to the science examinations section. A spokesperson has said that a thousand, I'm sorry I'll read that again, a hundred thousand candidates who took the November examinations will have to re-sit. A group of students is helping police with their enquiries.

Bad weather has caused the destruction of this year's spaghetti crop in Northern Italy. The crop was destroyed by exceptionally cold weather for this time of year. Farmers woke up this morning to find that the spaghetti had frozen on the branches of their trees. This means ruin for thousands of Italian farmers who were depending on this year's harvest to rescue them from economic difficulties. This is the third year that the spaghetti harvest has been a disaster and farmers must be wondering if they will be rescued by the European Community again.

UNIT 13

■ SET B   ■ PAGE 114

Living dinosaurs!

Part A

Pop Osborne: Hello Pat. What have you been up to?
Patricia: I've just taken Katie to an exhibition.
Pop Osborne: Oh, poor you, you must be tired.
Patricia: Tired! I'm exhausted!
Pop Osborne: Never mind. I'll make a nice cup of tea. So, what did you see?
Patricia: Well, it was called 'Living Dinosaurs'.
Pop Osborne: 'Living Dinosaurs'! You can't be serious!
Patricia: Of course they were models which look like dinosaurs. They're operated by computer. They do all the right things. Move and breathe and make horrible noises.
Pop Osborne: Katie must have been scared.

Patricia: Actually she loved it. One little chap was terrified. He can't have been more than four.
Pop Osborne: Oh dear, what a shame. He'll probably have nightmares.

Part B

Pop Osborne: So did you have a nice time, Katie?
Katie: Yeah. It was great. Can I tell you all about dinosaurs?
Pop Osborne: If you like, dear.
Katie: Well, they died a long time ago. Sixty million years.
Pop Osborne: Well fancy that.
Katie: I bet you don't know why they died.
Pop Osborne: You are going to tell me anyway, I expect.
Katie: Well, people used to think it might have been a change in the weather. You know an ice-age.
Pop Osborne: Oh really.
Katie: Nowadays they think it could have been a meteor.
Pop Osborne: A meteor, from outer space? Why's that?
Katie: 'Cos lots of other things died at the same time. They know that 'cos geologists dug up lots of fossils of things that died. So it must have happened suddenly.
Pop Osborne: Fancy that. People have some funny ideas, don't they?
Katie: So what happened is that it fell in the sea – splash – and made it boil.
Pop Osborne: Well I never.
Katie: There was lots of steam and stuff. It killed most of the plants. The 'vegetarian' dinosaurs died out so did the meat eaters – like tyrannosaurus rex – he was a meat eater – he's my favourite – well they all died. It got too humid too.
Pop Osborne: I don't like the heat either!
Katie: But you're not a reptile! Dinosaurs were reptiles; you know, cold-blooded like snakes. We're mammals.
Pop Osborne: That's nice.
Katie: So the dinosaurs couldn't cope. The heat made them slow.
Pop Osborne: Oh dear!
Katie: But the mammals, they were warm-blooded, they could control their temperature better. My dad says they were our ancestors. But the dinosaurs they died!
Pop Osborne: What a shame. Who would have imagined it? The poor old dinosaurs.
Katie: Well, mum says we shouldn't feel sorry for them. They did last over a hundred and sixty million years!
Pop Osborne: Even so it can't have been nice for them. Anyway, talking of vegetarians and meat eaters what do you want for lunch? Spaghetti or a hamburger?

Making intelligent guesses

Stress patterns

1 You must be tired.
2 It might have been a change in the weather.

■ SET D   ■ PAGE 119

The evolution of armour

Unfortunately human beings have always been very good at finding new ways of killing each other. When weapons improve and become more effective armour has to improve too.
(slide one)
In classical times most fighting was done on foot by soldiers fighting hand to hand with spears and swords. So armour had to

give protection but be fairly light so the soldier could move. That's why armour from this period only protects the head and upper body.

(slide two)

This shows a beautiful helmet from Greece. Even though it covers most of the face there's still plenty of room for the soldier to see through.

(slide three)

In Roman times better equipped soldiers wore body armour made up of strips of metal which was far more flexible – each piece moves – so they could move their bodies much more easily than in the armour made just from one piece.

(slide four)

During the Middle Ages, cavalry became more important and a lot of the fighting was done on horseback. This meant that armour could be heavier and give greater protection. A knight would wear a suit of chain mail which covered the whole body. Chain mail was popular for about four hundred years up to thirteen hundred. A knight would also have worn a heavy helmet like this one. It gave protection against heavy swords. Of course it was quite difficult to see because there was only a little hole to look through. However, as bows became more powerful they were able to penetrate chain mail so they had to find an alternative. The result was a return to plate armour.

(slide five)

For the next two hundred years, plate armour became more and more sophisticated. The best armour of all was made in Italy and Germany and shows remarkable craftsmanship.

(slide six)

The invention of gunpowder and guns changed the face of warfare. For a time it was possible to provide more protection by making thicker armour. But as guns improved armour became less and less effective. Look at this breastplate from the English Civil War of the sixteen forties. The bullet has gone straight through and must have killed the poor soldier wearing it.

(slide seven)

People quickly realized that the best protection against a bullet is to be a fast moving and difficult target. Because of this, over the next few centuries we see a return to fast and lightly armed soldiers with very little protection.

(slide eight)

However, the last fifteen years or so have seen new developments. Some new materials are so strong that they can offer protection against bullets and flying metal. Look at this picture of an American foot soldier wearing a flak jacket and a helmet.

UNIT 14

SET D   PAGE 127

The British Royal Family

1   Excuse me madam, have you got a moment?
    What do you think of the Royal Family?

I think they're absolutely marvellous. I mean they are wonderful ambassadors for this country and represent everything that is good and great in Britain … not to mention all of the wonderful things they do for charity. And just think of all the tourists who come here because of the Royal Family. I really don't know what we would do without them. And the royal babies, I think it's just marvellous when a new one comes along, bless them.

2   Could you tell me what you think of the Royal Family?

The royal family. What that lot? I mean they cost the country millions, don't they? There are so many of them too. Me, I'm unemployed and I have to live off fifty pounds a week but they've got millions and we still have to pay them. If I had my way I'd …

3   And you sir?
    Do you think the Royal Family does a good job?

To tell you the truth I don't think much about them at all. They're alright I suppose. They do a pretty good job … I wouldn't like to be one, I mean, they're always in the public eye, aren't they?

4   Would you mind telling me what you think of the Royal Family?

They're harmless, I suppose. The only thing is they're a bit out of date. They don't really mean much in the modern world, do they? It's not like in the old days when the king led his armies into battle. They're not much use but at least we know what we've got though. We don't have the circus the Americans have every four years when they elect a new president. That really makes me sick. The only real thing I don't agree with is that we have to pay for them. Taxpayers I mean. After all they're rich enough already.

Leading questions

Example: What do you think of the Royal Family?

1   Could you tell me what you think of the Royal Family?
2   Do you think the Royal Family does a good job?
3   Would you mind telling me what you think of the Royal Family?

Linking words in connected speech

1   It's not like in the old days when the king led his armies into battle.
2   Me, I'm unemployed and I have to live off £50 a week, but they've got millions.

SET E   PAGE 128

Henry VIII and his six wives

Interviewer: Henry VIII was the founder of the royal navy and established the Church of England. However, he is best remembered for his six wives. He was a difficult man but was he as cruel as some people think?

B: Certainly. He was capable of tremendous cruelty. His reign is full of dead bodies. Wife number two – Anne Boleyn – and Catherine Howard, wife number five, both had their heads chopped off. Most of Catherine's family was executed too. Many ministers met the same fate. It seems to be the way he solved problems. However, we should remember this was a cruel age and it was common for princes to use their powers in this way.

Interviewer: I see. And what made him marry so often?

B: Basically he was desperate for a son. His first wife, Catherine of Aragon, could only give him a daughter and so he had to re-marry. The Pope wouldn't let Henry divorce Catherine, so Henry formed his own church so that he could go ahead with it anyway. It also gave him the excuse to close down all the monasteries and steal all their enormous wealth. His chief minister, Thomas Cromwell, helped him with this.

Interviewer: And what sort of reward did he get?

B: Well, for a long while Cromwell was the second most powerful man in the kingdom. Even though the great lords looked down on him as the son of a butcher, they feared him. He made them obey the king and attend his special courts. But, as usual, in the end Henry turned on him and he lost his head.

Interviewer: How come?

B: Well, Henry finally got a son from wife number three, Jane Seymour. Sadly, she died shortly after the birth so he was on the lookout for a wife again. English families either couldn't keep up with his demands or were suspicious of Henry. Diplomats had to look abroad. She could not be a Catholic of course so there was a limited choice. Cromwell eventually talked the king into marrying Anne of Cleves. She looked OK from her portrait, so a diplomat married her on Henry's behalf.

Interviewer: So what went wrong?

B: Well, when she arrived Henry was horrified. He said that she looked like a horse and refused to have anything to do with her.

Interviewer: So that was the end of Cromwell. And wife number six?

B: Catherine Parr? Well she had the good luck to outlive him.

UNIT 15

■ SET C   ■ PAGE 135

What a bargain!

Liz Balfour: Well, here we are. Let me open the door for you. Mind the step. Here's the sitting room.

Miranda Short: Wow, it's really big isn't it?

Liz Balfour: Yes, but it could be really cosy. It needs to be redecorated.

Miranda Short: Are all the rooms this large?

Liz Balfour: Yes, but you could always divide them.

Miranda Short: It's been empty quite a while, hasn't it?

Liz Balfour: Only a few weeks.

Miranda Short: It's freezing. What's that funny smell?

Liz Balfour: Oh, just a little damp.

Miranda Short: Do you think you could turn the central heating on?

Liz Balfour: Actually, it doesn't have central heating.

Miranda Short: Oh doesn't it? I thought it did.

Liz Balfour: No, I'm afraid not. But the previous owners had the roof and the attic restored. That's why it's such a bargain.

Miranda Short: Oh really. I thought it was because of the stories.

Liz Balfour: Those silly stories. You don't believe those, do you?

Miranda Short: But there had been a murder, hadn't there?

Liz Balfour: Oh yes. But …

Miranda Short: And the other people. They only stayed six weeks, didn't they?

Liz Balfour: I'm not terribly sure. Anyway, let's look at the rest of the house … Let's begin with the cellar.

Miranda Short: OK then … as I'm here.

Liz Balfour: Watch out the door's a bit low. After you!

Miranda Short: Oh, thank you very much.

Checking and confirming

a It's really big, isn't it?
b They only stayed six weeks, didn't they?

■ SET D   ■ PAGE 137

Vampire rumours

Interviewer: Would you mind if I asked you some questions?

Vampire: Not at all, dear boy, after all that's why we're here.

Interviewer: How long have you been, um a creature of the night?

Vampire: Since 1327, that's six hundred and seventy years.

Interviewer: Wow! And how were you 'born', if I can say that?

Vampire: Well I happened to knock at the door of Count Dracula's castle in the middle of the night.

Interviewer: Why, were you lost?

Vampire: Not at all. I was a tax collector for the King at that time – so you can see I've always been a blood sucker, ha-ha. Anyway I wanted to catch the count at home.

Interviewer: I see. So he bit you and that was that.

Vampire: Quite.

Interviewer: Now I'd like to turn to your powers. Is it true that you can fly through the air?

Vampire: Absolute nonsense.

Interviewer: And what about being scared of crosses.

Vampire: Rubbish too – they have absolutely no effect on us.

Interviewer: But what are you scared of then? I mean, what about the sun.

Vampire: Ah yes, that's true. We have to be tucked up in our coffins before the first rays of sun otherwise we burn.

Interviewer: We have heard, do excuse me for bringing this up, that the only way to kill a vampire is with a wooden stake through the heart.

Vampire: Oh dear you have been watching too many horror films – but actually you are right.

Interviewer: And what about garlic, you know, protecting people against the attention of vampires?

Vampire: It depends on the tastes of the vampire – my English cousins can't stand foreign food, but I love a bit of garlic or paprika myself!

Interviewer: And finally, is being a vampire lonely?

Vampire: Not really. I have my family. There's my wife, Lucretia, and my boy, Vlad Junior …

Interviewer: Your wife … Where did you meet her?

Vampire: In Rome back in 1430 I think. Anyway, there she was across the room. I had to have her. It was love at first bite …